REVOLUTIONARIES, MONARCHISTS,
AND CHINATOWNS

Revolutionaries, Monarchists, and Chinatowns

CHINESE POLITICS IN THE AMERICAS AND THE 1911 REVOLUTION

L. Eve Armentrout Ma

University of Hawaii Press

Honolulu

Printed in the United States of America

90 92 93 94 95 96   5 4 3 2 1

Library of Congress Cataloging-in-Publication Data

Ma, L. Eve Armentrout.

Revolutionaries, monarchists, and Chinatowns :

Chinese politics in the Americas and the 1911 revolution /

L. Eve Armentrout Ma.

p.   cm.

Includes bibliographical references.

ISBN 0-8248-1239-5 (alk. paper)

1.   Chinese—America—Politics and government.

2.   China—Politics and government—1911–1912.

I.   Title.

E29.C5M3   1990

973'.04951—dc20   89–28021

CIP

University of Hawaii Press books

are printed on acid-free paper

and meet the guidelines for

permanence and durability of

the Council on Library Resources.

TO MY PARENTS,

EDWARD GOODWIN BALLARD AND

LUCY MCIVER WATSON BALLARD,

AND TO MY VERY PATIENT FAMILY

CONTENTS

Contents

NOTE ON ROMANIZATION

Generally, the Wade-Giles system of romanization following the Mandarin pronunciation has been used for Chinese characters in this book. In the case of proper names, where another romanization has become standard (for example: Foochow or Canton), I have used the standard. Where there are proper names with alternative forms that are not commonly known, such as the names of Chinese persons living in the Americas, I have included the alternative form in parentheses after the Wade-Giles form, where the name is first mentioned in the text.

In the case of publications, I have tried to keep in mind the convenience of future researchers. If a publication was readily available in a library, I have kept the romanization used by that particular library, and again, at the first mention of the publication in this text, the Wade-Giles spelling has been given in parentheses. For publications not readily accessible, Wade-Giles has been used, with any alternative romanization included in parentheses at the first mention of the title. Libraries may catalog many (but not all) Chinese-language newspapers according to an English added title or translation of the title; in this case, I have followed the library where the newspaper is located, but then have added the Wade-Giles romanization in parentheses at the first mention of the newspaper. If a library has used an alternative romanization, I have also used the alternative, and then put the Wade-Giles version in parentheses at first mention in the text.

ACKNOWLEDGMENTS

This book would not have been possible without the help and encouragement of many people and institutions. The original manuscript was my doctoral thesis prepared for the University of California at Davis. At that stage, I received much help from Don C. Price and Frederic Wakeman, Jr. Others whose support was important include Kwang-ching Liu, David Brody, and Benjamin E. Wallacker. In addition, I benefited from the financial support of the Committee on American-East Asian Relations, and also received a small grant from the Center for Chinese Studies of the University of California at Berkeley.

During the post-doctoral period, a grant from the Kellogg Foundation of the University of California at Davis helped me begin revising the manuscript. In addition, Edgar Wickberg gave the text a thorough reading, Don C. Price gave additional comments, Michael H. Hunt sent me his advice, and Richard J. Lee gave the first part of the manuscript a final reading.

A number of libraries have also been helpful: the Bancroft, the East Asiatic, and the Asian American Studies Libraries of the University of California at Berkeley; the San Francisco Public Library; the National Archives in Washington, D.C.; and the Hamilton Library of the University of Hawaii. The staff at *Shao-nien Chung-kuo ch'en-pao (Young China)* let me spend months reading early issues of that newspaper. Jung-pang Lo, Taam Wu, Him Mark Lai, and William Fong gave me important source material and in interviews provided additional facts. Others interviewed include Charles Mah, Chew Long, Howard Ah-Tye, Huang Yün-su, Ira C. Lee, and Lee Jit Sing. In addition, Edgar Wickberg and Wei Chi Poon helped locate some of the photographs.

Last but not least, Phyllis Killen gave some editorial advice, and the staff at the University of Hawaii Press, especially Pamela Kelley and freelance editor John Benson, were most helpful. My thanks to all those listed above, and to others whose names I may have overlooked. Any errors of fact or interpretation, and any infelicities of style, remain my sole responsibility.

INTRODUCTION

This is a book about an important period in the history of the Chinese in the Americas. (The designation Americas includes North America, Latin America, and Hawaii. The latter became a possession of the United States in 1898.) During this period, major social and political changes occurred in America's Chinese communities,[1] changes intimately linked to and to some extent reflecting developments in China, especially the Chinese revolution of 1911. It was a period in which Chinese in the Americas began to be politicized and became active for the first time in the national politics of their motherland. The politicization altered their social structure and social order in a way that was probably more profound than anything that has taken place in the Chinatowns of the Americas up until the late 1970s, when the modern Civil Rights movement caught up with them and the "new immigration" from East Asia began.

America's Chinese communities owed most of the direction and impetus for these changes to three Chinese statesmen who visited the Americas on several occasions between 1894 and 1911. The first was Sun Yat-sen, the major leader in the prorevolutionary camp and a proponent of a republican form of government for China. (He was later to become the first provisional president of the Republic of China.) The other two were K'ang Yu-wei and Liang Ch'i-ch'ao, the celebrated "reformers of 1898," best known for their efforts to establish a constitutional monarchy in China. These three, K'ang, Liang, and Sun, established China's first political parties—parties which operated in the Americas as well as within and on the borders of China. The first two of these parties were actually founded in the Americas: the Hsing-Chung hui (Revive China Society), founded in Hawaii in 1894 by Sun Yat-sen, and the Pao-huang hui (Chinese Empire Reform Association/Chinese Constitutionalist Party/Save the Emperor Society), founded in Canada in 1899 by K'ang Yu-wei.

I

Good documentation exists on the functioning and development in the Americas of these and later parties; on the interaction between the parties and preexisting social organizations such as surname associations, Triad lodges, and *hui-kuan* (fellow-regional associations); and on the competition between reform and revolutionary parties. Contemporary Chinese-language newspapers provide an especially rich source of information on these topics. A number of these newspapers were founded by the political parties themselves as a means of influencing overseas Chinese, and each newspaper reported its party's activities in great detail. In addition, there is much to be learned from the several usually politically unaffiliated newspapers of which San Francisco's *Chung Sai Yat Po* (*Chung-hsi jih-pao*, East-West News) was the most important.

Chinese in the Americas enjoyed a fair degree of political freedom, certainly more than their fellow citizens in Japan, Southeast Asia, and China itself. This freedom permitted the branches of the Chinese reform and revolutionary parties to develop with less outside interference than they encountered elsewhere in the world. It also allowed for more spontaneous political participation on the part of the members of the Chinese communities. As a result, Chinese in the Americas were able to sustain the political parties when these parties were restricted or came under attack elsewhere in the world. Moreover, the American environment permitted the growth of independent, unaligned political groups. In fact, a number of would-be revolutionary organizations in the Americas were not tied to the major political parties led by Sun Yat-sen or K'ang and Liang.

The greater political freedom among Chinese in the Americas, however, was accompanied by discriminatory laws and practices directed against Chinese as a group. Discrimination went a long way toward confining the Chinese to Chinatowns and to their own social organizations. It also greatly restricted the economic opportunities of Chinese in the Americas. As a result, not surprisingly, Chinese in the Americas held a somewhat jaundiced view of North America's liberal institutions. The more evenhanded functioning of the higher (federal and central government) law courts in the United States and Canada stood as a partial exception to this generalization. Chinese in North America were aware that at least the higher courts of the judiciary were not always against them.

American discrimination against Chinese also ensured that Chinese in the New World would retain a strong interest in their native land. In China itself, momentous changes were taking place. The Ch'ing dynasty of the Manchus was crumbling under the combined onslaught of encroachment by the Western nations and Japan, bureaucratic inefficiency and corruption, and new forces within China called into being in response to the possibility that the nation would be dismembered. These new forces included both a growing regionalism and, paradoxically, the birth of modern nationalism. A new emphasis on commerce as a means of achieving national wealth was matched in certain quarters by a desire to reinterpret Confucianism and turn it into a progressive philosophy or even an organized religion. Even more surprising, radical Confucianists wanted to eliminate China's Confucian examination system and institute a parliamentary, constitutional monarchy, while some of their opponents (or the radical Confucianists themselves, at a different stage) called for revolution and the establishment of a republican democracy. Whatever their means—or ends—the growing number of activists agreed that for China to survive and resume her rightful place in the world, fundamental changes were necessary in the body politic, changes leading in the direction of wealth, power, and broader political participation.

Parallel to these political and intellectual developments, China's traditional social system was changing and being redefined. This should be qualified: there was little net effect on the social status of the peasant in China's hinterland, other than a tendency for the gap between the haves and have-nots to become greater; but the peasant at this point had little to do with directing or refusing change. More significantly for our purposes, the social status of both commerce and the people involved in commercial and industrial activities were rising as it became clear that Western technology and Western manufactures, from weapons to cotton thread, were keys to Western strength. Furthermore, it now became socially acceptable to study and promote the development of military science, good generalship, and a modern army. Formerly marginal or even nonexistent groups now found themselves increasingly influential, and this was to have a profound effect on political development. For example, overseas Chinese—Chinese who sojourned abroad as laborers, merchants, or (especially after 1900) students—found new acceptance upon their return to China. Many of the students obtained jobs in the bureaucracy or the New Army after their return. Merchants, in their travels between China and their overseas businesses, discovered that their wealth and expertise were now valued, and their social prestige noticeably enhanced. Even returned laborers found that their ideas had an audience, often among the more progressive leaders of secret societies such as the Triads. Significantly, part of what the overseas Chinese brought back with them included new ideas with respect to the rights of citizens and the duties of government. The same tended to be true of "treaty-port Chinese"—Chinese residents of the ports of international trade along China's coast, opened up by Western nations through force of arms.

Of even greater importance, the traditional Confucian literati-gentry class, which staffed most of the government bureaucracy, began to change. As time passed, led by men like K'ang and Liang, more and more literati began to question and even challenge the existing order. As early as the Taiping Rebellion (1850–1864), literati ties to the court and to the traditional Confucian state had begun to weaken as a result of regionalism and localism. After the Chinese defeat in the Sino-Japanese War of 1895, progressive literati and even members of the imperial household criticized the Confucian examination system, and finally, in 1905, this system was permanently eliminated. The literati also began increasingly to take modern military and commercial developments seriously, and there was a growing feeling among them that the Manchurian rulers had an absolute obligation to provide the Han Chinese literati with an institutionalized means of expressing their views on government policy. A major thrust of the policy they desired to see implemented was a reassertion of national rights and a rejection of the special privileges that foreigners had extracted from China through the "unequal treaties" and the like. The imperial household sought to keep these movements within the existing framework of government, but the literati increasingly developed a willingness to go beyond it.

It was under these circumstances that some of the more radical Chinese political leaders, seeking safety, allies, funds, and other kinds of support, found themselves traveling to the Americas. The majority of Chinese in the Americas lacked a traditional Chinese education, and, to a certain degree, the Chinese political leaders who came to the Americas tailored their message to fit their audience. Sun Yat-sen, for example, talked little of his hoped-for party tutelage while in the Americas since the major Triad group there, upon which Sun had to depend, desired to become a political party in its own right. Liang Ch'i-ch'ao found his interest in revolution stimulated when he encountered prorevolutionary Pao-huang hui members in Canada in 1903. As early as 1899, K'ang Yu-wei claimed that the Pao-huang hui could help alleviate American mistreatment of overseas Chinese and would also bring material riches to party members.

As suggested above, the rise of the political parties within the favorable American environment had a truly profound effect upon Chinatown social organizations. A few examples will illustrate this point. By 1911, America's Triad organizations had become permanently politicized. A boycott declared by the largest and most powerful *hui-kuan* was first publicly flouted by hundreds of ordinary members, and then had to be called off and an apology issued. Old-style merchant guilds were superseded by Chinese chambers of commerce. Girls and women began to acquire more and better education. Personal habits changed. Many such innovations were influenced by the American environment, but all were precipitated by the activities of the political parties and had their origins in China.

There were, nonetheless, limits to both political movements and social change in the Chinatowns of that era. The dependence upon events in China could have a disastrous effect. For example, when in mid-1912 the political revolution in China ended with the militarist Yüan Shih-k'ai in control, radical democrats in American Chinatowns lost their grip over the local social organizations. These radical democrats had used methods (such as mass voting) new to the Chinatowns when they seized control, and their opponents were now strengthened by the conservative trend in China. Still, there was a slow but perceptible advance of new ideas even after the setback in 1912, thanks to the events of the preceding eighteen years.

Other aspects of the close association between Chinese politics in the Americas and politics in China also bear mention. Sun Yat-sen, for example, called overseas Chinese "the mother of the [Chinese] revolution." Chinese in the Americas certainly provided their share, financially speaking. Money from the Americas was especially important to an uprising in China in 1903 and again to the major efforts of 1910–1911. Huang Hsing's attempted coup in Canton in April of 1911 would not even have been possible without the financial

contributions of Chinese in North America. Going beyond uprisings, Chinese in the Americas contributed very large sums of money
for railroads, banks, mining ventures, land-reclamation projects,
steamship lines, and other modernization schemes in China, especially in Kwangtung province.

Finally, Chinese politics in the Americas of this period demonstrates the potential that Chinese had for political development along
liberal, democratic lines. From the point of view of Chinese history,
the competition among the several political groups in the Americas
underscores the importance of good organization and provides
another opportunity to examine the social and political implications
of the proposed alternatives, albeit in their Americanized forms.
This study thus crosses the Pacific and is offered as a contribution to
the history of Chinese in the Americas, of modern China, and of the
political and human relations between China and the Americas. It
invites comparison with similar situations in Southeast Asia and
other places where the Chinese were—and still are—to be found.

CHINESE IN THE AMERICAS

A number of factors made Chinese communities in the Americas potentially receptive to national (Chinese) political parties and to the reform and revolutionary politics that these parties espoused. Because of the discrimination that Chinese encountered in the Americas, coupled by the relative inattention of the Chinese government, overseas Chinese in the Americas were dissatisfied with their situation. However, they enjoyed somewhat greater political freedom than Chinese elsewhere, a circumstance which made it easier for them to express this dissatisfaction.

Their relative isolation from the American environment and political process ensured that Chinese in the Americas would focus their political concerns on China rather than on the American country of residence. For the most part, these immigrants intended their residence in the New World to be temporary. Their relatives usually remained behind in China, and with few exceptions the countries to which they immigrated denied them citizenship.[1] A multitude of discriminatory laws severely limited their economic and social opportunities, and the overwhelming majority of the immigrants were unfamiliar with the language and customs of the countries in which they resided.

At the same time, they were tremendously dissatisfied with the failure of the Chinese government to come to their aid. In 1880, a weak and somewhat reluctant China had been pressured by the United States into accepting a treaty permitting the suspension of the immigration of Chinese laborers into the United States. The treaty also denied Chinese the right of naturalization. Within the next two years, Congress passed a series of Chinese Exclusion laws to implement both of the above, laws due to expire in ten years. In 1892, Congress extended these laws over the objections of the Chinese government, and they were extended again in 1902. The blatant

7

racism of the treaty and laws was made even worse by the way in which they were interpreted. American immigration officials decided to exclude not only laborers, but all classes of Chinese not specifically granted the right of entry by the treaty—that is to say, all Chinese except diplomats, students, merchants and "travelers," or tourists. Furthermore, immigration officials intentionally made it a requirement to provide an almost impossibly high level of proof prior to granting entry to Chinese claiming to be members of one of the exempt classes.[2]

Contributing to China's inability to promote the interest of her citizens in an international context was her relative inexperience with the demands of modern international law. This could be seen, for example, in her failure to provide adequate diplomatic representation in the Americas. During the period in question, China had only one high-ranking official (the Minister to Washington) for the entire hemisphere. There were, it is true, consuls in Honolulu, San Francisco, New York, and (after 1908) in Ottowa, each with a small staff, but this level of representation was not sufficient for the task at hand. Since the right of these officials to "police" the Chinese communities was not clearly defined, the communities were able to develop, and were able to express their dissatisfaction, with a minimum of outside interference or direction.

Accidents of circumstance ensured that Chinese political organizers would take advantage of this situation. K'ang Yu-wei, Liang Ch'i-ch'ao, and Sun Yat-sen had to flee China between 1895 and 1898, and their exile forced them to pay attention to overseas Chinese. Furthermore, in addition to the points already noted, several aspects of the development of the Chinese communities in Hawaii and North America (and, to a lesser extent, Latin America) made these communities particularly attractive, although they also imposed tactical considerations on the operations of the political organizers.

Population Figures, Immigration, and Employment Conditions

By 1893, Hawaii and North America had a substantial and accessible Chinese population. Both areas were on a well-frequented shipping lane that stretched from East Asia to the Americas, and in North America the Chinese lived in cities that were linked by rail. A few figures will give a general demographic picture. In 1900, there were 119,050 Chinese in the United States, excluding the Philippines; about one-fifth (25,767) of these lived in Hawaii and one-half (67,729) lived in the western states. Of those in the western states, 45,753 lived in California, 10,396 in Oregon, and 3,629 in the state of Washington. The only East Coast state with a sizable Chinese population was New York; in 1903, Liang Ch'i-ch'ao said that 20,000 Chinese lived there, of whom 15,000 were in New York City and Buffalo combined.[3] In Hawaii, the Chinese population was concentrated on the island of Oahu, where there were more than 17,000.[4] According to Liang's 1903 figures, among the major cities San Francisco and its immediate environs had 30,000 Chinese residents, close to ten percent of the total population of that area. Several thousand Chinese also lived in Portland (10,000), New York City (8,000), Los Angeles, Boston, Chicago, and Seattle.[5]

Liang also estimated in 1903 that the Chinese population of Canada was 19,000; almost two-thirds lived in a small area of British Columbia on Canada's west coast, in or near the cities of Victoria, Vancouver, and New Westminster. In fact, Vancouver and Victoria together housed 9,000 Chinese, almost half the total Chinese population of Canada. A few thousand more lived in New Westminster and in the rural areas of nearby Vancouver Island. Between 2,000 and 3,000 Chinese lived on Canada's east coast, principally in Montreal and Quebec.[6]

Immigration restrictions and communications problems made Chinese in Latin America more difficult to reach, but if a political organizer made the trip, he could be rewarded with a sizable audience. Mexico's Chinese population was over 10,000 and still growing at this time. It was concentrated in Mexico City and the Torreón area.[7] And in 1911, there were some 15,000 Chinese in Peru, while several thousand more lived in Cuba.[8]

The overwhelming majority of these immigrants were adult males. Most were Cantonese: people who came from the city of Canton or its Pearl River delta hinterland, in the southern coastal province of Kwangtung. About ninety percent of this group in North America were Punti Cantonese. The next largest group was the Hsiang-shan, and the remainder were Hakka from Kwangtung.

In Hawaii, probably close to sixty-five percent were Punti, with Hakka coming next, followed by a considerable Hsiang-shan community. In Latin America, there seem to have been somewhat fewer Puntis and even more Hakkas.[9] Finally, in North America, there were also a few Chinese from outside of Kwangtung, four hundred to five hundred at most, principally students on government stipend.[10]

The preponderance of Cantonese in America held particular appeal for the political leaders, since K'ang, Liang, and Sun were also from Kwangtung. K'ang and Liang had the further advantage of being Punti. The unbalanced sex ratio may also have helped the political leaders since in China, adult males were supposed to be the decision makers. The small number of students and a dearth of gentry meant that literati such as K'ang and Liang could expect to be accorded great respect. It also meant that they would have to find issues that reached beyond gentry and student concerns if they were to win large numbers of adherents in the Americas.

From a purely logistical standpoint, by following the most convenient route from East Asia and staying on the main travel arteries, a political leader could reach over one-half of all Chinese in the Americas. This route was first by steamer to Honolulu and then to Vancouver/Victoria; then by rail from Vancouver/Victoria to Los Angeles (passing through Seattle, Portland, and San Francisco/Oakland), and back again from Los Angeles to San Francisco, before finally returning by steamer to East Asia. If the political leader added on a train trip across Canada, down to New York, and back across the United States, he could reach an additional 25,000 to 27,000 Chinese, bringing the total to about two-thirds of the Chinese in the Americas.

Not surprisingly, traveling political leaders usually followed one or the other of these routes. This meant largely ignoring Latin America: Peru was too far away, and on a different shipping route. K'ang Yu-wei was the only major leader to go to Mexico, and although he did involve himself in political activities there, the principal reason for those trips seems to have been to exploit certain financial opportunities which presented themselves. For the most part, as far as the political leaders were concerned, Latin America remained a backwater.

I should point out that the heavy urban concentration of the Chinese, which made the Americas a fruitful field for political organizations, was fortuitous. In the early days of immigration, many Chinese lived in the hinterland: in mining and railroad construction camps, agricultural areas, fishing villages, and the like. Between the 1880s and 1890s, however, most Chinese in North America moved to the cities because of changes in employment opportunities and the hostility of the indigenous population. In the cities, they were crowded into Chinatowns. Not surprisingly, by the turn of the century these Chinatowns supported a complex and dynamic social structure. To some extent, this facilitated the task of the political leaders. On the other hand, it also meant that these leaders had to compete with preexisting social organizations for the loyalty of the Chinese immigrants.

Chinese had begun immigrating to the Americas in large numbers between the late 1840s and mid-1850s. This first wave of immigration was as much the result of events in China as of developments in the Americas. Difficulties in China, which included severe economic hardship, the Taiping Rebellion of 1850–1864, the Red Turban revolt, and the Hakka-Punti wars in Kwangtung province, occurred roughly during the same period when there was an increasing demand for labor in the New World, and just as gold was discovered in California.[11] The Chinese who came to the New World did not intend their stay to be permanent, but the continuing instability in their motherland, the difficulty and expense of the return trip, and the obstacles to possible future reentry into the American countries (of which the notorious United States Chinese Exclusion laws provide only one example) eventually led about half to settle permanently in the Americas.[12]

The economic situation of Chinese living in the Americas was a matter of great concern to their political leaders. Although overseas Chinese contributed more than just money to political causes, K'ang, Liang, and Sun thought of them primarily as a source of income. Very few of the immigrants were wealthy, however, and many were quite poor. Most had had to borrow money to get to the Americas and spent the first several months, or even years, after their arrival simply paying off the debt. Many of those who went to Cuba and Peru had been kidnapped and placed aboard ships in Canton and (prior to 1877 when slavery was abolished) became slaves on their arrival. In general, non-Chinese businessmen in the Americas hired Chinese only as unskilled or semiskilled laborers;[13] more-over, individual initiative on the part of the workers was not gener-ally encouraged. The California gold rush was one of the exceptions to this rule.

By 1893, Chinese immigrants had to a great extent managed to rise above the unenviable condition they found themselves in on their arrival. However, most were still plagued by a dearth of capi-tal, an ignorance of the language of the country in which they lived, and, perhaps even more importantly, by the prejudice directed against them. Furthermore, they were subject to immigration re-strictions and laws designed to limit their economic opportunities.[14]

In Canada, around the turn of the century, at least eighty percent of the Chinese were laborers, and some fifty percent of the laborers in the Vancouver/Victoria/New Westminster area were unem-ployed. Chinese merchants, who depended on the spending power of these laborers, led a somewhat precarious existence. The most reliable source of wealth came from gambling and from smuggling opium and other Chinese across the border into the United States. Not everyone desired to engage in such occupations, and among those who did, only a few actually became wealthy from them.[15]

In the United States, in spite of all the restrictions, the level of unemployment was probably about fifteen percent, much lower than in Canada. But here again, as can be seen from Table 1, the major-ity were laundry workers, peddlers, fishermen, cooks in the homes of non-Chinese, waiters in Chinese restaurants, and clerks in Chi-nese stores. As in Canada, with few exceptions the proprietors of these stores depended upon the Chinese community for most of their business. Hawaii presented a more cheerful picture, largely due to the more amicable relations there between the three major ethnic groups (Chinese, Caucasian American, and Hawaiian), which per-mitted greater upward mobility for Chinese. The Chinese middle class was relatively large and more financially secure, but even in Hawaii, probably more than half of the Chinese were poor since they were agricultural laborers.[16]

In Mexico, Chinese were originally brought in to help build rail-roads. By the turn of the century, some were also working under contract as miners, while others formed associations to open up new agricultural land, and still others were engaged in banking, real

TABLE I
Means of Employment of Chinese in the
Continental United States, 1893–1911

Means of employment	Approximate number of people involved	Percent of Chinese in the continental United States
Laundry proprietors and employees	40,000	33.3%
Factory workers		
Canneries	15,000	12.5
Other	2,500	2.1
Shop owners and employees		
General stores	6,500	5.5
Clothing shops	3,000	2.5
Restaurant proprietors and employees	5,500	4.6
Farmers and agricultural laborers	4,500	3.8
Fishermen	3,000	2.5
Cooks and houseboys	2,000	1.7
Translators	500	.4
Medical doctors/practitioners	200	.17
Missionaries, pastors, priests	200	.17
Students	200	.17
Women	2,000	1.7
Children	3,000	2.5
Unemployed	10,000	8.3
Unknown (including more unemployed, gamblers, smugglers)	21,900	18
TOTAL	120,000	99.9

PRINCIPAL SOURCE: Liang Ch'i-ch'ao, *Hsin-ta-lu yu-chi*, pp. 392–393.

estate speculation, and the like. The standard of living of the majority was undoubtedly lower than these few examples might imply, but was probably about equal to that of the other inhabitants of Mexico.[17] In Cuba, a few Chinese had begun to go out and clear their own farms by 1900. In both Cuba and Peru, the Chinese communities' general economic situation was probably similar to that in Mexico, with perhaps fewer entrepreneurs.[18]

In order for the political leaders to tap what wealth there was, two possible approaches suggested themselves: seek to obtain large sums of money from the small number of wealthy Chinese, or try to persuade the far more numerous poor laborers, struggling shopkeepers, and laundrymen to contribute one or two dollars. Both the revolutionary and the reform parties tried both approaches with varying success.

Inside the Chinese Communities

Preexisting social organizations in America's Chinatowns had a profound influence upon the nascent political parties, helping to define the constituencies of these parties, their organizational alternatives, and even some of their political goals. Chinese communities in the Americas did not have a monolithic, or even a static, social structure. Several types of organizations had been competing for community leadership long before the political parties were founded. This competition had already engendered a gradual increase in the number of social organizations as well as periodic changes in the social balance. The fact that these preexisting social organizations performed quasi-political functions directed towards local concerns was itself a significant influence upon the political parties.

Elsewhere the history and functioning of these organizations has been described in some detail.[19] They may be divided into two different types, distinguished primarily on the basis of eligibility for membership. Organizations of the first type had a membership that was determined by accident of birth; these may be called organizations with restrictive entrance requirements. They included primarily the *hui-kuan* (or regional associations), the Chinese Six Companies and related *hui-kuan* federations, and the surname associations (family associations).

Organizations of the second type had a membership based primarily on occupation or personal choice. These may be called organizations with open membership requirements. They included the Christians, the merchant guilds, and the Triad secret societies. All of these groups, with either restrictive or open membership requirements, represented variations on organizations to be found in China.

Organizations with Restrictive Membership Requirements

By the 1890s, about ninety-five percent of the Chinese in the Americas belonged to *hui-kuan*. Moreover, throughout the Americas, in major centers of Chinese population, the regional associations would organize a federation. San Francisco's Chung-hua tsung hui-kuan (Chinese Consolidated Benevolent Association, called the Chinese Six Companies) is the most famous and has probably been the most powerful of these. It dates from the 1850s. San Francisco's *hui-kuan* and their federation, the Six Companies, early became the most influential of the Chinese organizations in the Americas. This was due in part to their partial control over the ability of immigrants to return to China.[20]

As was the case with certain of the *hui-kuan* in China,[21] America's *hui-kuan* provided many important social services. Most shipped the bones of deceased members back to China for proper burial (a service the immigrants regarded as extremely important). *Hui-kuan* also helped members find jobs, extended them credit when money was available, and maintained hostels in various American communities where transient members could stay for a small fee. Each *hui-kuan* also defended the interests of its members against nonmembers, whether Chinese or white American.[22]

Members of one *hui-kuan* needed protection against members of the others because Chinese from one region in China regarded those from other regions as potential enemies. These regional distinctions were often underlined by significant differences in the dialect spoken. The "regions" themselves were often very small in the geographic sense. *Hui-kuan,* organized along regional lines, institutionalized the regional distinctions and antagonisms. More than ninety-five percent of the Chinese in the Americas came from the city of Canton or its surrounding area. However, they divided themselves into three major regional groupings related to this relatively small area: Hakka, Hsiang-shan, and Punti. The Punti were further subdivided into *Szu-i* (Sai Yap, Szu Yup, or Four Districts) and *San-i* (Sam Yup, or Three Districts). The *San-i* early founded a San-i hui-kuan in San Francisco and, by the 1880s, in Victoria (British Columbia) as well. The *Szu-i* founded many *hui-kuan* in the Americas, the most important of which was the Ning-yang hui-kuan (today's T'ai-shan hui-kuan, or Toi-shan Association) in San Francisco. A similar

TABLE 2
Hui-kuan of the Continental United States, 1893–1911

Hui-kuan name	Members' area of origin
Yang-ho (Yeung Hop)	Hsiang-shan (Heung-shan, modern-day Chung-shan)
Ts'ao-ch'ing	Ts'ao-ch'ing prefecture except those from Hsin-ning district (modern T'ai-shan, or T'oi-shan)
En-k'ai (Yen Hoi)	En-p'ing and K'ai-p'ing (Hoi-ping)
Kang-chou (Kong Chow)	Hsin-hui (Sunwui) and Ho-shan
Ning-yang (Ning Yeung)	Hsin-ning (T'ai-shan) district except those of the Yü (Yee) surname
Ho-ho (Hop Wo)	Yü (Yee) surname of Hsin-ning district plus the Wangs of K'ai-p'ing (Hoi-ping)
Szu-i (Ssu Yap)	*Szu-i* people who were not members of the Ts'ao-ch'ing, Hsin-ning, Ho-ho, En-k'ai or Kang-chou *hui-kuan*
San-i (Sam Yap)	*San-i* districts (Nan-hai, P'an-yü, Shun-te)
Jen-ho (Yan Hop)	Hakkas

Sources: Liang Ch'i-ch'ao, *Hsin-ta-lu yu-chi,* pp. 386–387, and Chinn, Lai, and Choy, *History of the Chinese in California,* pp. 2–4.

Ning-yang association was founded in Victoria in the mid-1870s, but by the turn of the century the Vancouver branch of this organization had become more influential. Hakkas established the rather unimportant Jen-ho hui-kuan in San Francisco and in Victoria, along with a more important *hui-kuan* in Hawaii whose name is not known to us. Finally, Hsiang-shan people founded the Yang-ho hui-kuan of San Francisco.[23]

At the turn of the century, about ninety percent of the Cantonese immigrants in North America and seventy to eighty percent of those in Hawaii came from one of the groups mentioned above. Two-thirds were *Szu-i* and somewhat less than one-third were *San-i*. As a group, the *San-i* were the wealthiest and had the best business connections back in China. The *Szu-i* compensated for this by numbers and, by the late 1890s, had started operating big businesses of their own. The Hsiang-shan (often considered *Szu-i*) and the Hakka were small in numbers and relatively uninfluential in North America. However, there were significantly more Hakkas in Hawaii, where they did enjoy some power in the community.[24] Of the major political leaders, K'ang Yu-wei was a *San-i*. Liang Ch'i-ch'ao was a *Szu-i,* and Sun Yat-sen was a Hakka (a fact known in the Americas since he joined the Hakka Triad lodge in Hawaii in 1903).[25]

The *hui-kuan* also protected their members against individual (white) Americans and from the several American governments. Most whites were violently prejudiced against Chinese, and the Chinese government did not offer the immigrants much protection during this period, since it was more concerned with developments at home. The very number of *hui-kuan* made it difficult for them to present a unified front to white Americans, however. To overcome this difficulty, in the latter part of the 1850s, the *hui-kuan* in California established an umbrella organization called the Chinese Six Companies (Chung-hua tsung hui-kuan) to speak for the Chinese community. By the turn of the century, the Six Companies was generally accepted by Americans as the voice of all Chinese in the United States. In addition, the Six Companies helped resolve conflicts between the various Chinatown groups. Although many Americans regarded it as a government within a government, the Six Companies did recognize the superior authority of United States governmental organs in many types of cases.

The Six Companies attempted to be an island bastion of Chinese orthodoxy in the sea of the American environment. Its orthodoxy owed much to the practice of the regional associations of importing scholarly notables from China to act as *hui-kuan* presidents. (They were even able to obtain an occasional *chin-shih*.)[26] Many of the officers of the Six Companies were chosen from among the "imported" *hui-kuan* presidents. To encourage this practice, from the late 1880s the Ch'ing consul in San Francisco maintained an advisory board consisting of the imported *hui-kuan* notables, and established a traditional-style Chinese academy (Ta Ch'ing shu-yüan) in San Francisco, evidently staffed at least in part by these same notables. (Partly in response, by the early 1900s, the imported *hui-kuan* officials became involved in campaigns to solicit money from the Americas for educational institutions, capitalistic ventures, and famine relief in China.)[27] Thus, ideologically speaking, the Six Companies and the *hui-kuan* underscored the importance of the Confucian tradition and the examination system. They also helped strengthen the tie between the overseas Chinese and the Ch'ing government.

The Chinese Six Companies also institutionalized the actual

power structure. The labor contract and the credit-ticket systems were primary means through which Chinese obtained money for the passage to the Americas.[28] Through these systems, wealthy overseas (Chinese) businessmen with good social and commercial contacts back in China ("Kapitan China") located people in China who needed jobs. Then, they either arranged for them to sign a contract to work in the Americas for several years, or lent them enough money to purchase their passage. Sometimes, businessmen in the Americas simply acted as agent of the creditor (where the creditor resided in China).[29] Many American businessmen routinely approached the Kapitan China or his agents when they needed Chinese laborers. The Kapitan China in the Americas were highly respected by their fellow countrymen in the overseas communities. The Chinese-language press there called them "gentry merchants" *(shen-shang)*. The anti-Chinese movement in the United States hampered the efforts and lessened the influence of these Kapitan China after the mid-1880s, but they still had the wealth to be a major source of credit and to contribute generously to causes of community concern. Hence, although the *hui-kuan* and Six Companies were headed by imported notables, the middle rank of officers in both types of organizations were staffed by the Kapitan China.[30]

In the Six Companies, official position was normally reserved for the wealthy. Up until around 1900, the most important officers were usually *San-i* men because they dominated the important and lucrative import-export trade.[31] This trade included the transfer of cash remittances of Chinese in North America to their families back in China.[32] By the late 1890s, however, *Szu-i* merchants in the United States had begun to enter the import-export trade and to found major businesses and manufacturing concerns in the Americas.[33] This helped break *San-i* dominance of the Six Companies. Shortly after the turn of the century, the *Szu-i* forced the *San-i* to agree that the privilege of selecting the presidents of the Six Companies should rotate every three months among all the member *hui-kuan* (with the exception of the Hakka's Jen-ho hui-kuan, which was considered "too small").[34]

To clarify the Six Companies' new method of functioning, it drafted a new set of rules modeled on those of the United States during the federal period. By 1903, the *hui-kuan* had also drafted organizational rules patterned after the American model, which included the annual election of officers.[35] In spite of this, and in contravention of the decision to rotate the presidency of the Six Companies, from 1901 through mid-1903 only two of the *hui-kuan* (the San-i hui-kuan and the Ho-ho hui-kuan of people with the surname Yü) rotated the presidency of the Six Companies back and forth between themselves.[36]

The Six Companies had other shortcomings. Many *hui-kuan* officers were corrupt. Some were leaders of "fighting tongs" and maintained power in part through threat of violence.[37] This, naturally, spilled over into the councils of the Six Companies. In addition, the *hui-kuan* deliberately limited the power of the Six Companies in a number of ways. Most importantly, the Six Companies depended upon them for much of its finances. *Hui-kuan* sometimes refused to pay their allotted contribution in order to make a point.[38]

Still, at the turn of the century, San Francisco's Chinese Six Companies was formally acknowledged by most other Chinese organizations in the Americas as their official voice. Nonetheless, the Chinese communities in Canada, Hawaii, and several of the Latin American countries also had umbrella organizations which bore the name Chung-hua hui-kuan, to which their *hui-kuan* belonged and to which they paid more attention.[39] None of these rival Chung-hua hui-kuan dared use the all-inclusive term of *tsung* (all, chief), however.

The Chinese Six Companies performed a number of specific functions. It frequently acted as a soliciting and collecting organization: raising funds for disaster relief in Kwangtung, helping to finance a new library in Canton, and so forth. When major discriminatory legislation was pending, it conveyed the objections of the entire Chinese community to the relevant authorities or launched test cases to overturn the legislation. It made various attempts at avoiding friction between Chinese and Americans, establishing its own police force to protect San Francisco's Chinatown, and occasionally reprimanding those it thought had been cheating Westerners. It founded a school in San Francisco to teach Chinese "language, history, and philosophy," organized a Chinese hospital in the same city, and up until 1907, when the Chinese Chamber of Commerce was founded, it acted as witness to commercial contracts between Chinese in northern California.[40]

In addition to the *hui-kuan*/Six Companies, there was a second

major type of organization with restrictive membership requirements: surname associations ("family associations"). These reserved membership for all people of one or more particular surnames. The largest number of surnames in any given association
in the Americas was four. These associations appeared first and
were most prominent in North America. The earliest was the
multisurname So-yüan t'ang (Soo Yuen Benevolent Association),
founded in California in 1859.[41] Most of North America's surname
associations, however, were organized between 1870 and the mid-
1890s. Some of the more important ones were Ma (Mar) of Canada,
Li (Lee) and Huang (Wong) of the continental United States, and
the multisurname Lung-kang ch'in-i kung-so (Loong Kong Tin
Yee, or Four Brothers, Association) of Canada and the United
States, which united four surnames.[42] By the turn of the century,
most Chinese in the continental United States had joined a surname
association, as had many in Canada, Hawaii, and Mexico. They
were especially popular among *Szu-i* people. Liang Ch'i-ch'ao, who
traveled to North America in 1903, found twenty-four separate single
surname associations there at that time, the two biggest being the
associations for the Lis and the Huangs. The Liangs also had a large
association, but, interestingly enough, the surnames Sun (Sun Yat-
sen's surname) and K'ang (K'ang Yu-wei's surname) had none.[43]

In 1903, Liang also listed nine multisurname associations of which
the most important were the aforementioned Lung-kang ch'in-i
kung-so (extending up into Canada, down into Mexico, across the
continental United States, and possibly even into southern China)[44]
and the So-yüan t'ang of the continental United States. Interestingly, some of the groups which belonged to multisurname associations also had a surname association reserved for their own individual surnames. Most of the larger multisurname groupings claimed a
common ancestor in spite of their different names, and members of
constituent groups considered each other blood relatives.[45]

Many of the functions undertaken by the surname associations
were the same as those undertaken by the *hui-kuan*. They maintained
hostels for members and helped in the securing of jobs and loans.
They were supposed to defend their members against all comers,
and to that end, around the turn of the century, they organized
groups of young fighting men.[46] Surname associations, however,
had no control over Chinese returning to China, nor did they send

the bones of dead kinsmen back. And they had much less influence with Americans than did the *hui-kuan* through the Six Companies.

Surname associations cut across the membership of the regional associations. In China, the surname connection would probably have been accorded precedence—certainly so if a clan tie were involved. In the Americas, however, loyalty to the *hui-kuan* was often more important. Within the *hui-kuan*, however, surname affiliations were respected, and the privilege of choosing the president of the *hui-kuan* often rotated among the various internal surname units.[47]

The types of loyalties institutionalized by these organizations were important to the overseas Chinese. This was far more helpful to K'ang and Liang than it was to Sun: K'ang and Liang were Punti whereas Sun was Hakka. K'ang was a *San-i* man, the Liang surname was strong in North America, and so forth. Many other qualities that K'ang and Liang possessed also appealed to overseas Chinese in general and to the heads of the Six Companies and the *hui-kuan* in particular, such as their literary accomplishments and K'ang's interest in commerce and capitalism. Nor surprisingly, K'ang and Liang devoted great attention to these groups, and the Pao-huang hui attempted to entrench itself in them.

Organizations with Open Membership Requirements

There were several organizations in the overseas communities in which membership was more a matter of choice, and less determined by accident of birth. The most important of these were the Chinese Christians, the merchant guilds, and the secret societies. The proportion of overseas Chinese who were either Christian or belonged to a merchant guild was relatively small. But their influence was far greater than their numbers. Members of the merchant guilds (the Kapitan China) were a major economic force in the Chinese communities and, in the early years, a source of credit for the money required to get to the Americas. The Christian community included many of the most politically articulate and reform-minded of the overseas Chinese. Christians also frequently acted as interpreters of the Chinese community to the rest of America, and helped defend Chinese against Americans.

The secret societies, and particularly the Triad Chih-kung t'ang (or Chee Kong Tong), were important both because of their large membership and because of their functions. Like the *hui-kuan* and surname associations, the Chih-kung t'ang and affiliated lodges maintained hostels in various communities where members could find a place to sleep and food to eat. In addition, in certain localities and industries, jobs were reserved for the lodge brother. Just as importantly, however, the Triad lodge helped replace the family that the immigrant had left behind in China: surname associations, which might have fulfilled this need, failed at times because members were often not relatives in any meaningful sense of the word. In the secret society lodge, on the other hand, all were sworn brothers by choice and bound by oath to help and protect each other. Because of the complexity of the secret societies, we shall examine the Christians and merchant guilds first, saving the secret societies for last.

Adherence to a religion does not always constitute membership in a definite social group, but Chinese Christians were left by themselves and by the rest of the Chinese community to form a distinct social "organization." This feeling was unique to the Christians and was not manifest in the worshippers at surname shrines or Chinese temples in the Americas. Hence, for example, Chinese language works invariably called San Francisco's *Chung Sai Yat Po* (East-West News) a Christian newspaper.[48] This did not mean that the newspaper attempted to proselytize, which it did not. It meant that the entire staff from owner-manager to press runners were Christian, and the newspaper was convinced that it portrayed the political and social ideas shared by all of America's Chinese Christians.

Since Protestant Christians were more vigorous in their missionary efforts among Chinese in the Americas, Chinese Christians were far more important and numerous in North America and Hawaii than in Catholic Latin America. In North America and Hawaii, the Presbyterians, Baptists, Episcopalians, and Methodists had organized congregations in the Chinese community. Of these the Presbyterians were the most active. At first, missionaries and preachers were all white Americans, but by the turn of the century, these were rapidly being replaced by Chinese. There were only a few churches, however, principally in the San Francisco Bay area and around Los Angeles, Sacramento, New York, Honolulu, and Vancouver/Victoria. The congregations were small, consisting of anywhere from ten to fifty members, mostly adult men. Most of these churches also offered free instruction in written Chinese and in spoken and written English to both adults and children, a most important social service for a community dominated by the few people who either spoke English or could afford an interpreter.[49]

Another kind of major social organization was the merchant guild. In some cities, such as Victoria, a type of merchant association ran the entire Chinese community during the first few years of the Chinese settlement. Following San Francisco's lead, however, by the 1880s these had faded away and were replaced by the more purely commercial merchant guilds.[50] By the turn of the century, North America had two merchant guilds, each with independent branches in important commercial cities: the Shao-i kung-so (Shew Hing Association) for *San-i* merchants and the *Szu-i*-dominated K'o-shang hui-kuan (Guest Businessmen's Association), or Szu-i K'o-shang hui-kuan.[51]

Both of these guilds were rather traditional types of organizations, tied to the *hui-kuan* and conservative regionalism. Prior to the late 1890s, neither the guilds as a whole nor individual merchants within them engaged in any extensive capitalist endeavors, although there were some very large and lucrative businesses. Instead, the principal types of commercial endeavor were moneylending, the import-export business, investing in gambling and similar operations, and opening small shops (laundries, small groceries, and the like). Furthermore, wealthy businessmen generally preferred to use their excess capital for the benefit of the associations they belonged to and/or to buy property in Kwangtung, to hoard, or to help their villages and clans back in China.[52] Thus, at the turn of the century, the guilds were still a powerful center of traditionalism.

Secret societies were probably even more important than the Christians and the merchant guilds. They were widespread and a powerful force in the Americas, a force the political leaders could not ignore. The ideals of the secret societies bore many of the hallmarks that political parties are supposed to embody: they purported to transcend wealth, social class, family, and regional and "ethnic" divisions. They were a voluntary type of organization whose members theoretically were united by common aspirations. And the secret society Triads claimed the quasi-political aim of overthrowing the Ch'ing and restoring the Ming. Not surprisingly, the political parties early found themselves entangled in the secret societies. To a certain extent one can even say that the political parties were modeled on them.

Probably all, and certainly the overwhelming majority, of the Chinese secret societies operating in the Americas at the turn of the century, were offshoots of the Triads (also called San-ho hui, San-tien hui, T'ien-ti hui, I-hsing hui, Hung-shun t'ang, and Hung-men) in China. In a larger sense, to be a Triad member meant having passed through a certain initiation ritual in which one swore brotherhood to other members and also swore to overthrow the Ch'ing dynasty and restore the rule of the Ming.

By the late nineteenth and early twentieth centuries, the Triads emphasized the bond of brotherhood more than the aim of restoring the Ming dynasty. Anti-Manchuism, however (and/or feelings of antagonism toward the Chinese government and its officials), remained strong among them. Although proscribed by the government, Triad lodges were endemic in South China. They were also found among overseas Chinese in Southeast Asia, Australia, and, of course, the Americas. Liang Ch'i-ch'ao and Feng Tzu-yu, both of whom traveled to the Americas around the turn of the century and who had earlier been initiated into the society, estimated that somewhere between seventy and ninety percent of the Chinese in North America and Hawaii were members.[53] It may be presumed that a considerable portion of Chinese in Latin America belonged as well.

In North America the membership consisted primarily of *Szu-i* laborers, almost exclusively men. It had as members some Christians,[54] a few of the wealthy, and more of the middle-ranking merchants, and it included people of all regional backgrounds and many surnames. Lodge leaders within the same lodge usually had different surnames.[55] Lodge leaders were usually men of modest means who maintained their leadership by being sensitive to the needs of their members, rather than through direct economic domination or high social standing. The Triads in China had no central hierarchy, although there was a ranking system. Individual lodge members were usually people who shared common goals or grievances, or were simply interested persons of one small geographic area.

In the Americas, however, there was much greater centralization. Many "lodges" actually consisted of a head lodge (located in a major population center such as San Francisco, Honolulu, or Vancouver/Victoria) and sublodges scattered over a wide geographic area. In addition, at the turn of the century, one lodge (the Chih-kung t'ang) exercised a loose hegemony over all the others in North America. It was also acknowledged as leader by two of the three

Triad lodges in Hawaii and was actively involved in enlisting more lodges under its banner. The larger, inclusive organization can best be called the Chih-kung t'ang federation, to distinguish it from the Chih-kung t'ang lodge which headed it.[56]

The Chih-kung t'ang federation did not include any Triad lodge in Latin America until 1913 or all of the lodges in Hawaii until 1919, in part due to the enmity between Hakkas and Puntis. In Hawaii, for example, the Punti lodges joined the federation in 1892, whereas the Hakka lodge did not affiliate until 1919.[57] In addition, because of the distances involved as well as the large number of Hakkas in Latin America, the Triad lodges in Hawaii and Latin America developed independently of the Chih-kung t'ang, in contrast to the situation in North America. This meant that they could choose to join the federation or remain separate from it, instead of being automatically considered its members.[58]

The headquarters of the Chih-kung t'ang lodge and federation were located in San Francisco. From the turn of the century until the 1940s, the leader of both was a man named Huang San-te (Wong Sam Duck). Huang seems to have felt that his duties related to the Chih-kung t'ang alone required all of his attention, whereas many of the officers of the international headquarters were also the leaders of other, affiliated lodges. T'ang Ch'iung-ch'ang, for example, was an official in the An-i t'ang (On Yick Tong).[59] We shall encounter both of these men again when discussing K'ang, Liang, and Sun and their political parties.

The Chih-kung t'ang was an outgrowth of the first Triad lodge established in North America.[60] Federation leaders were usually *Szu-i* men from small surname groups, although by the 1890s, the rank and file included *San-i,* Hsiang-shan, and Hakkas, and people from large as well as small surname associations.[61] There were more than thirty lodges in the federation by the turn of the century. Lodges owed only limited obedience to the Chih-kung t'ang federation, although the federation was the only one with the right to conduct the official Triad initiation ritual. Hence all the members of affiliated lodges first had their names inscribed on the roles of the Chih-kung t'ang and only then with the lodge of their choice. In addition, the federation could collect certain fees from the members of the various lodges and was supposedly the arbitrator of conflicts between lodges.[62] With a few exceptions (such as affiliated lodges in Hawaii), headquarters of the member lodges, like federation headquarters, were located in San Francisco.[63]

In Canada, however, the Chih-kung t'ang lodge reigned supreme: there were no other Triad lodges. Canada's Chih-kung t'ang had branches throughout the country, and some time between 1886 and 1899 these Canadian branches set up their own semi-independent hierarchy in the Vancouver/Victoria area in defiance of the San Francisco headquarters. In Hawaii, two Triad lodges developed, one for Hakkas and one for Puntis. The Punti lodge later split into two and then three lodges, but there was no federation; and the three Punti lodges were reunited in 1892, at which time they affiliated with the Chih-kung t'ang.[64]

This rather elaborate organization differed significantly from the usual pattern in China, where fragmentation was the rule.[65] The relative centralization characteristic of the Americas was a result of various circumstances. Financial considerations and American policy drastically limited the number of Chinese women (and hence, of wives) who were able to come to America. Intermarriage with Americans was rare, so normally functioning family units were few and far between. The temporary nature of most forms of employment available to the immigrants, especially prior to 1880, made wanderers of the overseas Chinese and also taught them to change profession as dictated by circumstance. This situation, reinforced by other factors such as Triad entanglement with illegal pursuits (including smuggling Chinese into the United States) and even—according to one source—a surge of Red Turban refugees to the Americas in the 1860s,[66] gave the Chih-kung t'ang its original prominence.

After 1880, instability continued to beset the immigrants as employment opportunities diminished.[67] In North America the amount of discriminatory legislation directed against Chinese continued to grow, even as the Chinese Exclusion laws of the United States and various Canadian laws were directed at stemming the tide of immigration. During the last quarter of the nineteenth century, most Chinese in North America, except those who worked in agriculture, were physically driven from the countryside into urban areas by a hostile white population.[68] All of this helped perpetuate the unstable conditions and led to the continued flourishing of the Chih-kung t'ang and its affiliated lodges.

Because of the high rate of unemployment for Chinese in Canada, that country became something of a way station for Chinese wanting to enter the United States. Certain sublodges of the Chih-kung t'ang there specialized in smuggling Chinese across the border.[69] This probably accounts for the lack of independent lodges and the delayed organization of a federation in Canada: someone hoping to be smuggled across the border would scarcely attack the authority of the organization that was to do the smuggling.[70] This suggests in turn that the existence of independent lodges and the federation in the United States was an indication of greater social and economic freedom for Chinese there.

In Hawaii, so long as the Chinese population remained relatively small, there were only two lodges (one for each "ethnic" group) and no overarching organization. When the Punti population grew larger, its lodge split into several completely independent lodges. In 1892, however, the Punti lodges joined together into one large lodge (with sublodges) and later affiliated with the Chih-kung t'ang.

The Chih-kung t'ang federation contained two principal kinds of lodges: (1) "fighting tongs" and (2) all the others. "Fighting tongs" were the lodges which gained notoriety in the American press (and among local police departments) because of their proclivity toward violent disputes, which often resulted in "tong wars" and the killing of rival lodge members.[71] The total number of lodges which at any given time could legitimately be called "fighting tongs" seems to have been relatively small, perhaps six or eight at the most. They were usually involved in gambling, prostitution, opium smuggling, and (after Chinese Exclusion began in 1882) the smuggling of Chinese into the continental United States.[72] The popularity of gambling, the appreciation that people who were smuggled in often felt for the organization that assisted them, and the scarcity of respectable women available to the Chinese immigrants kept the illegal activities of the "fighting tongs" from appearing too distasteful; thus, many ordinary persons belonged to these lodges as well. As anti-Chinese sentiment began to interfere seriously with economic opportunity, the "fighting tongs" started quarreling over territory. These clashes, and, indeed, any fights within the Chinese community which involved physical violence, were referred to by Americans as "tong wars."[73]

"Fighting tongs" and "tong wars" were almost exclusively con-

fined to the continental United States. Several "tong wars" occurred there in the 1893–1911 period, particularly in 1901 and in 1910.[74]
In Canada there was far less violence, probably due to the poverty
which in turn made people anxious to be smuggled out of the country. This enabled the Chih-kung t'ang to maintain control. In
Hawaii, the lack of violence was due to low unemployment and the
greater degree of assimilation. Relations between Chinese, Hawaiians, and Americans in Hawaii were considerably more friendly
than between Chinese and others in the continental Americas. This
permitted some intermarriage and dual citizenship and also
minimized the isolation of the Chinese community. Low unemployment also meant that businessmen in the community did not see
their leadership challenged by the secret societies, as had occurred in
the continental United States.[75] Finally, since Chinese in Hawaii
were more able to participate in the island-wide government, the
tendency already present in the Chinese community to favor decision by consensus rather than violence was reinforced.

Even in the continental United States, most lodges in the Chih-
kung t'ang federation were not "fighting tongs." These other lodges
rarely engaged in open warfare and usually were not deeply
involved in any criminal activity. Many were organized along occupational lines, sometimes functioning as nascent labor unions with
rules for resolving grievances between employees and employers,
including the calling of strikes. One of this latter type of lodge consisted of workers in San Francisco's cigar industry. Another occupational lodge, called the Yang-wen Cheng-wu szu, was particularly
powerful around the turn of the century. Its members were the translators who worked for the other secret society lodges, for the American immigration officials, and for other United States government
offices.[76]

Another kind of lodge, including the Chih-kung t'ang lodge itself,
contained sublodges which governed the entire Chinese community
in their (usually rural) areas. *Hui-kuan* and surname associations
were generally confined to urban areas,[77] whereas the Triads organized sublodges in rural communities as well.[78] When a sublodge
acted as the community's governing apparatus, its rules would contain provisions for solving arguments within the larger community.
In Canada, for example, the rules of a Chih-kung t'ang sublodge
that flourished in a gold-mining community declared that the sub-

lodge was dedicated to the ideals of justice and fair play. In addition, it was supposed to afford security and profit to members. Members, however, were not to use the sublodge to extort money from non-members; nor were members to engage in claim-jumping; nor was any merchant member to lower wages drastically. The rules also specified that conflicts were not to be taken to the Canadian courts. Instead, conflicts would be arbitrated by the leaders of the sublodge, or, if arbitration failed, the leaders would dictate a solution.[79]

Although the power and prestige of the regional associations, Six Companies, and surname associations were very attractive to the political leaders, in the final analysis it was the Triad Chih-kung t'ang that proved to be most important to them. This was especially true for the revolutionaries. In part, the attraction was due to certain parallels between what a political party is supposed to do and what these secret societies actually did. Both valued the sharing of common goals and claimed that status in the organization should be a function of one's contribution to the organization rather than of one's status in the world outside the organization. In addition, the Triads professed to be interested in national politics. It is undoubtedly true that in 1893 their drive to change the government in China, epitomized by their slogan *"fan-Ch'ing, fu-Ming,"* was in fact minimal. But perhaps because their traditions encouraged it, by 1899 and 1900 many lodge and sublodge leaders had become actively concerned about China's fate.

Conflict with Americans

The hostility with which Americans regarded Chinese and the resultant difficulties suffered by Chinese living in the Americas were a major cause for the interest with which these immigrants came to regard political developments in their motherland. Between 1893 and 1911, various Chinatown organizations, including the political parties, attempted to ameliorate the condition of Chinese in the Americas and ward off the most serious attacks upon them. None of these efforts, however, met with any lasting success.

Examining the most important of these attacks that occurred between 1893 and 1911 reveals a great deal about the situation of the Chinese and the types of responses favored by the different types of

Chinatown organizations. It also shows graphically the social ferment in which the Chinese communities found themselves, ferment
that the political parties tried to turn to their own advantage. It clari-
fies why it was that Chinese in the Americas ultimately felt that the
only real way to improve their situation was to try to change the Chinese government. And it suggests that an astute political leader, particularly after 1905, would do well not to rely exclusively on Chinese
Christians or on Chinese Americans.

The attacks with which we are concerned occurred in 1893, 1900,
and 1905, respectively. All three were centered in San Francisco,
although Chinese elsewhere in the Americas were also involved. In
1893, the United States Congress passed a law called the Geary Act
which required all Chinese living in the continental United States to
register with the Department of Internal Revenue. Coming as it did
in the midst of the anti-Chinese movement, and not very long after
the onset of Chinese Exclusion, most Chinese felt that the Geary Act
was simply a prelude to their mass expulsion from the United States.
At that time, San Francisco's Chinese Six Companies was headed by
the president of the San-i hui-kuan, an educated and accomplished
fighting man "imported" from China by the dominant *San-i* community, a man named Ch'en Ta-chao.[80] Ch'en, as head of the Six
Companies, ordered Chinese not to comply with the Geary Act,
believing that the law would be ruled unconstitutional.[81]

The arrest of an individual who followed Ch'en's orders and did
not register led to a test case in which the Geary Act was upheld by
the United States Supreme Court. Those who had followed the Six
Companies' order became liable for immediate deportation; but at
the last minute, Congress, under pressure from various business
interests, passed a law extending the deadline for registration by
another six months. In the meantime, however, Ch'en, the San-i
hui-kuan, and the Six Companies had lost considerable prestige.
The Chih-kung t'ang federation and some of its subsidiary lodges
attempted to step into the vacuum, suggesting that people withdraw
from membership in the Six Companies by taking their names off
hui-kuan roles.[82]

The following year, *San-i* leaders in the Six Companies refused to
hire a lawyer for a *Szu-i* man accused in the San Francisco courts of
murder. In retaliation, *Szu-i* in the western United States declared a
boycott on all businesses owned by the *San-i*. Related to the boycott

was the fact, explained above, that *Szu-i* businessmen were finally able to challenge the *San-i* economic domination of the overseas communities and the Six Companies. The boycott was carried out in part through the Chih-kung t'ang federation and its affiliated lodges. Since many *San-i* residents were also members of a Triad lodge, the boycott led to strife and ushered in a period of virulent "tong wars." It also caused many *San-i* merchants to declare bankruptcy and leave the United States for Mexico and other Latin American countries.[83]

The violence was confined to the continental United States, but Chinese throughout the Americas were aware of what was going on. This must have produced a certain amount of tension between the various "ethnic" groups. In the continental United States, the "tong wars" and open confrontation only began to subside in 1900, when the San-i hui-kuan agreed to permit the presidency of the Six Companies to rotate between the various *hui-kuan*.[84]

The second major conflict between Chinese and Americans during this period raised the question of whether Chinese in the United States could be treated differently from people of other races in matters related to public health. In 1900, bubonic plague broke out in Honolulu. Local officials felt that Hawaii's Chinese residents were responsible for this menace. Accordingly, they forbade large gatherings of people of the Chinese race, refused to permit Chinese to board steamers bound for the continental United States, and set fire to a section of Honolulu's Chinatown. The fire subsequently got out of control, destroying much of Chinatown before it could be put out. Those whose property was destroyed sued for damages. However, they apparently did not question the original restrictions.[85]

At this point, officials in San Francisco became fearful that the plague might spread to their city. Once again, the white majority assumed that Chinese were responsible for the plague menace, and that the plague could be destroyed by taking action against the local Chinatown. San Francisco's Public Health Department decided to quarantine Chinatown, including all of its residents. Chinese there, however, decided to resist. Led by the local Chinese consul, the Chinese Six Companies, and the *Chung Sai Yat Po,* they decided to launch a legal battle and also to publicize their cause. The publicity was designed to increase solidarity within the Chinese community and gain outside support.[86]

Some outside support was forthcoming: the *San Francisco Morning Call* decided that the Chinese cause was at least partly just.[87] Various preachers and church groups who had missions in the Chinatown area also supported them.[88] Meanwhile, the legal battle was fought on two fronts. Wu T'ing-fang, Chinese Minister to the United States, presented their cause to the federal government, while the Chinese Six Companies hired an American lawyer to take their case through the local courts. These various efforts resulted in success: on June 19, 1900, Wu T'ing-fang learned that the federal government had wired San Francisco to say that the actions of the Public Health Department were arbitrary and unjust, and no quarantine could be effected without the permission of the Governor of California. The quarantine was then lifted and Chinese businesses were allowed to reopen. A few days later, the local judge also ruled in their favor and the issue was pretty much laid to rest.[89]

The third conflict between Americans and Chinese centered on the question of immigration. Many American countries, including most particularly the United States, desired to exclude Chinese— especially laborers—from the Americas. Predictably, Chinese deeply resented this. During the entire period 1893–1911, Chinese laborers (and their wives) were denied entry to the continental United States. Beginning in 1898, they were also excluded from Hawaii (and the Philippines). From 1897 on, the American officials charged with overseeing the immigration of Chinese to the continental United States also began a campaign to eliminate all Chinese, including merchants and other "permitted" groups.[90] At one point, this prohibition sparked a Chinese boycott of American goods, a movement in which Chinese in the Americas (especially in San Francisco) were deeply involved.

The opposition movement which ended in the boycott began in 1900 and 1901, when Chinese communities and Chinese officials in the United States called on the Ch'ing court to let the immigration treaty with the United States lapse in 1904 and negotiate a more favorable one to replace it. In 1903, the Chinese government notified the United States that it wanted a new treaty. But in 1904, the treaty lapsed while a new one was being negotiated, and the United States Congress passed internal laws reaffirming Chinese Exclusion. China and the United States were not able to come to an agreement on a new treaty, and in 1905, negotiations were broken off. At this point,

Chinese in the Americas along with merchants, students, and laborers in China called for and instituted a boycott of American goods. The Chinese government supported them at first, but after several weeks, changed its mind. Various circumstances caused the original boycott movement to become fragmented, and by 1906, the movement had lost its impetus.[91]

Right from the beginning, the *Chung Sai Yat Po* was in the forefront of this fight as it unfolded in the Americas. As early as 1900, this influential newspaper proposed that China should limit its trade with the United States if the immigration question were not solved.[92] In 1901, San Francisco's Chinese Christian community asked the Reverend Wu P'an-chao (Ng Poon Chew), founder and manager of the *Chung Sai Yat Po,* to make a national tour. An accomplished speaker in both English and Chinese, Reverend Wu was to inform American and Chinese audiences of the need for change in the immigration restrictions, along with the potential the Chinese had for contributing to American society and the American system of government. Various *hui-kuan* contributed money for this project through the Six Companies, but most of the funds and all of Reverend Wu's traveling companions came from San Francisco's Chinese Presbyterian Church.[93]

While Reverend Wu was on this tour (the first of many), the *Chung Sai Yat Po* continued its editorial attack. By 1902, the newspaper occasionally linked the United States' treatment of Chinese with the fact that Chinese (Han) were a subjugated race, and called for an anti-Manchu revolution in China to correct this.[94] In part due to the newspaper's efforts, by mid-1903, many Chinese in North America actively opposed renewing the immigration treaty. In October of that year, the Chinese Six Companies formally suggested that the Ch'ing government should terminate the treaty when it came up for review in 1904. Chinese Christians from the West Coast and Canada met to discuss modifications needed in the treaty. They ended by urging China to threaten a boycott of American goods.[95]

In November of 1903, while Liang Ch'i-ch'ao was in San Francisco, the local Chinese merchants drew up petitions to the Ch'ing court, an important provincial governor-general, and other officials saying that exclusion should be ended. The editor of Hawaii's official Pao-huang hui newspaper (along with Liang himself) agreed with these propositions, and the Pao-huang hui became identified with a portion of the antiexclusion forces.[96] When the Chinese government told the United States it desired to negotiate a new treaty, however, the Americans showed little flexibility. At this point, most Chinese in the Americas temporarily abandoned hope. The merchants and the churches let their earlier antiexclusion organizations die from inactivity.[97] But when the United States Congress enacted a new set of internal exclusion laws in 1905, the course of events spurred Chinese immigrants into renewed action.

By this time, the idea of a boycott had been picked up in China but had died in America. Instead, when Chinese in America learned that treaty negotiations had been abandoned, the Chinese Six Companies and the acting consul in San Francisco raised money for the legal defense of anyone arrested under the newly enacted exclusion laws. The Six Companies asked people to violate these laws so that a test case could be brought.[98] On May 10, 1905, a week after the Six Companies' action, word reached San Francisco that merchants in Shanghai had declared a boycott of all United States goods to begin in June. Soon, many of the most important Chinese organizations and groups in the Americas, including the Pao-huang hui, the Christians, and then the Six Companies, began to urge support of the boycott. Chinese in Hawaii, Canada, and Panama became active in the movement once San Francisco's Six Companies had announced its support.[99]

In the meantime, the Six Companies founded an organization in San Francisco called the Anti-Treaty Society (Chü-yüeh tsung-chü) to coordinate boycott activities in North America. In addition, a number of prominent Chinese toured the United States to gain support for the boycott movement and persuade Americans to sympathize with Chinese. The most important of these were K'ang Yu-wei (who spoke before both Chinese and American audiences), the Reverend Wu P'an-chao (who mainly addressed Americans), and Huang San-te of the Chih-kung t'ang (who confined himself to Chinese audiences).[100]

American intransigence gradually weakened the movement, however. Lack of success soon pitted the various Chinatown groups against themselves. The Chih-kung t'ang and the Chinese Christians accused K'ang Yu-wei and the Pao-huang hui of compromising on the question of exclusion by agreeing that laborers could be excluded if all nonlaborers were admitted. The boycott became more and more ineffective, and by the spring of 1906 had become a dead letter.[101] In 1907, the Pao-huang hui, *Chung Sai Yat Po,* and other groups attempted to revive the Anti-Treaty Society. They wanted to use it to institute a boycott against Japanese goods, but their attempted revival failed. (Ironically, this boycott was to have punished Japan for violating China's sovereignty when helping certain Chinese revolutionaries.)[102]

Much can be learned from these incidents. For example, when action was deemed necessary, more often than not, the initial reaction of the Chinese community was to try to solve the problem through judicial or diplomatic means. Lawyers were hired, legal (and constitutional) precedent pointed to, and diplomatic channels employed. The attempt was to show that the action desired by the Cninese was to uphold the law, and that the law had been violated by elements outside the Chinese community. In retrospect, it can be said that the initial reaction appears conservative, inasmuch as it remained within the confines of the existing social and institutional structure. In addition, it is evident that overseas Chinese felt some optimism concerning the ultimate justice inherent in the American system of government, particularly as regards the rule of law. Furthermore, Chinese were quite skillful at times in their use of the legal system. Interestingly, the major Chinese social organizations followed the American rather than the Chinese model when drawing up their rules and regulations. This could not but have benefited the political parties, who sought to make China conform more closely to the Western, and American, model.

Legal means were not the only ones employed by the Chinese immigrants, however. The boycott movement in particular sought to apply economic pressure to secure social and political aims. Boycotts had earlier been used by one portion of the overseas Chinese community against another, but this was the first time that Chinese in the Americas had used the tactic on a large scale against an outside group.

Another point of interest revealed by these incidents is that the presumed dominance of the Chinese community in San Francisco over all Chinese in the Americas (particularly in North America) had some basis in fact. Chinese in Canada and Hawaii did not officially proclaim their support for the boycott movement until San Francisco's Six Companies had given its approval. When Chinese

Christians in San Francisco held a meeting to decide what to do about modifying Chinese exclusion, Canada sent at least one representative. When the editor of Hawaii's Pao-huang hui newspaper decided a boycott should be instituted, he toured the continental United States and then wrote San Francisco's Chinese Six Companies for their approval of his idea. When Chinese in Los Angeles and other places in the United States wanted to participate in the movement, they also sought the approval of the Chinese Six Companies. The list of examples could go on and on. Obviously, the political leaders would find it worth their while to devote extra time and attention to San Francisco.

Our examination of the major conflicts between Chinese and Americans has also revealed that certain groups within the overseas community would be better able than others to afford the political leaders substantial aid. Chinese Christians, as devotees of a "Western" religion, were quite open to Western political ideals. The vast majority of the immigrants, however, looked upon the Christians as "un-Chinese." The important role that the Chinese Christians played in ending the 1900 quarantine of San Francisco's Chinatown increased their influence in the Chinese community. Much of what they gained, however, was lost in 1905 when their judgment of the potentialities of the boycott was proven by circumstance to have been ill-founded. Chinese Americans were even better acquainted with the American environment, but they tended to be young, were even fewer in number than were the Christians, and having never been to China were hardly considered Chinese by the immigrants. Clearly, organizations such as the Six Companies, the individual *hui-kuan,* the Chih-kung t'ang, and groups such as merchants potentially had much more to offer the political leaders.

Lessons Taught by America

The isolation from Americans suffered by Chinese in the Americas was a result of an active and deliberate policy on the part of the former. This was sometimes aided and abetted by a partial lack of interest on the part of the Chinese. At certain times and for certain groups the isolation was partially mitigated, but it was never eliminated: it seemed impossible to construct a lasting bridge between Chinese and Americans. The suggestion in 1900 that the American Christian congregations in San Francisco might become sympathetic to Chinese was undercut by the support from these congregations for Chinese exclusion in 1905. During the boycott, those Americans most favorably disposed toward relaxed immigration restrictions were businessmen, especially businessmen involved in the China trade or those who depended upon Chinese laborers. But since their long-range goals differed significantly from those of the Chinese community, they did not make reliable allies.

Other than from Christians and businessmen, the Chinese did not seem to have attracted the sympathy of any other groups of Americans. There are many cases of individuals coming to their aid, but community bonds must be based on a broader consensus. The United States courts were probably the most reliable ally that Chinese had, but even there, almost as many cases went against the Chinese—and often against justice as well—as went for them. Still, on several broad constitutional questions as well as in many more routine cases, the courts did go against public opinion and uphold the rights of Chinese.[103] As a result, Chinese continued to turn to the courts.

In spite of their isolation, we might expect Chinese to have learned something of "American ideals" from their stay here: equality, the rule of reason over force, the importance of democracy, the value of the vote, and the impartiality of justice. Although they did hear these ideals voiced, they did not often see them implemented, even in the United States. Certainly they were conspicuously absent in the average dealings between Chinese and Americans. Furthermore, it will be recalled that the turn of the century was in part still the age of the "robber barons." The power of Southern Pacific in the California state government had not been completely eliminated. And the Progressives, the people most anxious to end the stranglehold of big business, were, as a rule, virulently anti-Chinese. Finally, the Australian secret ballot was still an innovation adopted in only a few locations in the United States, and many elections were characterized by blatant corruption.

Of greater importance to the average immigrant was how to improve his (or her) difficult situation. His problems did not seem to admit to any direct solution. An alternative would be to approach the question indirectly, for it appeared that his plight could be attrib-

uted in part to the political weakness of his native land. Interest in
strengthening China gave rise to proreform and prorevolutionary
nationalism, and also suggested that racial arguments should be
applied to political problems. The immigrants hoped to see their
country become powerful, internationally respected, and sensitive to
their needs. Nationalism, an ideal espoused by Americans of the
time as well, became related to community and individual self-
respect.

Many problems encountered by overseas Chinese were related to
the racist attitudes of Americans. Already somewhat predisposed
toward emphasizing racial distinctions, Chinese learned in the
Americas that these distinctions were sanctioned by current scientific and social theories—with the twist, of course, that Americans
viewed Chinese as racially inferior instead of racially superior.
Americans and Westerners also argued that peoples of relatively
temperate climates (rather than those from either extreme northern
or southern latitudes) were innately superior.[104] Furthermore, some
maintained that a country must be ruled by the majority race.[105] All
of this could be interpreted by Chinese to support the idea that Chinese were, after all, among the world's most superior races. In addition, it suggested that it was to the disadvantage of the majority Han
to be ruled by the northern, minority Manchus. The influence that
these views had on Chinese in the Americas was reflected in the fact
that Sun Yat-sen often repeated them in his travels throughout the
Americas, and in the announcement by K'ang Yu-wei in Canada (if
we are to believe Feng Tzu-yu) that the Kuang-hsü Emperor was
actually Han Chinese.[106] Many editorials published by San Francisco's Chinese-language newspapers also noted the glorious attributes
of Chinese (especially southern Chinese) and the crudeness of Manchus.[107]

The Americas also taught Chinese that the strong, modern countries of the world respected wealth. North Americans attached great
importance to the business community, and the self-made million-
aire was held up as a model on which to base one's life. Americans
also felt more comfortable dealing with the wealthier men from the
Chinese communities rather than with the average poor laborer.

All of these lessons ultimately benefited the political parties, since
the lessons directed attention to the same concerns that the parties
attempted to address. The political parties all desired to strengthen

China. Sun Yat-sen's partisans found that Sun's *min-chu chu-i* closely resembled the kind of nationalism developing among overseas Chinese. Chinese saw that the Pao-huang hui of K'ang Yu-wei and Liang Ch'i-ch'ao was an organization respected by key figures in American governments as well as by local businessmen, especially in the period from 1900 to 1906.[108] This respect derived from the wealth and social standing of party leaders, the wealth and number of adherents the party itself possessed, and the party's moderate and progressive ideals. Furthermore, the Pao-huang hui was itself the standard-bearer of a certain kind of nationalism, a nationalism somewhat less colored by racial considerations. Nationalism of any stripe could also become a tool for ending the bloody strife that had broken out among Chinese in the continental United States—the *San-i* versus *Szu-i* conflict precipitated by the Geary Act fiasco in 1893. Not surprisingly, the Americas proved to be fertile ground for the political parties.

2

THE FOUNDING OF
THE POLITICAL PARTIES

The social instability of North America's Chinese communities during the 1890s and the rise of the *Szu-i* businessmen presented an especially good opportunity in which to establish political parties. Fortuitously, this was when Sun Yat-sen, K'ang Yu-wei, and Liang Ch'i-ch'ao made their first trips to the Americas. At the outset, K'ang and Liang enjoyed much greater organizational success than did Sun. In the Americas (as in China and Southeast Asia), K'ang and Liang elicited respect because they were prominent literati with administrative experience and well-deserved reputations as idealistic reformers. Chinese in the Americas also appreciated the fact that K'ang and Liang were Punti. Sun Yat-sen, on the other hand, was a relatively unknown Hakka nonliteratus from Hsiang-shan. Furthermore, when K'ang and Liang arrived in the Americas (in 1899 and 1900, respectively), the failure of the "Hundred Days of Reform" in 1898, the quickening pace of the scramble by the powers for concessions in China, and the outbreak of the Boxer disturbances ensured that overseas Chinese concern for China's future would be great. When Sun first traveled to the Americas (in 1894 and 1895), China's problems were of much less urgency. Finally, there were substantial similarities between Sun's Hsing-Chung hui and the early Pao-huang hui of K'ang and Liang. The similarities made considerations of personality and organizational proficiency (in which K'ang and Liang held the advantage) correspondingly more important.

The Founding of the Hsing-Chung Hui

In 1894, Sun Yat-sen went to Hawaii from Hong Kong with subversion in his mind. China's repeated defeats in the Sino-Japanese War then taking place revealed to Sun along with other treaty-port Chinese, and even some of the Confucian literati, evidence of what they felt to be fatal weaknesses in the government. Sun's remedy for the situation was to organize an uprising that would overthrow the Manchu government, give power to the Han majority, and direct that majority to work for the modernization (Westernization) of the country.[1]

The 1894 trip was not Sun's first to Hawaii. He had studied at a missionary school in Honolulu while in his teens and still had friends there. His wealthy, anti-Manchu elder brother Sun Mei (also called Sun Te-chang) lived in the Islands,[2] and the prospect of obtaining money from this brother was surely one reason Yat-sen traveled all the way to Hawaii to begin his political organizing. Several of Yat-sen's former acquaintances in the Islands were also anti-Manchu, and a number of them were quite prominent as well. Some were merchants, one ran a newspaper (the *Lung-chi pao*), and one was a translator for the Hawaiian customs bureau.[3]

The most prominent of these men was Sun Yat-sen's former classmate Chung Yü (also known as Chung Kun Ai). Chung was a friend of Sun Mei's, he was a Christian (Yat-sen's chosen religion), and he came from a family that hated the Manchus. He was wealthy and influential. In 1894, he had more than one business of his own, and was also the manager for an American entrepreneur. Chung frequently acted as translator and representative of the Chinese community, and by 1900 he had become an officer of Hawaii's United Chinese Society (Chung-hua hui-kuan).[4] Obviously, he was a man whose support could be very helpful.

On his arrival in Hawaii, Sun Yat-sen immediately began soliciting support from Chung Yü and others for the proposed revolutionary uprising. This soliciting was at first to no avail, however. Then he persuaded Sun Mei to write a public affirmation that the elder brother favored the younger brother's cause. After this, Yat-sen was able to interest some twenty people including Sun Mei, Chung Yü, and the newspaper owner Ch'eng Wei-nan. On November 24, 1894, these men officially founded the Hsing-Chung hui (Revive China Society).[5]

As far as Sun Yat-sen was concerned, the primary aim of the new organization was to raise money for his uprising. One-third of the society's original rules were related to fund raising. (The other two-thirds dealt with how officers were to be selected and new members initiated.)[6] The organization did succeed in raising a modest sum. Sun Mei's patronage enabled the Hsing-Chung hui to grow from its humble beginnings to a membership of one hundred and twenty by early 1895. Since it had a membership fee of five dollars (U.S.), this must have given Sun Yat-sen some six hundred dollars. More money was raised by selling $1,388 (U.S.) worth of "revolutionary bonds" at ten dollars each (repayable tenfold upon the success of the revolution). In addition, Sun Mei sold some of his livestock, and another Hsing-Chung hui member sold his shop and a field and gave the proceeds to Sun Yat-sen for the uprising. These latter two sources brought in five thousand dollars more.[7]

Sun also hoped that the Hsing-Chung hui would help secure soldiers and officers to "man the ramparts." Here, too, he achieved at least a bare minimum of success. Teng Yin-nan (Teng Sung-sheng), the man who had sold his shop and field, accompanied Sun to China to participate in the fighting. Teng was skilled in the use of firearms and archery, and even knew how to make explosives. Several other young men worked out in a drill team hastily organized by Sun and directed by a Danish drill master. Four or five of them returned to China with Sun and presumably participated in the 1895 uprising.[8]

Still, this was only six active participants out of a Chinese population of more than twenty-three thousand. Even the more than one hundred and twenty members of the Hsing-Chung hui would not be worth mentioning were it not for Sun's later achievements. There are several reasons for the organization's limited success. Chinese in those days did not ordinarily involve themselves in political movements of any stripe, since both the imperial government and the traditional Chinese social system discouraged political speculation. Sun was still a very obscure figure, of no great social standing by either Chinese or Western standards. He was neither *Szu-i* nor *San-i,* so he could not capitalize on the local quarrel to gain adherents for his organization. Harold Z. Schiffrin suggests that one reason for Sun's poor showing was that only "a few relatively educated" Chinese in Hawaii[9] even had an intellectual grasp of the meaning of the republican, anti-Manchu uprising for which Sun labored. This, however, seems unlikely since a few months prior to the founding of the Hsing-Chung hui, Hawaii itself had experienced a "revolutionary" coup d'état which established it as a republic. To participate in or contribute financially to an attack on the Chinese government, however, would put the participant and especially his family in China in grave danger of reprisals from Ch'ing officials. This was a risk that few, even if they sympathized with Sun's aims, would have been willing to run.[10]

The fact that Sun was not a secret society member also worked against him, since almost all Chinese in the Islands were members of one or another of the Triad lodges there.[11] Lacking this ritual bond of brotherhood made Sun Yat-sen more of an outsider than perhaps any of the other factors,[12] and helps explain why, in spite of Sun Mei's influence, even the Hsiang-shan and Hakka communities proved so unresponsive in relation to their total numbers in Hawaii.

But what of the people who actually did join the Hsing-Chung hui? The organization cut across surname lines, and probably across regional lines as well. About half of the members came from Hsiang-shan (Sun's native region), and another sixteen from Hsin-ning.[13] Of the society's first twelve officers, six were from Hsiang-shan, two from Hsin-ning, and one each from Nan-hai, K'ai-p'ing, and Hui-chou.[14] It is possible that the non-Hsiang-shan members were all Hakka. However, there are suggestions that some were Punti. If that is the case, their relative lack of attention to regional differences would have been a manifestation of their progressive spirit.

About half of the party members were merchants and several worked for the Hawaiian government. Somewhat under one-quarter were laborers. All twelve of the officers were merchants. Two officers were also translators for the Hawaiian government. One of these two was the Hawaiian government's chief undercover informer on affairs in the Chinese community, and the chief translator for Ch'eng Wei-nan's *Lung-chi pao*.[15] Another officer was a Christian, a naturalized American citizen, and the Chinese manager of the influential Bishop's Bank of Honolulu. As such, he was empowered to make bank loans of up to six hundred dollars without security to any individual.[16] Chung Yü was also a Hsing-Chung hui officer. His wealth (his most important firm was a lumber yard), influence, and Christian background have already been noted. These and the other merchants who joined were surely demonstrating their feeling that businessmen had the right to assume positions of political leadership. Although this idea ran directly counter to traditional Chinese ideas, these individuals were aware that the most powerful men in Hawaii's government were businessmen.

At least four of the officers and at least six of the regular members could speak English. Seven of the latter worked for Hawaii's govern-

ment. The special position of English speakers in the Chinese communities of North America has already been noted. This was true of
Hawaii as well, since by 1893 Hawaii was ruled by Americans, and
English had become the official language. Chinese in Hawaii had
been better received and had experienced a greater degree of assimilation than in the continental Americas, but still the English speakers among them were few and far between.[17]

In addition to the Western-orientated businessmen, progressive
merchants, forward-looking community leaders, Hawaii government agents, and English speakers, the party contained some Triad
members. One of these was an officer *(chih-shih)* of Hawaii's Chih-
kung t'ang. Circumstantial evidence suggests that Sun Yat-sen's
elder brother was also a Triad member, and that one small Triad
sublodge joined as a body.[18]

After establishing the Hsing-Chung hui and collecting funds, Sun
Yat-sen returned to China with the few enthusiasts mentioned
above. There, he launched his Canton coup of 1895. Ch'eng Wei-
nan's newspaper provided some political support for his cause.
However, Sun's coup failed. This turn of events chilled the enthusiasm of Hawaii's Chinese. When Sun returned to the Islands late in
1895, he could not find any new recruits for the Hsing-Chung hui,
and the old members were content to let the organization remain
inactive. Sun is supposed to have enjoyed some success in fund-raising, so fear may have been one factor which discouraged potential
recruits. Another factor was that the uprising, which Sun had
claimed would easily result in victory, had collapsed without even
one major battle to its name. Schiffrin's claim that the 1895 uprising
made Sun Yat-sen feared and famous seems in fact an overstate-
ment.[19]

Hawaii having proved unresponsive, in 1896 Sun traveled to
North America. Unfortunately for Sun, he arrived there just after
the Ch'ing official Li Hung-chang began a tour of the same continent to request that American officials improve their treatment of
Chinese. Sun spent several months touring the United States and
Canada, speaking in Chih-kung t'ang halls and trying to gain
recruits. The Chih-kung t'ang granted him the privilege of speaking
in lodge halls because of his "credentials" as one who had organized
an antigovernment uprising. He asked his audiences to join his society or to form an alliance with it, but since his uprising had failed

and he was not a Triad member, they were uninterested. Sun claimed that his difficulty was that the Chih-kung t'ang had no interest in politics in 1896,[20] but this is disproved by the alacrity with which Chih-kung t'ang members joined the Pao-huang hui three years later. The only followers Sun acquired during his 1896 visit to the Americas were a small handful of people (less than fifteen) mostly in San Francisco, people to whom he appealed as a fellow Christian. These were the total additions to the Hsing-Chung hui in the Americas until late 1903.[21]

The Founding of the Pao-huang Hui

Many elements of the pattern revealed in the founding of the first branch of the Hsing-Chung hui were repeated in 1899 when K'ang Yu-wei founded the Pao-huang hui in Vancouver, Canada. Both founders were "outside agitators" rather than immigrants. Both also felt, at least at first, that their political goals could not be achieved unless they could get an army to support them and attack their opponents in China.[22] Both welcomed all interested people into their party, regardless of background, and neither man seems to have realized that he was setting up a permanent organization through which overseas Chinese could express political views. Instead, both were seeking money, manpower, and support on a short-term basis to help with the matter immediately at hand.

At the outset, both party leaders obtained the active participation of several wealthy and influential merchant-businessmen. K'ang, unlike Sun, was able to hold the loyalty of these men for an extended period of time, and his successes were not just limited to one community. This difference should not be overemphasized, however, as will soon be clear. Finally, in both parties, members of the Chih-kung t'ang and independent Triad lodges provided a large number of early recruits and a forum through which Sun, unsuccessfully, and K'ang, successfully, expended much of their organizational efforts.

K'ang Yu-wei first touched ground in the Americas when he landed in Canada in April of 1899. This was just a few short weeks after the Empress Dowager's coup d'état had ended the Kuang-hsü Emperor's "Hundred Days of Reform," put a temporary end to moderate modernization, and launched China on a collision course with the West. The coup also made outlaws of K'ang and his chief disciples, including Liang Ch'i-ch'ao, forcing them to flee China. One of the prime movers in the "Hundred Days," K'ang planned to cross Canada and go to Washington, D.C., where he hoped to persuade President McKinley to field an army in China. This army was to deny power to the Empress Dowager and restore it to the Kuang-hsü Emperor, with K'ang as his advisor. Since K'ang was a prominent man with an international reputation, leading figures of the Chinese community in Canada arranged for him to deliver a couple of speeches. On each occasion, he attracted a very large audience (over one thousand people on each occasion), but he made no attempt to form any kind of association at this time. He spent several weeks on Canada's west coast, mostly in the city of Victoria, where many wealthy Chinese merchants and Canada's main branches of the Chih-kung t'ang and Chung-hua hui-kuan were located. He also visited Vancouver, the Canadian city with the largest Chinese population. In both places, some of the wealthiest and most influential members of the Chinese community sought his patronage, including most notably Li Fu-chi (Lee Fuk Ki) and Yeh En (Yip On), both of whom were *Szu-i* men from Hsin-ning.[23] Li Fu-chi spoke English and had access to the English-language press. Yeh En was a translator for the Canadian customs, a former manager of a Canadian company, and a wealthy businessman.[24] He may also have been one of the founders of Victoria's Chih-kung t'ang.[25]

In spite of various maneuvers and a letter of recommendation from the American ambassador to Japan, K'ang was ignored by the United States government. When he realized he would not even be permitted to enter that country due to Chinese Exclusion, K'ang went to England to plead his cause before Parliament. He was politely received in England and did address Parliament, but he was not given any aid. Returning to Canada's west coast, K'ang gave more speeches and he and his supporters (Yeh En, Li Fu-chi, and others) then decided to organize a political association to further his political aims in China. K'ang claimed that his aims were identical with those of the Kuang-hsü Emperor. He produced the famous "secret memorial" to buttress this contention, a memorial supposedly written by the emperor, asking K'ang and all progressive Chinese to come to his aid. K'ang saw the role of his nascent political association as twofold: it should be a vehicle through which hundreds or thousands of overseas Chinese could petition the court for the restoration of power to the emperor,[26] and it should be a fund-raising organization, the funds evidently being earmarked to pay for the assassination of the Empress Dowager or to field an army against her. Once a model petition had been drafted and suitable names for the organization had been chosen, K'ang turned matters over to his supporters and retired to an island near Victoria owned by a prosperous backer. He reappeared only once, to attend the lavish birthday celebration in honor of the Kuang-hsü Emperor given by the new society. Even so, his supporters raised seven thousand dollars for him to take to China, money above and beyond the sum used for the birthday celebration and regular operating expenses.[27]

K'ang's leading supporters in Canada showed themselves willing to raise funds to restore power to the emperor, and some even agreed to sign his petition. These men were just as concerned with local problems as with court politics, however. The mistreatment of Chinese in Canada was a matter that directly affected them, and they held that the new organization would be dedicated to alleviating this condition as well as to saving the emperor. The two aims were linked by saying that the former was dependent upon the national-strength-through-modernization that would develop if the emperor were allowed to rule.[28]

Canada's Chinese were also interested in the politico-economic aims of furthering the cause of merchant capitalism and the merchant capitalist in China and the Americas. This interest diverged somewhat from K'ang's views and led to an argument over the title that should be given to the newly emerging society. K'ang proposed the formal title of Chung-kuo Wei-hsin hui (Chinese Progressive Society), with the informal title Chiu-kuo hui (Save the Nation Society). K'ang's most influential supporters in Victoria and Vancouver, however, preferred the informal title of Pao-shang hui (Preserve Commerce Society), since those leading the move to organize the society were businessmen.[29]

Many other Chinese in Canada disliked the title of Chiu-kuo hui because they were afraid it sounded too much like K'ang's earlier organization, the now-illegal Pao-kuo hui (Preserve the Nation Society). To resolve the impasse, someone proposed the compromise title of Pao-huang hui (Preserve the Emperor Society), which was acceptable to those with enough influence to have a voice in the debate.

Accordingly, on July 20, 1899, the society was officially founded with the English title of Chinese Reform Association and the Chinese names of Wei-hsin hui and Pao-huang hui (the latter being the shorter form of the alternate title of Pao-chiu Ta-Ch'ing Kuang-hsü huang-ti hui: Society to Save the Kuang-hsü Emperor of the Great Ch'ing Dynasty). The idea of the Pao-shang hui, however, was perpetuated in the Pao-shang chü (Preserve Commerce Bureau), which was organized as a subcommittee of the Pao-huang hui in various cities, including San Francisco.[30]

All of this helped give the party a strong commercial bias. The bias was, however, tempered by several factors. In the first place, according to Feng Tzu-yu and others, most early Pao-huang hui members also belonged to the Chih-kung t'ang, and the early party leaders were most often Chih-kung t'ang officers. Chih-kung t'ang members who had had some education had already started to become politically conscious, especially since the coup d'état.[31] Moreover, since K'ang had been made an official of the secret society Ko-lao hui (Society of Elders and Brothers), it is probable that he was a secret society initiate.[32] This would have further predisposed the Chih-kung t'ang in his favor. Letters written by Canada's Pao-huang hui leaders to K'ang Yu-wei in 1900 also claimed that a majority of the party members were poor. Poor members would certainly have expected the Pao-huang hui to do something besides protect someone else's commercial activities; and in fact, most of the letters reflect an overwhelming interest in the fortunes of what they believed to be the Pao-huang hui army in China.[33]

From the time of its inception, then, the Pao-huang hui included rich and poor, men for the most part united by their membership in the Chih-kung t'ang and their interest in having an influence on China's political development. Branches were soon established in the continental United States as well as in Canada. The party cut across surname lines, as is evident from the names of the members given above.[34] It also cut across regional lines: of the eight original founders (not counting K'ang Yu-wei), at least five were *Szu-i* and at least one was a *San-i*.[35] In San Francisco, at least one leader (T'ang Ch'iung-ch'ang, the Chih-kung t'ang officer) was a *Szu-i* man. Hawaii's first chapter, organized in 1900, included people from Hsiang-shan, Hsin-ning, the *San-i,* and other areas.[36]

It is significant that in communities heretofore controlled by *San-i* men, communities in which a power struggle was then taking place between *San-i* and *Szu-i* (the boycott in the continental United States was still in effect), a *San-i* literatus could come over from China and draw such enthusiastic support from the *Szu-i* community. This is partly because K'ang directed his appeal to all Chinese, not to any one "ethnic" subgroup. The "secret memorial" ostensibly written by the emperor added weight to the appeal. Since K'ang himself was a *San-i,* asking overseas Chinese to rise above regional antagonisms in their nationalism was in fact inviting *Szu-i* men to join in the leadership of the community (as well as in the leadership of China).

This becomes even clearer with an examination of the idea behind the Pao-shang chü (and earlier Pao-shang hui). In being attached to a party which sought to rise above regionalism, the Pao-shang chü would have superseded the *hui-kuan* and "ethnically" inclined merchant guilds such as the Shao-i kung-so and the K'o-shang hui-kuan. Naturally this would have been of greatest benefit to the *Szu-i* merchants.

The *San-i* community could also profit from such an organization, for their prestige would be increased by the fact that the Pao-huang hui and the Pao-shang chü were founded by one of their coregionalists. Furthermore, since *San-i* merchants in the continental United States were being ruined by the *Szu-i* boycott, *San-i* support of the Pao-huang hui and the Pao-shang chü and the cause of Chinese unity could help resolve the fight between *San-i* and *Szu-i* without causing too much loss of face. This fight was, in fact, partially resolved and the boycott brought to an end between 1899 and 1901.[37]

In October of 1899, K'ang left Canada and returned to China. By that time, the Pao-huang hui was well established in western Canada, and organizers like Yeh En, Li Fu-chi, and Liang Ch'i-ch'ao's relative Liang Ch'i-t'ien had gone out to other communities in Canada as well as to San Francisco, Seattle, and Portland, Oregon. (K'ang himself had hoped to organize a branch in Hawaii on his way back to Hong Kong, but he could not get permission to land,[38] so the Hawaii chapter was not founded until January of 1900, when Liang Ch'i-ch'ao went there.) Many of the Pao-huang hui's peripatetic organizers found that branches of the party had sprung up in advance of their arrival. In San Francisco, local Chinese founded their own branch on October 26, 1899. Its first president was a Chinese medical practitioner and T'ang Ch'iung-ch'ang was its secretary.[39] T'ang, in addition to his Chih-kung t'ang (and An-i t'ang) duties, was manager of a local newspaper, the *Wen-hsien pao*. His espousal of the Pao-huang hui cause helped turn his newspaper into a Pao-huang hui organ.[40] In New York and Cuba as well, probably influenced by renewed perils to China, local Chinese communities took the initiative and organized their own Pao-huang hui branches in the summer of 1900.[41]

These renewed perils were a result of the decision by the Ch'ing court, under the Empress Dowager, to side with the antiforeign, anti-Christian Boxer "armies" of north China. The Boxers killed hundreds if not thousands of Christians (some of whom were foreigners). In June, Boxers and regular Ch'ing armed forces beseiged the diplomatic legations of the powers in Peking, and the court declared war on the powers. In response, the latter (chiefly Great Britain, Germany, France, Japan, and the United States) sent a large joint military force which fought its way up to Peking and occupied that city on July 14. Meanwhile, in the name of national preservation and enlightened rule, Chinese governors-general in central and south China had refused to acknowledge the court's declaration of war or to tolerate the massacre of Christians and foreigners. Also in the name of national preservation and enlightenment, both K'ang and Sun decided to organize and support military movements in China to bring down the Empress Dowager.

In the midst of all this activity and confusion, the Pao-huang hui began to appeal to more and more of America's Chinese as an intelligent means of forcing national salvation and modernization on a reluctant China. Still, the Pao-huang hui was not able to carry all before it. Of the numerous branches in Canada, Victoria's was probably the largest. Still, in a letter to K'ang written in the fall of 1900, Li Fu-chi estimated that only one-third of Victoria's Chinese had joined the organization.[42] In Hawaii, however, almost ninety percent of the Chinese community joined during the six months in 1900 that Liang Ch'i-ch'ao was in the Islands, as we shall see later. In August of 1900, San Francisco's Chinese consul-general (no friend of the Pao-huang hui) estimated that there were only two thousand members in that city. T'ang Ch'iung-ch'ang replied on behalf of the Pao-huang hui, claiming five thousand members in San Francisco, ten thousand more in the rest of the United States, and millions (four-fifths of the population) in southern China.[43] His figure for southern China obviously represented his hopes rather than reality. It may be assumed that the actual number of members in San Francisco was somewhere between the consul-general's figure and T'ang Ch'iung-ch'ang's number (perhaps three thousand five hundred to four thousand). Assuming T'ang may also have been over-generous with his United States estimate, it might be hazarded that this should have been about eight thousand. If these calculations are anywhere near correct, in the summer of 1900 approximately one-eighth of the Chinese in the continental United States belonged to the Pao-huang hui.

External Attacks on the Pao-huang Hui

The rather substantial response that the Pao-huang hui elicited from the Chinese in North America made the party a threat to the Ch'ing court. Ch'ing authorities, and people loyal to the Empress Dowager, made various attempts to weaken it. In the long run, these attempts proved to be unsuccessful. Detectives and agents infiltrated the society so as to obtain the names of its most ardent and prominent supporters. The Chinese government used these names to threaten, and in some cases destroy, the families and property that Pao-huang hui members had left behind in China. Another device was to levy a tax on a Pao-huang hui member's home village, hoping that other overseas Chinese from the same area would bring enough pressure on the member to force him to resign. Ch'ing agents also tried to force the host governments to expel the major Pao-huang hui organizers: Chinese minister Wu T'ing-fang tried but failed to get the United States to expel Liang Ch'i-t'ien, claiming Liang's presence was in violation of Chinese Exclusion. (Wu's action was intended to prevent Liang Ch'i-t'ien from going to San Francisco to strengthen the local Pao-huang hui chapter.) Another Ch'ing official requested (unsuccessfully) that the British government withdraw its protection of K'ang Yu-wei in Singapore on the grounds that K'ang had raped his host's wife during K'ang's visit to Canada. Even another accused the American headquarters of the Ho-ho hui-kuan (whose members had the surname Yü and came from Hsin-ning *hsien*) of importing a Pao-huang hui leader from China to lead their organization, and reprisals were threatened.[44]

Opponents of the Pao-huang hui tried to confuse people as to what was going on in China and to discourage political speculation in general. During the Boxer Rebellion, an anonymous individual sent a letter to the _Chung Sai Yat Po,_ a newspaper which at that time strongly supported the Pao-huang hui. The writer of the letter criticized the _Chung Sai Yat Po_ for concerning itself with political matters, and for stirring up and deceiving people. The deception referred to was the _Chung Sai Yat Po_'s accurate report that the armies of the powers were in Peking. The letter writer maintained that, to the contrary, the powers' armies had been defeated near Peking and that the powers were at that moment earnestly suing for peace.[45]

Finally, when the Pao-huang hui in Hawaii tried legally to incorporate, the Chinese consul in Hawaii prevented this from happening. Two months after Liang Ch'i-ch'ao left the Islands, the party's officers had applied for its incorporation as a social and benevolent society. A Pao-huang hui organizer sent from San Francisco was the man behind this move. At first everything appeared to be proceeding smoothly—so smoothly that the society's officers did not even bother to draw up an English-language version of the regulations. The Chinese consul in Honolulu, however, notified Hawaii's Executive Council that the organization was not social and benevolent, but instead was a subversive political society. Authorities in Hawaii had little interest in whether or not it was subversive, but felt obligated to turn down the charter if the society was primarily political. Six weeks of investigation ensued, an investigation characterized by charges and countercharges (the Chinese consul suggested that permitting the Pao-huang hui to incorporate would cause a wave of crime and bloodshed, similar to what was then going on in San Francisco). The final result was that the petition for incorporation was denied.[46]

The Pao-huang hui tried to counteract these measures. Li Fu-chi of Canada, blaming Ch'ing agents for the party's difficulties in gaining recruits in Victoria, characterized his opponents as behaving "as if they had neither father nor emperor." More significantly, Li suggested that if K'ang's supporters were successful in China, these opponents should be shown no mercy. Party agitators in various cities publicly accused nonmembers of conniving with Americans to attack the Chinese community as a whole, a rather serious charge. The _Chung Sai Yat Po_ printed a series of editorials ridiculing the claim by the anonymous letter writer that the armies of the powers had been defeated. The newspaper maintained that political associations and political discussion were vital to the well-being of a nation and its citizens, and gave its editorial support to those whose home areas had been taxed in an attempt to generate the public pressure necessary to force them out of the Pao-huang hui. Both Li Fu-chi and the *Chung Sai Yat Po* wanted to believe the incorrect reports that Li Hung-chang, then governor-general of the two southern provinces of Kwangtung and Kwangsi, would not persecute the families in China of Pao-huang hui members. The newspaper and Li Fu-chi encouraged and applauded all attempts on the part of K'ang, Liang Ch'i-ch'ao, and others to win Li Hung-chang over to the Pao-huang hui cause. The Pao-huang hui in Vancouver and San Francisco even wrote Li asking for his support.[47]

Finally, the Pao-huang hui in Hawaii threatened to assassinate its chief opponent, the Chinese Consul Yang Wei-pin. He was the consul whose vigorous efforts had resulted in Hawaii's Pao-huang hui being denied permission to incorporate. In addition, Consul Yang had written to the Chinese authorities in Kwangtung asking them to arrest the family of one of Hawaii's most prominent Pao-huang hui members. In retaliation, the Pao-huang hui sent an anonymous letter to Consul Yang threatening his life. Yang responded by taking the letter to the Hawaii authorities, who dutifully notified Yang's bodyguards to be on the alert for an attack. Learning that the Hawaii officials were now at least minimally involved, San Francisco's Pao-huang hui published the claim that the Pao-huang hui in Hawaii was not actually planning to kill Yang (as in reality they did not fear him), but that they had only wanted to scare him. This seems to have been the end of the affair.[48]

Internal Problems and the Nature of the Early Pao-huang Hui

Problems for the Pao-huang hui did not all come from outside, however. Within the organization there was considerable disagreement and conflict that was separate and distinct from the problem of Ch'ing agents infiltrating and sowing discord. One involved Li Fu-chi's faction and a certain Tom Chhui Pak (also known as Tom Cheu

Phom or Tom Chhu Pak). Tom, a Protestant Christian who lived in New Westminster, British Columbia, was a leader and fund-raiser for the Pao-huang hui. He was an ardent backer of "K'ang's" military uprising (actually, T'ang Ts'ai-ch'ang's forces). He also felt that many Pao-huang hui members looked down on Christians, a situation he deplored. He accused Pao-huang hui leaders in Vancouver of "caring only for profits. They were not able to subscribe [funds for K'ang's army] and wish to embezzle." Finally, he advised K'ang to enlist bandits and common foot soldiers in his army, as both groups "are willing to lay down their life whenever they can find food and clothes."[49]

Li Fu-chi violently objected to Tom Chhui Pak, writing K'ang that Tom and others were "extremely 'savage' and causing a lot of trouble and that we must not trust them in the future."[50] Li's objections were based in part on the fact that Li was not a Christian. Furthermore, he was less interested in K'ang's army and more in favor of gaining power through winning people such as Li Hung-chang to their cause. Besides, Li Fu-chi was a businessman and a chief representative of that faction of the Pao-huang hui which ardently favored the development and protection of capitalism in China. Perhaps it was some of Li's friends that Tom suspected of embezzling. Finally, rather than wait for K'ang to approach bandits and common soldiers, Li Fu-chi suggested that the Pao-huang hui try to win over rich families in the interior of China, and generally try to rely on influential and respected individuals.[51]

This dispute raises the question of the nature of the early Pao-huang hui. That it was not an entirely homogeneous organization should come as no surprise in view both of the number of its adherents and the variety of aims that, by 1900, K'ang Yu-wei had assigned to the party: to promote commerce and industry; to save the Kuang-hsü Emperor through a military coup and/or assassination; to improve the situation of overseas Chinese; to change, extend, and modernize the educational system in China; to promote equality and "people's rights" through the gradual improvement of the citizenry; slowly to change the social system; to modernize the military; and so on. In addition, K'ang added a financial incentive for joining the party. Any person who contributed money to the Pao-huang hui coffers would be given shares in an as yet nonexistent gold or iron mine in China.[52]

The character of the Pao-huang hui was greatly influenced by its close association with the Chih-kung t'ang. (In Southeast Asia, it was loosely connected with the Triad I-hsing kung-szu.) As the Chih-kung t'ang federation was not a monolithic entity, its involvement need not have included all affiliated lodges. The Chih-kung t'ang lodge itself was in 1900 an enthusiastic supporter of K'ang Yu-wei, and especially of T'ang Ts'ai-ch'ang's proposed uprising. This enthusiasm was generated in part by the personal predilections of a few of the officers of the San Francisco headquarters, including most particularly Huang San-te (the head of the lodge and federation) and T'ang Ch'iung-ch'ang.[53] Part of the reason for Huang's and T'ang's interest in the Pao-huang hui may have been that they desired to place the Chih-kung t'ang at the head of the rising tide of nationalist sentiment and thereby increase their influence. After all, the Chih-kung t'ang had made a similar attempt in 1892 in the Geary Act fiasco, and was to do so again in 1904 when it permitted Sun Yat-sen to rewrite its regulations (see chapter 4). Another reason for their joining the party, of course, was that they were sincerely distressed by China's plight, and wanted to help rectify the existing situation.

The Chih-kung t'ang lodge and the federation leaders were not the only ones to throw their lot in with the Pao-huang hui. The "translators" lodge seems to have been an early supporter of the reform party. Since T'ang Ch'iung-ch'ang was its founder, the An-i t'ang must have favored the Pao-huang hui as well. Many of the lodges which supported the Pao-huang hui operated as units within it and attemped to use the Pao-huang hui to extend or maintain their power, not only in the Americas but even in China. For example, a Chinese naval commander on the Yangtze reported to Shanghai's *Shen pao* that the head of a Chih-kung t'ang-affiliated lodge in San Francisco had joined the Pao-huang hui and in his capacity as a Triad leader was having proreform tracts distributed around the Yangtze.[54]

The secret-society influence on the Pao-huang hui is very evident in one of the two remaining Chinese-language versions of a Pao-huang hui chapter's rules and regulations. These rules, or bylaws, were prepared for the Hawaii chapter in January of 1900. They note that "All members are brothers, no matter whether they are rich or poor, old or young," and "Those who have been admitted as members are termed 'brothers.' They ought to love each other as brothers from the same parents so as to exert themselves to take necessary steps in regard to political affairs of the country. If anyone do any harm or injury to our brothers we must retaliate the same &. &. [sic]." This was sworn to in the name of "Heaven our Emperor and Earth our Empress."[55] This is highly reminiscent of the type of brotherhood championed by late Ch'ing secret societies (especially the Triads), and even the language is similar to that used in Triad oaths.

The second remaining Chinese-language version of the Pao-huang hui's rules was evidently written by K'ang Yu-wei and used in Canada. In addition to promising to work to help both the emperor and overseas Chinese, and noting that anyone could join the party, the rules—Triad-like—required that all members must aid each other. As Sun was later to do, K'ang promised subsequent financial remuneration to anyone who gave money to the party. (Funds not needed in China could go towards the establishment of schools, hospitals, and the like in the overseas communities.) Peripatetic organizers for the party were guaranteed reimbursement for travel expenses and K'ang urged that party headquarters be established where weekly meetings could be held. The rules even gave details of Ch'ing imperial court life and court intrigues, the flattering implication being that overseas Chinese had the right to know such details. Finally, the rules urged overseas Chinese to forget their differences, take their destiny in their own hands, and work for the good of all China.[56]

The English-language versions of the bylaws show how the Pao-huang hui hoped to be viewed by Americans, and they also contain some of the ideas of the English-speaking, more Westernized party leaders. Of these versions, the one submitted in San Francisco during the process of its incorporation is perhaps the most revealing. It states that the purposes of the Pao-huang hui included: "elevating" Chinese to a level "equal that of any other civilized race," securing for them equal treatment by foreign countries and nationals, vigorously promoting "commercial enterprise," and inculcating the spirit of nationalism. The reason for promoting nationalism was that it was "an all sufficient blessing" which would enable Chinese to receive "that recognition from other nations which it is justly manifest should exist." Finally, the society would seek "to impress upon the Chinese people, the urgent need of a revival of reform in governmental affairs of China," which would help both China and overseas Chinese, the latter by placing "them on a footing of equality as is at this point enjoyed by the citizens of the United States."[57] The latter version once again underlines the fact that the positive response of Chinese in North America to the Pao-huang hui was related to their mistreatment by Americans. Obviously, also, at the outset it was the same strain of nationalism seen in the revolutionary party that expressed itself in the Pao-huang hui.

In the Chinese-language version of Pao-huang hui rules for the Hawaii chapter, the tone was militant and strongly influenced by secret society ideals. The regulations contained various protestations of dedication and activism including a stirring song written by Liang Ch'i-ch'ao which encouraged all to go and fight for the emperor and the nation. The Chinese-language rules for the Canada chapter were somewhat more moderate and the English-language charter in San Francisco seems even more so. Although the latter was primarily intended to look good to the American authorities, it also points up a legitimate split between militant radicals and moderate capitalists. Bound together by nationalism, party leaders disagreed as to how to make the nation strong and whom this strong nation was to benefit. The moderate merchants (Li Fu-chi, Yeh En, the *Chung Sai Yat Po*'s editor, Reverend Wu P'an-chao, and others) tended to favor an alliance with reform-minded officials such as Li Hung-chang, and generally resisted K'ang Yu-wei's pleas for money, arms, and volunteers. They were not happy with T'ang Ts'ai-ch'ang's Ko-lao hui connections—and in fact were not terribly enthusiastic about T'ang Ts'ai-ch'ang himself. The radicals supported T'ang Ts'ai-ch'ang and even looked with favor on Sun's Hui-chou uprising of 1900. This radical camp included T'ang Ch'iung-ch'ang, Tom Chhiu Pak, many members in Hawaii, and the Chih-kung t'ang federation headquarters in San Francisco.[58]

In the beginning, or at least in 1900, the radicals may have had the upper hand as K'ang Yu-wei had permitted himself to be named *Ta-lung-t'ou* (that is, supreme chief) of T'ang's Ko-lao hui associates, and titular head of the Tzu-li Chün (Independence Army). After the ignominious failure of T'ang and his associates in 1900, however, the moderate procapitalists became increasingly powerful. The radicals were demoralized by T'ang Ts'ai-ch'ang's failure, and many left the party. In addition, the moderates strengthened themselves by establishing a Commercial Corporation (Shang-wu kung-szu) in 1902 as a subsidiary of the Pao-huang hui. Founded by Li Fu-chi in Victoria with the help of Yeh En and others, the purpose of this corporation was to invest Pao-huang hui party funds and the money of wealthy party members in capitalistic enterprises. The profits would go partly to member-shareholders and partly to the financing of other Pao-huang hui ventures.[59]

In addition to the divisions noted thus far (between radicals and moderates, between those interested in commercial activities and those who were not, and between members of rival secret society lodges), there was one more that was of some importance: the division between Christians and non-Christians. This was particularly acute in Canada.

K'ang himself wanted the support of Christians as well as non-Christians. One of the staff members of the *Chung Sai Yat Po* (a kinsman of Reverend Wu P'an-chao) reports that when K'ang was founding the Pao-huang hui, K'ang wanted to include an article on revering Confucius and Confucianism *(pao-chiao)*. Desiring also to have the support of Chinese Christians, particularly Reverend Wu P'an-chao and other editors of a successful Christian newspaper in Los Angeles, K'ang wrote Reverend Wu to ask him to join the Pao-huang hui. The latter replied that he was interested, but wanted K'ang to abandon his talk of *pao-chiao*. If K'ang would do this, then Reverend Wu would change the orientation of his newspaper from a Christian news sheet to a political daily. When K'ang agreed, Reverend Wu and the other editors moved up to San Francisco (with its larger Chinese community and more important branch of the Pao-huang hui), and in February of 1900 began publishing the *Chung Sai Yat Po* as a pro-Pao-huang hui newspaper.[60] Again, in the summer of 1900, while K'ang was in Singapore, Chinese in New York established a branch of the Pao-huang hui in that city. The main branch in Singapore wrote the fledgling New York branch its congratulations in the name of the "sages" Confucius and Jesus. Evidently, K'ang was concerned with gaining the support of the Christians.[61]

Before entirely leaving the question of the nature of the early Pao-huang hui, one other type of member should be mentioned: the Americans. The most important American member of the Pao-huang hui was Homer Lea, a hunchbacked Stanford University student who had an apparent obsession with war and military strategy. He and the friends he was sometimes able to enlist in the cause gave strength to the radical wing of the Pao-huang hui: seeing himself as a latter-day Byron, Lea had every intention of leading an army in China—an army that was opposed to the conservative and reactionary faction of the Chinese court. In 1900, during his summer vacation, he and his friends organized a drill squad and let it be known that he wanted to fight the Empress Dowager. Hearing of this, a local Pao-huang hui leader invited him to join that organization and sent Lea from his family's home in Los Angeles up to San Francisco with Reverend Wu P'an-chao, who by that time was a Pao-huang hui stalwart. In San Francisco, Lea was initiated into the Pao-huang hui and the Chih-kung t'ang, and then was packed off to China with money, collected by the San Francisco Pao-huang hui, which he was to deliver to K'ang Yu-wei.[62]

Before embarking for Hong Kong, Lea solicited American volunteers to meet with him in China and fight the Empress Dowager under his command. This was the year of the Boxer Rebellion, and many Americans did volunteer. Yung Wing, then in China and associated with both the reformers and the revolutionaries, told British authorities that K'ang Yu-wei would have four hundred seasoned American veterans in his army. Lea, along with Liang Ch'i-ch'ao and Sun Yat-sen (and possibly Yung Wing as well), favored the tactic of coordinating the military efforts of the Pao-huang hui and the Hsing-Chung hui—a policy ardently opposed by K'ang Yu-wei. K'ang's wishes were eventually honored, but both uprisings failed. None of Homer Lea's American volunteers actually seem to have arrived in China. Lea himself, because of a variety of mishaps, only participated in a few minor skirmishes before the uprising of T'ang Ts'ai-ch'ang and the reformers had completely collapsed, and Lea was forced to return to the United States.[63]

With T'ang's collapse, the Pao-huang hui's first major attempt to force a radical change in Chinese politics and society had resulted in ignominious public failure. Still, the growth of the organization as a political party had been impressive. In spite of the quarrels and factions, it had started two newspapers in the Americas, one in Vancouver, called the *Jih-hsin pao* (New Day News), and one in Honolulu, the *Hsin Chung-kuo pao* (New China News), founded by Liang Ch'i-ch'ao in 1900.[64] The party had also persuaded two newspapers in San Francisco to affiliate with it: the *Wen-hsien pao,* whose affiliation remained permanent, and the *Chung Sai Yat Po,* whose support was temporary. Branches of the party existed on the west coast of Canada, throughout the continental United States, in Cuba, and in Hawaii (as well as in Japan and Southeast Asia).

The Situation in Hawaii

By mid-1900, as a result of Liang Ch'i-ch'ao's trip to the Hawaiian Islands, the Pao-huang hui had been able to destroy what little remained of the Hsing-Chung hui in Hawaii. Many of the Pao-huang hui's officers were drawn from the Hsing-Chung hui. These included the Pao-huang hui's president (Huang Liang, the Bishop's Bank officer), its treasurer (Chung Yü), an advisor (formerly the translator, and by then the editor, of Honolulu's *Lung-chi pao*), and one of its secretaries. Several of these men had formerly been officers in the Hsing-Chung hui. At least thirteen merchants switched from the Hsing-Chung hui to the Pao-huang hui in January of 1900. Others who switched included two translators for the Hawaiian government, and one of Sun Yat-sen's sworn brothers. Several of these people were from Hsiang-shan and at least one was Sun's former classmate.[65]

This, however, does not give a full picture of Sun's loss and the Pao-huang hui's gain. For example, Chung Yü in 1900 was already a manager of the United Chinese Society and in the following year became its president. The defection of the *Lung-chi pao*'s chief editor turned that newspaper from what had once been a Hsing-Chung hui into a pro-Pao-huang hui organ. Finally, Sun Mei (Sun Yat-sen's older brother) was so impressed by Liang Ch'i-ch'ao that he not only joined the Pao-huang hui but also asked his eldest son to revere Liang as an older brother. Sun Mei sent this son to accompany Liang in Honolulu and later sent him to the Pao-huang hui school in Japan.[66]

Why did these important former Hsing-Chung hui members and officers join the Pao-huang hui? Sun Yat-sen has said it was because he had given Liang Ch'i-ch'ao a letter of introduction to his friends, his brother, and the Hsing-Chung hui in Hawaii. Sun believed Liang had been won over to the side of revolution and wanted an alliance between the Hsing-Chung hui and the Pao-huang hui. While Liang was in fact interested in revolution, he continued to obey his teacher K'ang Yu-wei; so the Pao-huang hui in Hawaii, although militant, favored restoring the Kuang-hsü Emperor and was definitely a rival to the Hsing-Chung hui.[67]

Sun's opinion as to why Liang was so successful, however, is not the only view. Some, like Loretta Pang, say that the Chinese in Hawaii were simply confused about the aims of the two parties and were also unsure as to what was the best solution to China's problems. This is undoubtedly true. But Liang Ch'i-ch'ao saw his success as a direct result of his joining a branch of the Chih-kung t'ang in the Islands. Significantly, perhaps, one of the first people in Honolulu to join the party was a high-ranking officer of the Chih-kung t'ang. Chung Yü writes that his own interest was aroused by hearing Liang's gossip about the plight of the emperor and the doings of high officials. In other words, Chung (and presumably others as well) was flattered that so famous a figure as Liang Ch'i-ch'ao would seek Chung's friendship, and that the emperor himself ostensibly wanted overseas Chinese to come to his aid.[68] In addition to all these factors, the *Szu-i* members of the Hawaiian community must have been impressed by the fact that Liang was both a *Szu-i* and of high social status. And finally, since 1895 there had been no viable political organization for them to join.

Not surprisingly, at its first formal meeting the Pao-huang hui in Hawaii had almost one hundred members, nearly two-thirds as many as the Hsing-Chung hui there had ever acquired. By the fall of 1900, one party leader estimated that nine-tenths of the Chinese in the Islands had joined, including merchants and laborers. The Chinese consul in the Islands partially corroborated this by noting that Chinese in Hawaii were far more "traitorous" than those in San Francisco, and that many Christians had joined and made very generous financial contributions. Huang Liang, the Catholic head of the society, made the largest single contribution of one thousand U.S. dollars—for which reason his family in China was later harassed. In addition, the Pao-huang hui commanded enough capital to let Liang Ch'i-ch'ao found the *Hsin Chung-kuo pao,* and the newspaper in turn helped win new adherents to the Pao-huang hui.[69]

Thus, between 1894 and 1900, two political parties were estab-

lished among overseas Chinese in the Americas. Of these two parties, only the Pao-huang hui was viable. Various factors in addition
to their respective political ideologies caused people to join one or
the other, or one then the other, or neither. In fact, to the extent that
the Pao-huang hui had its radical faction and the Hsing-Chung hui
solicited merchants, and to the extent that cooperation between
reform and revolutionary leaders in China had occurred in the past
and continued to occur until the middle of 1903, it can be said that
politics was confused and diffuse enough to make the two parties
seem in many ways rather similar.

There are five principal ways in which the Hsing-Chung hui was
clearly distinguished from the Pao-huang hui, however. First was
the social standing (by Western as well as by Chinese standards) of
their respective founders. Social standing here includes the matter of
"ethnic" affiliation. Second was the Pao-huang hui's intimate relationship with an even higher-ranking, and certainly sympathetic,
individual: the Kuang-hsü Emperor. This association added an aura
of great legitimacy to the party.

Third was the willingness of Pao-huang hui leaders to join the
Chih-kung t'ang and work with it. Fourth was the matter of timing:
although Sun's second trip to the Americas was made after China's
defeat by Japan, when K'ang and Liang arrived some three years
later, China's position had deteriorated, and the need for change
became even more pressing. Finally, the Pao-huang hui had at its
disposal, and was able to attract, dedicated men who went from one
place to another organizing party branches, helping to clarify policy,
and encouraging members when times became difficult. In other
words, it had a reasonably high level of organization. It may be that
the idea of using peripatetic organizers (K'ang Yu-wei himself,
along with Liang Ch'i-ch'ao, Liang Ch'i-t'ien, Li Fu-chi, Yeh En,
and later Hsü Ch'in, Ou Chü-chia, and others) was not part of
K'ang's original plan. But whether it was K'ang or overseas Chinese
in Canada who started the practice is irrelevant. The practice was a
valuable one, and one that Sun Yat-sen and the Hsing-Chung hui
learned only relatively late.

From an examination of the founding of the Hsing-Chung hui
and the Pao-huang hui, it is further evident that many characteristics usually ascribed to the revolutionaries also applied to the Pao-
huang hui—and sometimes even more to the latter than to the for-

mer. Hence, it can be seen that the Pao-huang hui was strongly influenced by its Triad connections, that it had special appeal to overseas Chinese merchants, that it was a nationalistic organization tied to the mistreatment of Chinese abroad, and that certain factions within it championed revolutionary action and military uprisings.

Huang San-te (Wong Sam Duck), head of the Chih-kung t'ang federation in San Francisco. (Author's collection)

The Reverend Wu P'an-chao (Ng Poon Chew), founder and publisher of San Francisco's *Chung Sai Yat Po*. (Asian Studies Library Archives, University of California, Berkeley)

Honolulu's Chinatown as it was when Sun Yat-sen and Liang Ch'i-ch'ao first visited the islands. (Hawaii State Archives)

Vancouver's Chinatown, 1904. (Vancouver Public Library)

K'ang Yu-wei (right), Liang Ch'i-ch'ao (left), and the Kuang-hsü emperor (center). (Janette Moffat)

Liang Ch'i-ch'ao (standing) with Pao-huang hui leaders in Vancouver, 1903. (Mrs. Hilda Cumyow)

Stock certificate issued in 1908 for the Pao-huang hui's bank in Mexico. (Author photo, original in the archives of the Asian American Studies Library, University of California, Berkeley)

Sun Yat-sen with supporters in Chicago, 1909. Sun is seated directly to the right of the table. (Archives, Asian American Studies Library, University of California, Berkeley)

附錄檀山正埠帝國憲政總會公啟

公啟者○○去年曾奉康會長命○於本報佈告公文○嗣後凡屬我會○有招股振

與實業等事○有總會會長之六厶文認可方作公辦○各同志之入股者○將來興敗

○本會可任其咎○不然○即與本會無涉○此佈告諒亦早已深悉○近因振華

廣美公司招股以來○未嘗有隻文佈告爲我會公辦○我同志想亦早已洞悉

公私瞭然○○事出有因○無怪我同志來函詢問○今再聲明○振華廣美公司

自有振華廣美公司之辦事人○於本會無涉○幸勿誤會○謹此敬請　義安

一千九百零九年六月廿九號　　　　　檀山正埠帝國憲政總會公啟

按讀代理督辦徐勤等之佈告書○其破壞振華公司招股之鐵証明矣○又檀

山正埠帝國憲政總會之公啟○康會長亦未曾代振華招股事飛一字鼓舞矣

○更顯然與徐勤等無涉矣○現因徐勤任意造詞○四處函告○誣攻振華創

辦諸熱心實業愛國人○是以再將其佈告原書附印成套○想諸公持平○一

閱如見其肺肝然○○

康徐等平日所謂具有愛國之大名○○請其反躬自問○○豈是此佈告書誠救國

Open letter to Hawaii's Pao-huang hui/Hsien-cheng t'ang trying to calm fears aroused by the scandals and financial difficulties of the Commercial Corporation in 1909. (Author photo, original in the archives of the Asian American Studies Library, University of California, Berkeley)

"Success to the Revolution," scene from a San Francisco parade. (California State Library)

Flag of the new Republic of China on parade in San Francisco, 1911. (California State Library)

3

THE PAO-HUANG HUI

TAKES ROOT

In August of 1900, when Ch'ing officials put down T'ang Ts'ai-ch'ang's uprising, they thereby ensured that neither K'ang Yu-wei nor the Pao-huang hui would take control of China's destiny. T'ang's defeat led to a series of ideological and organizational changes in the Pao-huang hui's American branches, as conservatives and radicals jockeyed for control of the party. The factionalism and power shifts were related to economic, geographic, and secret society rivalries, as well as to differing political views. In a sense, this internal difficulty can be thought of as the natural fermentation needed to enable the party to take root in the Chinese communities. By 1902, it had produced what seemed to be a party in which prorevolutionaries had achieved a balance with commercial-minded moderates, a party with which almost all of the major social organizations were satisfied.

The Reaction to Events in China

Chinese in the Americas were slow to learn what was taking place in China, both because of the confused situation in China and because the trans-Pacific cable was not yet complete. T'ang Ts'ai-ch'ang's uprising failed in the month of August, but it was not until early October of 1900 that Chinese-language newspapers in North America began publicizing this fact. At first, they did not even associate the failure with the Pao-huang hui, but by November 7 they noted that several reform leaders had been executed, and finally, on November 27, they were able to clarify the connection between T'ang Ts'ai-ch'ang, K'ang Yu-wei and the uprising.[1]

While Chinese in North America were learning of the collapse of K'ang Yu-wei's military schemes, they were also hearing that Sun Yat-sen and the secret society San-ho hui, in alliance with certain reformers, had launched a more successful uprising near Hui-chou in Kwangtung province. Other reports indicated that several prominent reformers in China and Southeast Asia were again trying to affect an alliance with Li Hung-chang.[2]

In the face of these confusing reports, many moderate Pao-huang hui members felt that their leaders, especially K'ang and T'ang Ts'ai-ch'ang, had failed them. They deplored K'ang's (and Sun Yat-sen's) alliance with secret societies and called on the southern governors-general to suppress the Ko-lau hui (on whom T'ang Ts'ai-ch'ang depended) as well as the San-ho hui, the Hsing-Chung hui, and Sun's own Hui-chou uprising.[3] An editor of the *Chung Sai Yat Po* called T'ang a "rebel chieftain" *(ch'ü-k'uei)*, and in Vancouver a Pao-huang hui leader claiming to be the "secretary of the Chinese Reform Association in the Americas" told the *New York Tribune* that Chinese in the Americas were "loud in their expressions of disapproval of the conduct of the [military] campaign by their leaders."[4]

Perhaps a bit jealous of Sun Yat-sen's geater success, this moderate wing of the Pao-huang hui ridiculed Sun and the Hui-chou uprising. They were particularly scornful of the Triad slogan "*fan-Ch'ing, fu-Ming* (overthrow the Ch'ing, restore the Ming)." They declared the revolutionary supporters to be a generally ignorant lot. Even before Sun had failed, they predicted that inevitably he would, just as the Taiping Rebellion before him had failed. He would fail because revolution was not what the times called for. This was the period of *hsiao-k'ang* (small strength), when the imperial system was still needed. By ignoring this, Sun had given the powers an excuse to send more troops to China, and (so moderate Christian members indignantly claimed) had even permitted his followers to burn down several churches.[5]

The criticisms of K'ang, T'ang, and Sun because of their willingness to make alliances with secret societies is most interesting in view of the fact that many members and leaders of the Pao-huang hui in North America were also Triad members. Why did they scorn secret societies in China and the Triad rallying cry of "*fan-Ch'ing, fu-Ming*"? At least some of the critics were Triad members themselves,[6] so it would seem that those who belonged to the Triads in the Americas considered themselves better educated, more sensible, and better qualified to understand events than their secret society "brothers" in the hinterland (relatively speaking) of China. The opposition of moderates to *"fan-Ch'ing, fu-Ming,"* for example, was based on the argument that there was no Ming dynasty left to be restored, nor had the Ming imperial house always ruled with justice and foresight.[7]

Many Triad members in the Americas were shocked by the violence of the secret-society Boxers during the Boxer Rebellion. The *Chung Sai Yat Po* editors at first sympathized with the Boxers and even suggested that they were incipient Chinese nationalists. But later, when they learned that the Boxers were burning churches, killing Christians, and laying siege to the foreign legations in Peking, the editors reversed themselves. They went so far as to declare that the powers had a moral right to send an army to Peking to break the siege.[8] The *Chung Sai Yat Po* editors were moderates, but even T'ang Ch'iung-ch'ang, who was not, was so upset by the destructiveness of the Boxers (and the American reaction to it) that he started an English-language newspaper in San Francisco to try to persuade Americans that Chinese in the United States deplored the bloodshed caused by the Boxers.[9]

Chinese in the Americas were unanimous in their opposition to the Boxers, but not all Pao-huang hui members were moderates opposed to T'ang Ts'ai-ch'ang, Sun Yat-sen, and their secret society allies. The party's radical camp, which backed T'ang, Sun, and others like them, did not control any newspapers, but some radicals did send editorials to the existing moderate publications like the *Chung Sai Yat Po*. In these editorials, the radicals castigated governor-general Chang Chih-tung for having suppressed the "Pao-huang hui" army. They also declared that Sun and his allies were not anti-Christian, and moreover they were not only competent militarily, but their treatment of the local populace and their inherent governing ability had won most of the uncommitted to their side in the region in which they were operating.[10]

Sun's Hui-chou uprising failed, of course, but before Chinese in the Americas learned of his failure, news came that Liang Ch'i-ch'ao had announced that the Pao-huang hui was going to unite with the Hsing-Chung hui. The two parties together would then raise a new army in China to seize control of the government.[11] The more radical members of the Pao-huang hui in the Americas must have greeted this news with enthusiasm (as did Chinese in Australia, where Liang was then staying). The moderates, however, did not and publicized a rumor instead that the Kuang-hsü Emperor would soon return to power without the aid of an army, and reinstate the 1898 reformers.[12]

The suggestion that another army might be raised helped delay for a time an exodus of radicals from the Pao-huang hui. In addition, it still seemed possible that Li Hung-chang would ally with the Pao-huang hui and lead an army against the Empress Dowager. As late as January of 1901, there was a man in San Francisco with a letter he claimed was from Li Hung-chang soliciting funds for just such an army. In January, however, after this man had already spent several months in San Francisco, another letter arrived from Li rejecting the idea of cooperation and disowning the first letter.[13]

The Temporary Rise of the Moderates

By the end of January 1901, the Pao-huang hui and its leaders had no further suggestions as to how either the reformers or reform principles were going to triumph in China. In the meantime, the powers were withdrawing their armies from China, and the danger that the country might be dismembered began once again to recede. The court, under the Empress Dowager, embarked on a program of moderate reform, but at the same time launched another campaign to weaken the Pao-huang hui. K'ang Yu-wei, for his part, began to work actively to prevent any future involvement of the Pao-huang hui in any military venture. Under these circumstances, many individuals—especially radicals—left the party. Those radicals who remained behind found their influence noticeably diminished. Events, in a word, conspired to strengthen the moderate wing of the party.

The moderates, although opposed to violent change, were no mere proponents of the status quo. They did want China to be led by a strong emperor; they did feel that the base of political power should remain narrow; and they did lack confidence in the ability of the Chinese people as a whole to exercise self-government; but they also felt that they, themselves, should play a leading role in Chinese politics. This, of course, went counter to prevailing Chinese law and tradition. The moderates desired to lead, both because they felt it to be their right and because they felt that the policies they favored would benefit China. The type of role they sought in some ways resembled the traditional gentry role of aiding, advising, and partially staffing the government—but was more active, as shall be seen.

The moderates particularly favored policies designed to encourage commerce, manufacturing, and free-market capitalism in China. In October of 1900, they took a daring step to promote these policies: the Pao-shang chü stalwarts of the Pao-huang hui in San Francisco managed to secure the official backing of the Chinese Six Companies for a memorial to the Ch'ing court. This memorial consisted of sixteen suggestions as to how the Chinese government should deal with commerce, foreign travel involving Chinese nationals, and merchants engaged in overseas trade.[14]

A number of suggestions concerned the procedure for issuing passports. The memorial asked that passports be issued through local government officials in conjunction with merchant organizations such as San Francisco's Chinese Six Companies, and requested in general that the procedures involved be changed to approximate more nearly those of the United States government. The memorial also suggested that people returning to China should pay a fee to the official or merchant group handling their papers. It further specified that three classes of people should be denied passports: "unemployed vagabonds" *(wu-yeh yu-min)*, those who cheated on their entrance or import-export taxes, and those who illegally smuggled Chinese into other countries.[15]

In China, the memorial suggested, chambers of commerce should be established consisting of local merchants in free association to help both Chinese and foreign merchants. Members of these chambers of commerce (who were called *shen-shang*, "gentry and merchants") should not be permitted to adopt "official" airs and should be available to whomever wanted to see them. Business ventures and the property in China of overseas-Chinese merchants should be protected by the government, and their property outside China should also be protected when they were in China. Merchants should pay taxes, but they should help decide the tax rate in newly opened ports. Finally, the government should actively encourage merchants and businessmen in general by giving them a larger role in the development of commercial and economic policy.[16]

The fact that this memorial was formally sanctioned by the Six Companies is as interesting as are the sixteen suggestions it contains. By 1901, leaders of several *hui-kuan* were looking with favor on the Pao-huang hui. These were the Kang-chou hui-kuan and San-i hui-kuan, both of which were dominated by merchants, and the Ho-ho hui-kuan, an organization actively attempting to increase its influence in the community. Since the memorial was introduced to the Six Companies by Pao-shang chü members, there is a strong possibility that Pao-huang hui moderates from these three *hui-kuan* were using the memorial to increase their power in the Six Companies.

Several aspects of the memorial appealed to the self-interest of the Six Companies, particularly the suggestion that the Six Companies be given some formal authority in the matter of issuing passports. Furthermore, the proposal suggesting a fee for those returning to China, if adopted by the Chinese government, would have granted legal sanction to the customary fee required by the Chinese Six Companies of any Chinese leaving the United States, a levy it considered of great importance.

The proposal that smugglers should be denied passports tells something about factions within the Pao-huang hui. Some of the party's most prominent moderates in Canada, probably including Yeh En (who, in 1900, was head of Canada's Pao-huang hui), were involved in smuggling.[17] It would have been difficult as well for smuggling to be done without the knowledge and connivance of the "translators' " lodge, for after all, its members were located at border stations, were officially connected with these stations, and would have known if a large number of Chinese mysteriously appeared in the Chinese community. Yet in 1902 and 1903, the "translators' " lodge was a staunch supporter of the Pao-huang hui. Unless we make the illogical assumption that the Pao-huang hui leaders were deliberately proposing policies that ran against some of their own interests, we must assume that the Pao-shang chü in San Francisco represented one faction of the Pao-huang hui, and those associated with the smuggling, a rival faction.

Several additional factors lend weight to this argument: even before 1900, there is evidence that a good deal of friction existed between Chinese in Canada and in the United States, with both San Francisco and the Vancouver/Victoria/New Westminster area seeking to speak for all Chinese in the Americas. Since the Pao-huang hui was founded in western Canada, Chinese there may have seen the reform party as a vehicle for capturing the leadership from San Francisco, whose Chinese Six Companies and Chih-kung t'ang lodge were then claiming supremacy. It is also quite likely that one reason Chinese in San Francisco organized their own branch of the Pao-huang hui before K'ang's official emissary could get down from Canada was to retain the leadership for San Francisco. And finally, a great deal of enmity existed between members of the "translators'" lodge and other lodges in the Chih-kung t'ang federation, enmity which in 1903 led to an open fight.[18]

Before discussing the effects of the memorial on Chinese in the Americas, the implications of one other section of this memorial should be pointed out. Not only is the use of the term *shen-shang* significant, but also the provision that the *shen-shang* members of the proposed chambers of commerce should not be allowed to adopt "official" airs. What these and other parts of the memorial suggest is that overseas merchant-businessmen had acquired self-respect, had expectations that the government and its organs would serve them, and had come to favor the free enterprise system. These ideas were undoubtedly at least partly due to their living in an American environment.

The day after the *Chung Sai Yat Po* had published the full text of this memorial on its front page, it aroused so much support among both merchants and laborers in San Francisco's Chinatown that the Six Companies called an open meeting for the same afternoon to discuss it. More than three hundred people attended; several San Francisco policemen came as well, wanting to break up the meeting because it was "too crowded." Apparently the Six Companies elders agreed because they adjourned the meeting for two hours until more spacious quarters could be found to house it, but when they reconvened, none of the elders appeared, and so it had to be canceled.[19] Evidently the idea of self-government had only limited support among community leaders. It also seems likely that the Pao-shang chü partisans wanted self-determination for merchants, but did not seek to extend this to laborers.

As the triumph of the conservative faction at the Ch'ing court became evident, all parties connected with the memorial began to have second thoughts. Not too long after it was sent off (via the Chinese consul in San Francisco), some Pao-shang chü adherents suggested that the memorial would make it easy for the Ch'ing government to identify America's Pao-huang hui leaders. Whether or not this was the case, it took two years for the Ch'ing court to react formally to this memorial. This formal reaction was highly unfavorable and even threatening, and in response the Chinese Six Companies renounced any connection with it, claiming that although the memorial purported to be endorsed by all of the Six Companies officers,[20] a reexamination of their records indicated that a few people (presumably Pao-huang hui members) had falsely borrowed the name of the whole organization in order to further their own ends. By this time, none of the Pao-huang hui/Pao-shang chü partisans were willing to acknowledge their connection with the memorial. In the end, the Six Companies requested Chinese minister Wu T'ing-fang and San Francisco's Chinese consul to intercede for them with the court so that only the guilty original authors of the memorial (whose identity should be ascertained by an investigation) would be punished.[21]

By the time everyone had disavowed the memorial, the Pao-huang hui was no longer the vital political party it had been in 1900. This was due not only to the failure of all military attempts but to the confused situation in China and news that the major political leaders of the parties could no longer agree on political goals. None of the Pao-huang hui's major leaders came to the Americas between 1900 and 1902, and this further contributed to party weakness.[22]

The New Organizational Drive

In addition to its decline, between 1900 and 1902 the Pao-huang hui in the Americas was increasingly beset by factionalism. This began when certain agents of K'ang Yu-wei made a new drive to strengthen the moderate, royalist, procapitalist faction of the Pao-huang hui against the remaining radicals. The most important of these was Liang Ch'i-t'ien, who toured the Americas in 1901.[23] Liang Ch'i-t'ien was no stranger to Chinese in the Americas. As K'ang

Yu-wei's emissary and a member of the Chih-kung t'ang, he had visited Canada and the continental United States in 1900, helping to organize and reorganize branches of the Pao-huang hui. When in San Francisco, he met with the Pao-huang hui branch that had spontaneously arisen in that city, confirming some of its officers in their posts and appointing new ones to other positions.[24]

In 1901, his duties were to help revive old chapters of the Pao-huang hui, organize new ones, and ensure that the branch societies were pursuing the proper political goals. In one community in western Canada, he persuaded eighty to ninety percent of the Chinese residents to join. Another small community, hearing that Liang was in the area, spontaneously established a branch, then invited Liang to come and instruct them in proper ideology. In both of these communities, the most ardent swore "peach garden" oaths that they would die trying to restore the emperor to power.[25]

Everywhere he went, Liang Ch'i-t'ien stressed the theme of loyalty to the emperor. In Baker City, Oregon, a chapter of the Pao-huang hui founded by Liang during the 1901 organizational drive sent an open communication to other Pao-huang hui chapters noting that before Liang's arrival, they thought they should not, could not, and would not try to preserve the emperor. Liang, however, convinced them that the emperor must be saved before reforms could be introduced, and that unless China were saved, their own lives and families would be forfeited.[26]

Through this means, the ideas of nationalism and preserving the emperor were linked together. One effect of this linkage was the further erosion of interregional and interclan barriers. People most inclined to admire the West were appealed to directly through nationalism. For the benefit of the more traditional, Liang Ch'i-t'ien and the other Pao-huang hui moderates also stressed loyalty and other traditional virtues (*chung* and *chung-ai, jen,* and *te:* loyalty, benevolence, and morality), hoping that this would persuade people to transcend their regional and clan orientation and work for all of China. Ironically, then, many of the party's most ardent members (those who swore "peach garden" oaths of loyalty) must also have been the most conservative, but their swearing of the oath was taking them in a more Western direction. Liang's approach had great appeal, enough to permit Yeh En to call a meeting in Vancouver of all Pao-huang hui members in western Canada. The meeting was well attended, and in view of the political situation in China at the time, this act of attendance must have taken considerable courage.[27]

Not long afterwards, however, the Pao-huang hui split into two rival camps. In one camp were those who emphasized power to the people *(min-ch'üan),* favored a democratic revolution patterned after those of France and the United States, and wanted to promote egalitarianism by eliminating the power and status of the elite *(chün-chu kuei-tsu).* In the other were the "royalists" *(tsun ti-kuo),* who wanted to strengthen the monarchy after the example of Japan (and perhaps Peter the Great), believing that the promotion of *min-ch'üan* could destroy the country through the disorder it would cause. The revolutionaries countered the latter argument by saying that destruction must precede construction.[28] This split was also related to the fact that K'ang and Liang Ch'i-ch'ao were at that time engaged in a similar argument, K'ang taking the side of the monarchy and Liang adopting an anti-Manchu, prorevolutionary, and prodemocratic stand.[29]

The tension in the quarrel between the two factions in the Americas became so acute that Liang Ch'i-t'ien was forced to end his tour early, and the more diplomatic Hsü Ch'in (or Hsü Shih-ch'in, a student of K'ang's) was sent to replace him. Hsü arrived in San Francisco in August of 1901,[30] in time to help celebrate the Kuang-hsü Emperor's birthday there. His presence seems to have put an end to the discord: over one hundred people attended the birthday dinner given in honor of the emperor, including representatives of the *Chung Sai Yat Po* (which had recently sided with the revolutionaries), San Francisco Bay area Pao-huang hui partisans, and even a handful of Americans.[31]

Hsü was the principal speaker at the birthday dinner. He discussed China's problems, adding that these problems would not destroy her. Surprisingly enough, in the *Chung Sai Yat Po*'s report of the speech, the Kuang-hsü Emperor was never mentioned, although Hsü did list twelve reasons for believing that China would survive. Hsü felt that China's large population and vast territory, the native intelligence of its citizens, and its people's unity were the chief causes for hope. Two of the types of unity he noted were racial unity (there was no mention of a distinction between Han and Manchu or, of course, between *San-i, Szu-i,* and Hakka) and religious unity, for Hsü could discern only two real religions in China: Confucianism and Christianity (all others were dying out!). In order to save China, Hsü called for such generally accepted measures as the nurturing of nationalism, the instituting of reforms, and the encouraging of a positive frame of mind.[32]

Like Liang Ch'i-t'ien, Hsü's assignment in the Americas was to revive the Pao-huang hui. Judging from his speeches, he seems to have gone out of his way to avoid offending any faction, and he reported that he was able to solve the quarrel between local moderates and nationals.[33] Hsü's conduct was also notable for his giving a public accounting of the money he received from Pao-huang hui chapters. His first four months in the Americas were spent in San Francisco, after which he toured the rest of North America. He was especially well received in New York, and in fact founded that city's branch of the Pao-huang hui. October found him in the Vancouver/ Victoria area, where he discovered that Pao-huang hui members were especially interested in learning what progress had been made towards opening the mine mentioned in the Pao-huang hui rules.[34] After Canada, Hsü's itinerary was to return to the United States and visit the Chinese communities located in the central and eastern part of the country. Finally, he was to go to Latin America.[35] His long tour produced a general revival of the Pao-huang hui and led to the establishment of Pao-huang hui chapters in many areas of Latin America. Torreón in Mexico, and Havana, Cuba, were two cities where the Pao-huang hui achieved immediate success, enrolling several tens if not hundreds of members by the end of 1902.[36]

Hsü's ability to make peace between the various factions of the Pao-huang hui and increase its membership—both numerical and active—had the partial effect of bringing radicals such as San Francisco's T'ang Ch'iung-ch'ang back into the party's councils.[37] But grounds for further conflict remained since both the royalists and those who favored the protection of commerce over revolutionary schemes continued to exercise influence in the party. In addition, the Vancouver/Victoria branches did not completely lose their dominance over the Pao-huang hui in the continental Americas, although they were only able to retain this dominance by allowing California, and San Francisco in particular, to have greater independence.

As a result, the year 1902 saw Homer Lea (with the blessings of California's Pao-huang hui radicals) prepare to go to China to help organize a revolutionary coup while Ou Chü-chia came to San

Francisco to generate more support for the same coup. Simultaneously, in the Middle West of the United States, Pao-huang hui chapters organized drill teams and self-defense corps to protect the Chinese communities against outside (American) aggressors.[38] Between
1902 and 1904, Homer Lea turned many of these corps into cadet
training schools designed to prepare their members for military duty
in China. In the midst of all this radical activity, the more moderate
Vancouver/Victoria branches of the Pao-huang hui under Yeh En
and Li Fu-chi founded the Commercial Corporation (Shang-wu
kung-szu) as a subsidiary organ of the Pao-huang hui and a logical
byproduct of the Pao-shang chü.

The Commercial Corporation was perhaps the least politically
inclined branch of its parent political party. It helped pave the way
for the later corruption that permeated the organization and encouraged the conservatism usually associated with the Pao-huang hui. Li
Fu-chi is the official founder of the corporation. He organized it in
the winter of 1902 in Victoria, with the cooperation of Yeh En;[39] it
will be recalled that the Chinese community in Victoria was dominated by businessmen and was the home of Canada's central branch
of the Chih-kung t'ang.

Li Fu-chi and Yeh En intended for the Commercial Corporation
to sell one million dollars in stocks to raise capital, and to use this
capital to further the stockholders' political and capitalistic aims.
The one million dollars was to come in part from Pao-huang hui coffers, and in part through private subscription.[40] It can immediately
be seen how such an arrangement might blur the line between the
political goals of the Pao-huang hui on the one hand, and the personal goals of the directors and stockholders of the Commercial Corporation on the other. Indeed, as we shall see below, the temptation
was to prove irresistible, with devastating effects upon the party's
strength.

This problem, however, lay in the future. In 1902, the Pao-huang
hui appeared to be thriving. While the capitalistic faction was being
strengthened through the development of the Commercial Corporation, the radicals were being encouraged by the prorevolutionary
pronouncements of Liang Ch'i-ch'ao. Having started out in 1899 as
an alliance between radicals and moderates, it was composed of
approximately the same factions in 1902. In spite of the disagree-

ments between its members and leaders, their conflicting interests, and the political changes that had occurred in China, the organization was not only viable but still growing. It had weathered the setbacks and failures of late 1900 and 1901. In a tentative fashion, it had even begun directing the Chinese community away from social groupings based on regionalism, clan affiliation, and secret-society lodge. Instead of these divisions, the Pao-huang hui organizers emphasized ideological commitment and, by supporting first the Pao-shang chü and then the Commercial Corporation, distinctions based on means of livelihood and economic status.

It would be incorrect to overemphasize the party's ability to render insignificant the earlier social divisions. But in 1902, factionalism and community distinctions were temporarily muted as Chinese in the Americas, through the Pao-huang hui, were beginning to develop and express a growing interest in national politics. The party members themselves were bound together by nationalism, an interest in becoming politically effective, and a desire to see China adopt a more Western outlook and policies. And by 1902, they were increasingly learning to expect to have a politically active role in society.

4

THE BEGINNING
OF DIFFERENTIATION

During Hsü Ch'in's visit, the Pao-huang hui in the Americas had managed to preserve its unity by refusing to adopt a consistent ideology. Between 1902 and 1904 this situation reversed itself. First the party became prorevolutionary; then, in a final about-face, all of the party's major leaders turned decisively against revolution. The result was that by 1904, the Pao-huang hui had become the Reform Party in fact as well as in name. Simultaneously, as in Southeast Asia, leadership of local branches increasingly devolved upon progressive businessmen.

The growing ideological coherence of the Pao-huang hui (as well as its rapid about-face) had some unexpected repercussions. By 1904 Chinese in the Americas no longer accepted the Pao-huang hui as the only vehicle for political opinion and protest. The Hsing-Chung hui managed to revive, presenting the Pao-huang hui with a viable rival in the Americas for the first time.[1] Furthermore, a sizable proportion of the Pao-huang hui's membership in the United States broke away from the party. These people became "independents" (people with no party affiliation who still expressed opinions on what should be done to save China). In 1904, the independents claimed that they were more numerous and commanded more respect than the Pao-huang hui. There was no need to compare themselves with the Hsing-Chung hui, for although contemporary newspapers reported that speeches by Sun Yat-sen attracted large and enthusiastic audiences,[2] the actual membership of America's Hsing-Chung hui in January of 1905 was under fifty people.

The Chih-kung t'ang also became more politicized during this period. As one sign of this development, it founded and supported a political newspaper in San Francisco. In addition, it gave material support to prorevolutionary movements in China and broke with the Pao-huang hui when the latter turned against revolution. It even took steps that effected a partial alliance with Sun Yat-sen on the basis of its support for revolution.

The Pao-huang Hui Opts for Revolution

Late in 1902, another disciple of K'ang Yu-wei arrived in North America to further the Pao-huang hui organizational drive. Named Ou Chü-chia, he landed in San Francisco and shortly afterwards published a revolutionary tract entitled *Hsin Kwangtung* (New Kwangtung). The popular Hsü Ch'in was credited with being a coauthor.[3] *Hsin Kwangtung* enjoyed wide distribution, not only in the Americas but also in other overseas Chinese communities and even, to the extent that this was possible, in southern China. In the tract, Ou proclaimed that Kwangtung province belonged to Cantonese in the same fashion in which a company belongs to its stockholders. He declared that since the government in Kwangtung was being poorly run, the province should have a revolution to make it independent and to give Cantonese the power of self-determination. A few far-sighted scholars and the secret societies (the latter, according to Ou, had become true revolutionaries ever since the downfall of the Ming dynasty) should spearhead the province's revolution. Several of Ou's friends and associates (including Hung Ch'üan-fu, the putative brother of the Taiping leader Hung Hsiu-ch'üan) were at that moment organizing just such a revolutionary attempt in the Canton area, which would certainly have influenced Ou's audience. Chinese in the Americas would also have appreciated the fact that most leaders of the attempted uprising, including Hung Ch'üan-fu and Yung Wing, had spent many years abroad. Hung and Yung Wing, in fact, had lived in the United States.[4]

Enthusiasm for *Hsin Kwangtung* and its revolutionary, pro-secret society theme was widespread throughout the Americas (as well as in other overseas Chinese communities). An official Chinese government report captured by the British noted that one of Hung Ch'üan-fu's chief backers was a man who lived in California and was "very rich with a very bad character."[5] In 1903, after Hung's uprising had failed, Liang Ch'i-ch'ao commented that Chinese, and Pao-huang hui chapters, in Oregon and the Vancouver area were still so prerevolutionary that his own interest in revolution was revived. (Leaders in Vancouver even wrote the Hong Kong headquarters asking that party rules be changed.)[6] Liang tried to persuade Pao-huang hui leaders in Hong Kong and Southeast Asia that the party must launch a successful rising in the immediate future, in order to preserve the allegiance of America's Chinese.[7] In San Francisco, one faction of the Pao-huang hui became violently anti-Manchu in addition to favoring Cantonese independence. It also talked of *min-ch'üan* ("people's power") as opposed to *chün-ch'üan* (oligarchy), and even suggested social equality between men and women.[8]

It was mainly due to the character and background of Ou Chü-chia that the prorevolutionaries were able to reestablish their dominance over the Pao-huang hui so rapidly. Ou was a student of K'ang Yu-wei and a man of high social standing and proven literary ability. He was a secret society member and believed that secret societies had traditionally been a progressive, prorevolutionary force in China. He was familiar with and espoused the modern principles of Western learning. And he addressed a strongly provincial people declaring that Cantonese were inherently superior to all other Chinese. (Ou said Cantonese superiority was partly the result of native ability and party due to Kwangtung's long contact with the West and progressive ideas.) Chinese in the Americas, moderates as well as radicals, had no trouble accepting these views. In fact, the *Chung Sai Yat Po* had been publishing editorials on Cantonese superiority ever since its founding.[9]

Ou's credentials as a rebel were impressive, and harmonized well with the claims of many members of the Chih-kung t'ang federation. His family had been actively involved in the Taiping Rebellion on the Taiping side. Ou had joined a secret society at a very young age and the Triads in 1899 or earlier. His close association with the organizers of the uprising in Kwangtung has already been noted. Finally, Ou had been involved not only in the "Hundred Days of Reform" of 1898, but also at least peripherally (says his biographer) in the Hsing-Chung hui's Waichow uprising of 1900.[10] With such an illustrious and influential leader on the prorevolutionary side, the moderates seem to have been either converted or reduced to silence.

Ou's skill, prestige, and connections, however, were not all that persuaded Chinese in the Americas to espouse revolution. They were also worried about Chinese Exclusion and the treatment of Chinese immigrants in the Americas. The *Chung Sai Yat Po* felt that the Chinese government had no interest in them, and that their difficulties were exacerbated by China's weakness. The newspaper claimed on one occasion that the real problem was that China was ruled by a minority race instead of the Han Chinese, and that as a result Americans despised (Han) Chinese as weaklings. Only a revolution could improve the situation. A revolution might also persuade the powers (especially Japan, Great Britain, and Russia) to be fairer and more respectful when dealing with China.[11]

The Chih-kung t'ang's prorevolutionary attitude also contributed to the enthusiasm for the uprising in Kwangtung. The Chih-kung t'ang's interest in revolution derived in part from the personal conviction of leaders such as Huang San-te and T'ang Ch'iung-ch'ang. T'ang's revolutionary ardor came partly from a desire for revenge: Chinese government officials had destroyed his family in China in 1901 for political reasons.[12] Also contributing to the prorevolutionary tendencies of the Chih-kung t'ang was the Triad motto, which called for the violent overthrow of the Ch'ing dynasty. The penchant for violence on the part of the "fighting tongs," the Triad emphasis on the knight-errant ideal, and the unstable situation in the Chinese communities made it even easier to turn the organization toward revolution. When Ou Chü-chia brought news that a large-scale uprising was pending, Chih-kung t'ang members reacted with great enthusiasm. Even after the news arrived in March of 1903 that the uprising had failed, the Chih-kung t'ang did not lose interest in revolution. With Ou's help, it established a newspaper, the *Ta-t'ung jih-pao* (Great Unity News) to help spread revolutionary propaganda. Ou's *Hsin Kwangtung* was the first series of editorials to appear in the paper.[13]

Community Fights and Party Splits

Ch'ing officials stopped Hung Ch'üan-fu's uprising on January 17, one day before it was to start.[14] Chinese in North America did not know until the end of March about Hung's difficulties, so revolutionary fervor grew unchecked through the first few months of 1903.

When news arrived that Hung had failed, the reaction was immediate, although divided. Within twenty-four hours, San Francisco's *Chung Sai Yat Po,* which probably had the largest circulation of any Chinese-language newspaper in the Americas at that time,[15] came out strongly against the coup. The newspaper said that misguided people who organize uprisings (including both Hung Ch'üan-fu and the supporters of Sun Yat-sen in the 1900 Waichow uprising) made life unbearable for other Cantonese: greedy and vengeful officials used the uprisings as excuses to persecute the innocent.[16] This opinion is significant not only because of the newspaper's large circulation, but also because of its long association with the Pao-huang hui. In Canada, however, the Pao-huang hui continued to favor fielding an army in China to wrest power from the government.[17]

In part, the *Chung Sai Yat Po'*s disaffection was related to party organization and methods of control rather than simply national politics. Ou Chü-chia was the first major leader of the Pao-huang hui to reside for an extended period in one city in the Americas.[18] His long stay in San Francisco gave him an excellent opportunity to try to seize control of its Pao-huang hui branch and mold it to fit his own ideas. In addition, by helping establish the *Ta-t'ung jih-pao* and then retaining editorship for himself, Ou made himself the official spokesman for the Chih-kung t'ang. His jockeying for power led him to quarrel with Reverend Wu P'an-chao, however, and later contributed to the estrangement of T'ang Ch'iung-ch'ang.

The quarrel with Reverend Wu and the *Chung Sai Yat Po* erupted near the end of April when the *Chung Sai Yat Po* published editorials that were highly critical of the Pao-huang hui.[19] The attack was soon broadened to include the Pao-huang hui's *Wen-hsing pao,* edited by Ou. Reverend Wu was particularly unhappy with a report appearing in the *Wen-hsing pao* which claimed that the United States government would require all Chinese in the United States to register with the Department of the Treasury, then use this information to force Chinese to leave the country. The *Chung Sai Yat Po* said that the story was false, and only a ploy to build up the circulation of the *Wen-hsing pao.*[20] The *Wen-hsing pao* denied the charge and accused the *Chung Sai Yat Po* of having no ideology. The latter responded that its aim was to broaden people's knowledge, and accused the *Wen-hsing pao* of using underhanded means to curtail the *Chung Sai Yat Po'*s circulation in New York. After several days, the fight ended at the request and under the mediation of various San Francisco merchants. There seem to have been no public retractions.[21]

In the meantime, Liang Ch'i-ch'ao (presumably Ou's "superior") had decided to come to the Americas. He arrived in Canada shortly prior to the outbreak of the quarrel between the *Chung Sai Yat Po* and the Pao-huang hui.[22] He had come to further the Pao-huang hui's business and educational concerns, recruit more members, and raise money for other projects. The projects seem to have included funds for military contingencies (Liang was still interested in revolution, and K'ang Yu-wei wanted money to hire assassins to eliminate the Empress Dowager). Ironically, a further reason for Liang's trip was to assuage the wrath of K'ang Yu-wei. K'ang was angry that Liang had espoused revolutionary rather than reform goals under the influence of the organizers of the Canton coup. He hoped a trip to the Americas might keep Liang out of trouble.[23]

But near the end of April, Liang wrote from Portland, Oregon, that he continued to favor revolution, and that his enthusiasm had been increased by the ardor with which Chinese in the Americas espoused this cause. Liang was especially interested in the views of Pao-huang hui members, and those he hoped to convince to join the Pao-huang hui. In another letter shortly afterwards, he noted that although he was prorevolutionary, revolution was not something he mentioned publicly, but only in private conversations with Pao-huang hui leaders.[24]

At the same time Liang was soliciting new members for the organization. He was most interested in enlisting the support of the wealthiest members of the overseas Chinese communities. This was partly because these men had the kind of business sense needed to keep the Pao-huang hui solvent. The party operated three newspapers in the Americas: San Francisco's *Wen-hsing pao,* Honolulu's *Hsin Chung-kuo pao,* and Vancouver's *Jih-hsin pao* (New Day News). In addition, the largest Pao-huang hui chapters owned their own buildings, and payments (or at any rate, taxes) had to be kept up on these. It may be presumed that those chapters that did not own a meeting hall would have liked to acquire one. Then, the emperor's birthday had to be celebrated every year, the party operated two schools in western Canada, and both Liang and K'ang ardently hoped that vast sums of money would be left over to contribute to "central headquarters." Finally, one of the tenets of the Pao-huang

hui was the commercial modernization of China; who would be better qualified to advise on this than businessmen? These considerations also led Liang to endorse, and draft, an official set of rules for
the Commercial Corporation while he was in Canada.[25]

One effect of persuading more businessmen to participate actively
was to give the party a more conservative cast. Any one businessman might be an ardent radical, but as a group they generally
favored either the status quo which had permitted them to acquire
their fortune, or evolutionary change, which would enable them to
enlarge their opportunities without upsetting the social order or
marketing system. In the Americas, they tended to prefer evolutionary change. This was partly because they owed much of their status
and influence to the American environment: in China, the mer-
chant-businessman was supposed to be at the bottom of the social
order.[26] The Chinese businessmen's conservatism, in other words,
was not the conservatism of traditional, Confucian China but rather
a combination of Chinese and American elements.

Liang Ch'i-ch'ao was also becoming more conservative as the
length of his stay in the Americas increased. After a brief trip to
Canada, during which time he wrote a more formal set of rules for
the Commercial Corporation and established branches of the Pao-
huang hui in Toronto, Ottawa, and Montreal, he reentered the
United States and spent six weeks in New York, making side trips to
Boston and Philadelphia. In all three cities, he spent most of his time
talking to Pao-huang hui leaders and giving speeches. His letters no
longer contained mention of revolution. In an interview with the
New York Times, he claimed he felt little attachment to the Kuang-
hsü Emperor, but wanted China to have a parliament, a constitution, and modern education. It is assumed that these were the same
goals that he espoused in his speeches to Chinese, speeches which
were enthusiastically received. Evidently, many Pao-huang hui
members as well were losing interest in revolution.[27]

Not everyone was happy to switch to more moderate policies,
however. More than one hundred Chinese resided in Hartford,
Connecticut, where Yung Wing (a leader of the recently stifled
uprising in Kwangtung) lived, and all were members of the Pao-
huang hui. Subject to Yung's influence, they were probably more
inclined to back another uprising than to adopt the evolutionary
approach. Other die-hard revolutionaries included the Pao-huang

hui members who financed or joined the cadet school in Los Angeles organized by Homer Lea and his deputy Ansel O'Banion in June of that year, a school established to train its participants (mostly Triad braves) for antigovernment military duty in China.[28] This cadet school and its affiliates will be discussed in detail in chapter five.

Of equal significance, the Chih-kung t'ang's newly founded (in April of 1903)[29] *Ta-t'ung jih-pao* was still publishing prorevolutionary editorials under the editorship of Ou Chü-chia. T'ang Ch'iung-ch'ang, always prorevolutionary, also played an active role in the newspaper. It was well received, even taking readers away from the Pao-huang hui's *Wen-hsing pao.*[30]

In July of 1903, however, while Reverend Wu and his paper were at the height of their quarrel with the Pao-huang hui, the Chih-kung t'ang's international headquarters, with its prorevolutionaries, began breaking away from the Pao-huang hui. First, the *Ta-t'ung jih-pao* joined the *Chung Sai Yat Po* in criticizing the *Wen-hsing pao's* reports of a plot to force all Chinese in the United States to register. For its temerity, the Pao-huang hui demanded and received an "apology" payment of close to seven hundred dollars from the *Ta-t'ung jih-pao.* ("Pao-huang hui" in this case means Ou Chü-chia and T'an Shu-pin, a leader of California's Pao-huang hui and one of the founders of the San Francisco chapter.)[31]

There is no direct indication of how they were able to force the Chih-kung t'ang (meaning T'ang Ch'iung-ch'ang?) to give them this payment, but in view of Ou's later association with the "translators' " lodge, either force or blackmail was probably involved. Liang Ch'i-ch'ao reported that in 1903, the "translators' " lodge dominated the Chinese community by virtue of its influence with American officials. Unhappy with this situation, toward the end of 1903 all the other lodges in the Chih-kung t'ang federation (including the Chih-kung t'ang lodge) formed an alliance to break its power, and a "tong war" broke out.[32]

In the meantime, Liang continued his tour of the United States, stopping in St. Louis and New Orleans before heading out West. While in Cincinnati, Liang organized a chapter of the Pao-huang hui. Presumably, the new members contributed further to the strength of the moderate element. Liang himself was becoming more and more antirevolutionary, in part because of what he had observed in the Americas, in part because of K'ang Yu-wei's influence, and in part because of events in China (such as the famous *Su-pao* affair). The violence and frequent shortsightedness of Chinese in the Americas—particularly in San Francisco—helped persuade him that only gradual reform would succeed in changing so benighted a people. Liang also looked with disfavor upon the corruption he observed, both in the functioning of government in the United States and in the activities of Chinese modernizers *(hsin-tang),* including members of the Pao-huang hui.[33] The Chinese modernizers who disturbed him most were those in Yokohama and Hong Kong, but he was also dissatisfied with many of those in the Americas.[34]

On September 25, Liang arrived in San Francisco accompanied by Yeh En, the Canadian Pao-huang hui leader. After Liang's arrival, Ou ceased to espouse publicly the cause of revolution. Liang's presence briefly reunited the Chinese community in San Francisco, partly because he confined his speeches to an appeal for unity and national strength. The *Chung Sai Yat Po* forgot its former enmity and gave Liang favorable coverage for the length of his stay. The quarrel with the Chih-kung t'ang subsided. T'ang Ch'iung-ch'ang even went to welcome Liang at the train station in Oakland and escort him to San Francisco.[35] Still, within days of Liang's arrival, the "tong war" of the Chih-kung t'ang federation against the "translators'" lodge broke out.[36]

By the time Liang arrived in San Francisco, he had decided that fund-raising for newspapers, schools, and bookstores was his major duty while in the Americas. He abandoned the call for revolution, and even criticized the desire of many Pao-huang hui members (including K'ang Yu-wei) to hire assassins to kill the Empress Dowager and others. In his letters, Liang reported that he received many contributions for the reformers' Yokohama school, the Ta-t'ung hsüeh-hsiao (Great Learning School), a far cry from the solicitations of Ou Chü-chia for Cantonese revolution. While Liang was in San Francisco, however, Sun Yat-sen arrived in Hawaii. That the *Chung Sai Yat Po* gave Sun almost as much coverage as Liang Ch'i-ch'ao suggested the turn that events would take.[37]

Liang left San Francisco in the middle of October for Sacramento, where he founded another branch of the Pao-huang hui. He went to Los Angeles, where he was met by both American and Chinese friends of the Pao-huang hui in a gala parade organized by Homer Lea. Lea's Pao-huang hui cadets were present as well. Liang was far more interested in the Americans, partly because he was led to believe that some of Lea's wealthy friends might give him financial backing. They did not, and Liang returned to San Francisco.[38]

As far as Chinese in the United States were concerned, Liang's return to San Francisco in November of 1903 was the high point of his trip. This was when Liang helped formulate and agreed to help deliver petitions to officials in Kwangtung and at the Chinese court complaining of the mistreatment of Chinese in the Americas and asking the officials to seek redress.[39] Chinese in the United States particularly wanted to end Chinese Exclusion by having the immigration treaty between the United States and China renegotiated. The treaty was subject to review in 1903 and possible renegotiation in 1904, so the petitions were intended to be a timely reminder of the immigrants' plight.

Those who participated with Liang in drawing up the petitions were primarily merchants, but interest in this question was virtually universal. Chinese Christians were discussing treaty revision before the San Francisco merchants held their meetings, and a delegate from Canada proposed a boycott of American goods if no satisfaction could be obtained from the United States government. The Chih-kung t'ang was also interested in the problem, as demonstrated by the fact that Huang San-te went on a national tour in 1905 to encourage participation in the boycott. The editor of the Pao-huang hui's Honolulu newspaper wanted either treaty revision or a boycott, and came to the continental United States in 1903 to try to get the backing of San Francisco's Chinese Six Companies. (The Six Companies, however, preferred appealing to the Chinese government.) Liang noted that the communities whose Chinese residents were most strongly committed to the Pao-huang hui were also those in which Chinese had received the worst treatment at the hands of Americans. The Pao-huang hui had managed to make itself appear as a champion of the Chinese cause, enabling it to grow: there were over thirty major branches and 103 subbranches by the time of Liang's departure, including branches in Peru, Panama, and Mexico as well as those in Canada and the United States.[40]

After the petitions were drafted, Liang traveled to Vancouver and boarded a ship bound for Japan. In his diary, he noted that he deliberately chose a ship which would not stop in Hawaii, since he felt that the Chinese and the Pao-huang hui there were evil (*e*), a national humiliation. (Unfortunately, he did not give any specifics concerning their evil ways.)[41] Liang's distaste for Chinese in the Americas (he found San Francisco particularly repulsive[42]) did not bode well for the continued growth of America's Pao-huang hui. Western Canada, especially Vancouver/Victoria, was something of an exception. There, the Chih-kung t'ang possessed unity and control over both its members and the Chinese community. Pao-huang hui membership overlapped with the Chih-kung t'ang membership, and the Chih-kung t'ang leaders were also the leaders of the Pao-huang hui. Liang responded favorably to the order and peace evident in these communities. In San Francisco, however, although the Chih-kung t'ang leaders in the past had been strong supporters of the Pao-huang hui, they could not control their branch lodges or the affiliated lodges.

After Liang's departure, Ou Chü-chia was freed from his restraint. Relations between the Chih-kung t'ang in the United States and the Pao-huang hui once again became strained. An argument developed over something referred to in the *Chung Sai Yat Po* as the "T'an Chin-yung case." Once again, the Pao-huang hui (meaning principally Ou and T'an Shu-pin) was able to force an apology and a payment of several hundred dollars from the Chih-kung t'ang.[43]

In the meantime, the moderate politics of Liang Ch'i-ch'ao contributed to the founding of the New York Pao-huang hui's *Wei-hsin pao* (Reform News) in 1904.[44] The moderates also managed to replace Ou as *Wen-hsing pao* editor by the spring of that year,[45] although he remained on the newspaper's staff. San Francisco's *Chung Sai Yat Po,* espousing the same moderate policies as the *Wei-hsin pao,* did not renew its former sympathetic relationship with the Pao-huang hui as a party, partly due to anger over Ou's and T'an's high-handed manner. Furthermore, after Liang returned to Japan, he published his travel journal, *Hsin-ta-lu yu-chi* (Record of a Trip to the New World), in the *Hsin-min ts'ung-pao* (Journal of the "New Man").[46] This work was not only highly critical of Chinese in the Americas in general, it was downright offensive concerning the community in San Francisco. Questions of communications make it difficult to know exactly when San Francisco residents had a chance to read this work—certainly no later than July of 1904. Probably it arrived well prior to that date, because after March 17, 1904, the *Chung Sai Yat Po* never again published an editorial that praised the reformers.[47]

Sun's Second Trip to North America

On March 23, 1904, Sun Yat-sen arrived in San Francisco. Huang San-te had gone to the docks to meet him (as Sun was now a bona fide member of the Chih-kung t'ang), but no Sun was to be seen. The Chinese translators for the American immigration officials were members of both the Pao-huang hui and the "translators' " lodge. At the instigation of one faction of the Pao-huang hui (most sources attribute it directly to Ou Chü-chia), these translators informed the American officials that Sun's document claiming United States citizenship was fraudulent. Consequently, Sun was detained immediately on his arrival, so Huang did not see him.[48]

Huang wrote the Triad leaders in Hawaii to find out what had happened. Sun, in the meantime, smuggled a message to Reverend Wu P'an-chao telling the latter of his predicament. Reverend Wu, in turn, informed Huang and T'ang Ch'iung-ch'ang. These three obtained the aid of the Chinese consul in San Francisco, who was the brother of an ally of Sun's, and together the four worked secretly to secure Sun's release, hiring lawyers and presenting Sun's case to officials in Washington, D.C. They were successful, and on April 6, Sun was released.[49]

For the next few weeks, Sun stayed with Reverend Wu and negotiated with the Chih-kung t'ang. Capitalizing on the antagonism between the "translators' " lodge and the Chih-kung t'ang lodge, he arranged a formal alliance with the latter, which gave him the prerogative of rewriting its rules and using it to raise funds for him. The new rules emphasized greater centralization (good for the Chih-kung t'ang—that is, Huang San-te and T'ang Ch'iung-ch'ang), revolutionary ideals (good for Huang, T'ang, and Sun), and emphasized Sun's close relationship with the Chih-kung t'ang (good for Sun). Sun was very much interested in the money he hoped would be forthcoming. T'ang also asked Sun to provide the *Ta-t'ung jih-pao* with a new editor to replace Ou Chü-chia; the latter took the hint and returned to China. T'ang did not expect Sun to choose the new editor, however. Instead, Sun was to relay the request to Feng Tzu-yu (a longtime member of both the Triads and the Hsing-Chung hui). Sun did so, and Feng found and sent to T'ang a suitable prorevolutionary, secret-society editor.[50]

After his consultations with the Chih-kung t'ang had been proceeding for several weeks, Sun began giving public speeches to the

Chinese community in San Francisco. Like Liang Ch'i-ch'ao, he also paid his respects to all the *hui-kuan* heads. Contemporary reports in the *Chung Sai Yat Po* state that Sun's anti-Manchu, prorevolutionary speeches were very well received. The *Chung Sai Yat Po* also printed several hundred copies of Tsou Jung's *Ko-ming Chün* (Revolutionary Army) for Sun, which Sun distributed in San Francisco and elsewhere in the United States. The tract increased enthusiasm for revolution among Chinese in the Americas (as it had among other overseas Chinese), and the *San Francisco Examiner* remarked that the *hui-kuan* heads and wealthy merchants had all come to approve of Sun.[51]

When he tried to organize a branch of the Hsing-Chung hui, however, Sun ran into trouble. The only group that showed even the faintest interest were the Chinese Christians. At a meeting called by Sun, many Christians expressed their support for his goals, and quite a few even made financial contributions. Still, almost no one was willing to join, although some twenty or so were finally persuaded to sign up. The others said they were too afraid that membership might endanger their families and property back in China.[52] Since people did not hesitate to join the Pao-huang hui even though it also was proscribed in China, this might seem to be a specious argument. In fact, however, since 1902 the Pao-huang hui had become a relatively safe organization to join. Not surprisingly, this gave a real advantage to the reformers.[53]

Near the end of May, Sun and Huang San-te went to Sacramento to raise money and introduce the new rules. The local Chih-kung t'ang chapter invited Sun to give a speech in their meeting hall. Sacramento's Pao-huang hui had only been organized a few months earlier by Liang Ch'i-ch'ao. Certain Pao-huang hui leaders notified the members that they were not to go hear Sun speak, but according to the *Chung Sai Yat Po*, the membership did not obey these orders. One half of the Pao-huang hui in Sacramento was composed of people who sincerely believed in the moderate, reform goals of K'ang Yu-wei and Liang Ch'i-ch'ao. Others tended toward revolution. The proreform members went to hear what the opposition had to say; the prorevolutionaries went to see if they really wanted to belong to the Pao-huang hui. Apparently, after hearing Sun, they decided that they did not.[54] Once again, however, this does not seem to have led to any rush to join the Hsing-Chung hui. Furthermore,

Sun was not able to raise any large amount of money either in Sacramento or in the rest of the Americas.

While Huang, T'ang, and the Chih-kung t'ang managers associated with them were happy to cooperate with Sun, they had no interest in helping him organize what they viewed as a competitive organization.[55] The Chih-kung t'ang's attitude toward the Hsing-Chung hui is significant because Huang, T'ang, and their supporters had not viewed the Pao-huang hui as a competitor in 1900. This was primarily because at that time neither K'ang nor the other Pao-huang hui organizers had tried to use the Pao-huang hui to control the Chih-kung t'ang, whereas Sun evidently took the opposite tack. By 1903, of course, the Pao-huang hui also desired to control the Chih-kung t'ang (although in Canada, the opposite seems to have taken place). As a result, another open break between the Chih-kung t'ang in the United States and the Pao-huang hui was inevitable. On July 14, while Sun and Huang were still on their national tour, a Chih-kung t'ang lodge in Walla Walla, Washington, formally accused the Pao-huang hui (especially Ou and T'an Shu-pin) of having cheated the Chih-kung t'ang. Once again bringing up the question of registration and the "T'an Chin-yung case," the lodge said that since Ou had now left America, it unfortunately would have no redress for its grievance.[56]

In the meantime, once Sun had appealed to Reverend Wu P'an-chao for aid, the *Chung Sai Yat Po* and many Christians began leaning towards revolution. By mid-May the newspaper suggested that revolutionaries ("people's party," *min-tang*) should take advantage of an uprising then in progress in Kwangsi, allying themselves with the Kwangsi rebels and reform-minded officials. The newspaper claimed that the *min-tang* was not like rebellious secret society groups of the past. Instead, it worked unselfishly for the people's benefit trying to secure a constitution, the rule of law, and an end to the racial discrimination suffered by the Han Chinese at the hands of the Manchu rulers. Other editorials reiterated that revolution was necessary and that the Manchus had no right to rule the Han; it was also claimed that Cantonese were inherently superior.[57] Still others championed the cause of young men who refused to obey their fathers and young women who, like Florence Nightingale, helped society instead of trying to please their husbands and parents. The newspaper ran a series of editorials praising freedom, in the course of which one of the editors stated that freedom *(tzu-yu)* was more important than life itself. Those who opposed it, specifically, fathers and elder brothers *(fu-hsiung)* were absolutely wrong—although it was not correct to assert that "freedom" meant the right to break the law.[58]

Toward the end of May the *Chung Sai Yat Po* noted the split that Sun's presence in Sacramento had caused in the Pao-huang hui there. Between June 10 and July 23, at the same time that the rift between the Pao-huang hui and the Chih-kung t'ang broke out into the open again, the newspaper engaged in another public quarrel with the Pao-huang hui and the *Wen-hsing pao*. From that time until well beyond January of 1905, the *Chung Sai Yat Po* was consistently prorevolutionary.

In spite of the permanent loss of the Chih-kung t'ang in the United States and of the *Chung Sai Yat Po,* the Pao-huang hui remained strong. It continued to harbor some dissidents and prorevolutionaries, although these no longer had access to the party's inner councils. The most important of the dissidents were the members and supporters of General Homer Lea's Western Military Academy, incorporated in California on November 28, 1903. By early 1905, the Western Military Academy had over twenty branches established in various cities in the United States. Its Pao-huang hui supporters (principally the Triads' Ping-kung t'ang and Hsieh-sheng t'ang) were supposed to have provided a salary of $140 a month to all the American trainers employed, and they also purchased the uniforms, arms, flags, and other training equipment. Lea and his drill master, Ansel O'Banion, intended that their military cadets would see military duty in the field against the Ch'ing armies. Perhaps they stayed with the Pao-huang hui because there was no other organization that could or would support them.[59]

Between 1902 and 1904, after flirting with the idea of revolution, most Pao-huang hui members espoused reform policies and accepted the implication that this would make their party more authoritarian, conservative, and concerned with commercial affairs. One reason for the turn toward reform was the inability of radicals in China to launch a successful antigovernment uprising. Another was because Liang Ch'i-ch'ao and K'ang Yu-wei publicly supported the attempts by Chinese in the Americas to change Chinese Exclusion and the treatment of Chinese in the Americas. Finally, Liang had great appeal for *Szu-i* leaders and, partly because of his support of the Commercial Corporation, for conservative merchants.

In spite of the long list of putative members, however, between 1902 and 1904 the Pao-huang hui seems to have reached its peak. Ou Chü-chia's high-handed methods offended many, and the party's more consistent conservatism alienated others. Some of this conservatism had been imposed upon the party from the top, and did not completely reflect the views of the rank and file.

The Chih-kung t'ang's continuing evolution had a tremendous impact on the course of events. As the political parties moved from national to local concerns, the Chih-kung t'ang moved from the local to the national, inadvertently helping to prepare the ground for the further development of the political parties. The Chih-kung t'ang's evolution was occasioned in part by the political inclinations of Huang San-te and T'ang Ch'iung-ch'ang, in part by their ambition, and in part by the somewhat explosive nature of the Triad membership.

By 1904, national politics revolving around moderate/radical alternatives had become a major (but not the only) factor in the party affiliation of Chinese in the Americas. From 1903 onwards, the Pao-huang hui on the one hand and the Hsing-Chung hui on the other increasingly made clear the political distinctions between them. The independents remained independent, not joining either party but also not attempting to form their own. The Chih-kung t'ang lodges and sublodges vacillated and then split over the issue, but by 1904 the federation was officially committed to revolution (although not necessarily to Sun Yat-sen's revolutionary party).

5

REFORMERS AND REVOLUTIONARIES,

1903–1908

Just as the Pao-huang hui acquired political rivals in the continental United States between 1902 and 1904, it acquired one in Hawaii late in 1903, as will presently be shown. In spite of the existence of these rivals, the period from the tumultuous 1903–1904 realignment to 1908 was characterized by gradual political growth rather than sudden changes. The Pao-huang hui settled into a pattern of continuing strength accompanied by continuing factionalism. The Chih-kung t'ang sought to add greater centralization to greater political involvement. The Hsing-Chung hui[1] and Sun Yat-sen began to interest themselves in local issues and to work more closely with pre-existing organizations, factors which were to help them pick up strength and then triumph in 1911.

One of the burning issues of the day was the 1905 boycott of American goods and the question of treaty revision. Every group that had political pretensions became involved in the boycott, and the question of reform versus revolutionary politics soon arose. Although the boycott movement was suppressed more quickly in the Americas than in China (partly because the determination of the United States not to renegotiate the treaty was clearest on the eastern side of the Pacific), concern over the treaty and the boycott helped forge a clear link between local and national (Chinese) concerns.

Other events which significantly spurred politicization were the Japanese defeat of Russia in 1905 in the Russo-Japanese War and the post-1905 movement in China, tolerated and even encouraged by the court, to plan for a parliament, a cabinet, and a constitution. The Russo-Japanese War showed that a suitably "modernized" Asian nation could defeat a European power. The projected parliament, cabinet, and constitution were to be steps toward China's own modernization. Finally, even the abolition of the Confucian examination system in China in 1905 helped tie America's Chinese more tightly to China and encouraged their politicization, since it made them and their familiarity with the West more socially and intellectually acceptable in China.

Sun's 1903 Trip to Hawaii

The furor caused by Sun's 1904 visit to the continental United States first surfaced in Hawaii when Sun visited the Islands late in 1903. It has been shown already that the shifts and realignments brought about by Sun's presence in the continental United States were partly a reflection of past problems within the Pao-huang hui, and between the Pao-huang hui and other organizations. Although there is less information concerning Hawaii, the evidence suggests a similar situation there. Once again, Hung Ch'üan-fu's failure must have been a contributory cause, especially in view of the fact that one of Hung's chief lieutenants was a young radical from Hawaii who had gone to China with Sun Yat-sen in 1894.[2]

Sun's 1903 visit to Hawaii was his first since 1896. On his arrival, he tried without success to persuade the former members of the Hsing-Chung hui (most of whom still belonged to the Pao-huang hui) to return their loyalty to him.[3] Next he went to Maui to appeal to Sun Mei for aid. The latter suggested Yat-sen should devote more attention to his medical practice. Sun Mei did give Yat-sen a small sum of money for traveling expenses, and he and another kinsman helped Sun Yat-sen to join the Triads. The kinsman introduced Yat-sen to a Triad elder, and in the process described below, Yat-sen was initiated into Hawaii's Hakka lodge, the Kuo-an hui-kuan (Ket On Society). Sun Mei also helped Yat-sen obtain (false) papers declaring that Yat-sen was a United States citizen by virtue of his being born in Hawaii.[4]

Reviving Hawaii's Hsing-Chung hui was another matter. Fortunately for Sun Yat-sen, a prorevolutionary Christian preacher lived in Hilo on the island of Hawaii. This preacher had participated in an attempted bombing/revolutionary uprising in 1895.[5] After the attempt failed, the preacher had returned to Hilo to champion God and revolution. In 1903, he invited Sun to Hilo, rented a theater for Sun to speak in, and persuaded twelve people to join the Hsing-Chung hui even before Sun arrived. Sun gave several speeches in Hilo which, when added to the preacher's support, convinced "several tens" more people to join the Hsing-Chung hui.[6]

The new members joined in groups, and certain recruits were more important than others because they were able to lead others in with them. Most of the new members were Triads.[7] In view of this, it seems likely (although we cannot be certain) that the groups consisted of Triad lodges following their lodge leader into the Hsing-Chung hui.

While in Hilo, Sun added a new objective to the Hsing-Chung hui's goals of expelling the Manchus, reviving China, and establishing republican government. The new plank was the equalization of land rights (*p'ing-chün ti-ch'üan*), pointing up Sun's long-time interest in some form of socialism and the just reapportionment of wealth.[8] Most Chinese in Hilo were agricultural laborers, so the new plank must have held great appeal for them.[9]

After Sun had been in Hilo for a few days, the preacher persuaded one of his own kinsmen, a resident of Honolulu, to support Sun as well. Sun then returned to Honolulu, where the preacher's kinsman persuaded several other people to join the Hsing-Chung hui. After this, a number of former Hsing-Chung hui partisans returned to the fold. One of these was the owner of the *Lung-chi pao*.[10]

With the owner's return to Sun's revolutionary fold, the *Lung-chi pao* once again inclined towards revolution. At Sun's request, the paper was reorganized and renamed the *T'an-shan hsin-pao* (New Honolulu News). Most of the former managers and editors (including a number of erstwhile Pao-huang hui stalwarts) agreed to stay with the newspaper. The owner invited Sun to write some editorials, and permitted him to ask Feng Tzu-yu in Hong Kong to send the newspaper a suitable "revolutionary" editor from China. The first man Feng chose was unable to secure an entry visa from the American authorities, but Feng had better luck with his second choice.[11]

Disturbed by this turn of affairs, the Pao-huang hui's *Hsin Chung-kuo pao* launched an editorial attack against Sun, the Hsing-Chung hui, and Sun's supporters in Honolulu.[12] In response, Sun wrote two editorials for the *T'an-shan hsin-pao* to make clear the difference between the Pao-huang hui and Hsing-Chung hui, and to persuade people to join the latter.[13]

In these editorials, Sun directed his appeal to the Triads' presumed anti-Manchu prejudice. He wrote that only he and his followers understood consistent opposition to the Manchus, whereas the Pao-huang hui claimed to want both to overthrow them and to preserve them in the form of the Kuang-hsü Emperor. Pao-huang hui members, said Sun, were criminals and cheats because of this. The Manchus (including the Kuang-hsü Emperor) should be removed from power. They were racially inferior "barbarians" and they were a minority race in China ruling the majority race.[14] They had proven weak in the face of foreign aggressions, they had permitted other races and nations wrongfully to gain control over Chinese, and they had been willing to sacrifice China's territorial sovereignty in order to buttress their own rule.[15]

In Hawaii, continued Sun, Pao-huang hui leaders had manipulated the Chih-kung t'ang, joining the latter organization under the guise of being prorevolutionary. The *Hsin Chung-kuo pao*'s editor had revealed himself to be a racial traitor *(Han-chien)* by saying Chinese were not fit for self-government. This editor was also guilty of subservience to the Americans in Hawaii, opposition to Sun Yat-sen, and loyalty to the Kuang-hsü Emperor. The reformers' plan of having constitutional monarchy develop into a republican government was unworkable. It would require two revolutions instead of one, and the final step in fact would never be achieved. Sun also declared that it was ridiculous to ignore Darwin's findings by trying to prevent Chinese from rising up against foreigners (Manchu and otherwise). Furthermore, this was not a time for traditional virtues. Only nationalism and racial solidarity would solve China's problems.[16]

Sun's public attack won few new adherents to the Hsing-Chung hui, and influential people such as Chung Yü continued to oppose Sun. Disappointed, Sun abandoned Hawaii in favor of the continental United States. In retrospect, however, the trip to Hawaii was not really a failure. Sun did gain new recruits and allies in Hilo, he managed to turn the former *Lung-chi pao* into something of a propaganda organ, and, most important of all, he was able to join the Triads.

Sun's relatives had arranged for a man who in 1900 had been one of the "trustees" of the fledgling Pao-huang hui[17] to sponsor Sun's Triad candidacy. The lodge does not seem to have given Sun any special treatment: sixty other men were initiated at the same time as he was. It is true that Sun was given the high rank of "elder brother" *(ta-ko)*, but that was because he had helped to organize an antigovernment uprising.[18] It is to be presumed that there were many "elder brothers" in the Triads, although perhaps more in China than overseas.

Sun's right to initiation was challenged by an influential reformer, the manager of a company intimately associated with the Triad lodge. Sun's sponsor counterattacked, pointing out that the ostensible aim of the Chih-kung t'ang was to overthrow the Ch'ing and restore the Ming, an aim similar to what Sun stood for. This speech carried the day, and Sun was initiated.[19]

The Reorganization of the Chih-kung T'ang, 1904

Sun's arrival in the continental United States and its initial effects have been dealt with in chapter 4. To recapitulate briefly, Sun left San Francisco with Huang San-te in the spring of 1904, and traveled across the country with him, stopping in each town and city that had a Chinese population (and Chih-kung t'ang or Chih-kung t'ang-affiliated sublodge). There they gave speeches, raised money, and organized. When they reached New York, they parted company, Sun going on to Europe and Huang recrossing the United States, still organizing.

Sun raised little money through the Chih-kung t'ang. Outside of San Francisco he does not appear to have attracted any new members into the Hsing-Chung hui, and Huang's account of their organizational drive does not even acknowledge the existence of the Hsing-Chung hui. Perhaps Sun promised Huang not to engage in any recruiting for his own party. Huang, on the other hand, claims that his own efforts to strengthen his hold over the Chih-kung t'ang and increase the influence of the San Francisco "international head-quarters" were relatively successful. He recruited a large number of new members, raised a lot of money for Sun (which Sun, himself, had been unable to do) and arrived to lavish receptions for himself and Sun in all the major cities.[20]

One aim of Huang and Sun was to get all the lodges and sub-lodges to accept the new Chih-kung t'ang rules that Sun had just helped to compose. These new rules represented a compromise between Sun and Huang. They are quite different in tone from the editorials Sun had so recently written in Hawaii, embodying much more sophisticated ideas concerning nationalism and democracy. The attack on the Pao-huang hui was more pointed, reflecting Huang's recent disagreements and knowledge of the local situation. It is unclear which parts of the new rules were written by Sun and which by Huang. Still, they provide evidence that Sun would present more "advanced" ideas when given the opportunity, and suggest that Huang San-te and the Chih-kung t'ang leaders under him were considerably more sophisticated than the agricultural laborers to whom Sun appealed in Hawaii. Furthermore, in Hawaii, Sun was writing what he thought his audience wanted to hear, whereas in San Francisco his "audience" helped him to write.

The new set of rules was divided into two parts. First came a long preamble which explained why new rules were necessary, and that Sun Yat-sen would be writing them. Then came the actual rules. The preamble first noted that the purpose of the Chih-kung t'ang was to ensure Han solidarity and avenge the wrongs visited upon the Han. Then, it listed and elaborated upon its specific aims: to unite overseas Chinese so as to improve their lot, to revive China, and to eliminate "Han traitors" and foreigners (including Manchus). The preamble castigated the Pao-huang hui in great detail, stating that all of the reformers' schemes (banks, mines, railroads, schools, and the like) were just devices for seeking personal gain. It claimed that the main interest of Pao-huang hui members was to make money, a fact that the Chih-kung t'ang had early come to realize and which had led to its break with the Pao-huang hui. This break, declared the preamble, had caused the collapse of the Pao-huang hui. The preamble also stated that the reformers were the slaves of the Manchu thieves, and said that it was the duty of the Han in general and the Chih-kung t'ang in particular totally to destroy them.[21]

In other parts of the preamble, a great deal of space was devoted to characterizing the unfortunate position of Chinese in the Americas, much of which was attributed to the lack of strong community organizations and central direction, two things that the Chih-kung t'ang hoped to remedy with its revised rules. Finally, there was a section which discussed how to revive China. This section noted that overseas Chinese wanted to help and had the financial means to do so, but lacked a strategy. Sun Yat-sen would remedy this lack, for he had contacts with revolutionaries *(ko-ming chih-shih)* as well as the knowledge of a solution to China's weakness. This was the age of competition and struggle (a competition and struggle that so far the white race was winning), and since the Manchus could not even retain control of their ancestral land, and since China under the Ch'ing dynasty was known as the "weak man of Asia," a revolutionary struggle on the part of the Han race to take control of China from the Manchus would restore China to her rightful place in the world.[22]

The individual rules, of which there were seventeen, provide the most striking contrast to Sun's Hawaii editorials and are suggestive of the sophisticated ideas concerning popular sovereignty to be found in Ou Chü-chia's *Hsin Kwangtung*. The rules have the flavor of a government constitution, since the Chih-kung t'ang saw itself as an *imperium in imperio*. Borrowing heavily from the United States Constitution, they provide for three branches of government: the executive (headed by a *tsung-li*—chief executive officer—which was Huang San-te), a legislature, and a judiciary that at its highest levels was to be independent. Executive and legislative posts were elective, and the terms of office were limited. The *tsung-li,* for example, was to have a term of four years, although evidently he could succeed himself. The legislative branch does not appear to have been independent, nor were the branch lodges to be so. The latter could choose their own officers, but their rules had to be approved by the *tsung-li* and his legislators *(i-yüan)* in San Francisco. Chih-kung t'ang sublodges were to send San Francisco two dollars for each new recruit they initiated, and non-Chih-kung t'ang lodges in the federation were urged to dissolve themselves and merge with the Chih-kung t'ang. All Triads were required to reregister individually with the Chih-kung t'ang. If they did not, they would lose the right to vote for the various officers, especially the legislators.[23]

To make plain its political commitment, the head lodge in San Francisco ordered each Chih-kung t'ang sublodge publicly to condemn the Pao-huang hui. The rules also announced that the Chih-kung t'ang would help those in China whose aims agreed with those of the Chih-kung t'ang. These aims were listed in phrases drawn from Hawaii's new Hsing-Chung hui oath (later used for the T'ung-meng hui): "This lodge is dedicated to the principals of eliminating the Manchus, reviving China, establishing a republican form of government, and equalizing land rights."[24]

It may well be asked to what extent these rules were carried out, since one of their purposes was to further centralize the Chih-kung t'ang and increase Huang San-te's own power. For example, in spite of the stipulations concerning elections, the leadership at the top did not undergo a change every four years. Elections were undoubtedly held, but most probably once a sublodge had been organized, the normal procedure would have been to nominate only the incumbent and then elect him by a landslide. In other words, the election process was probably used to demonstrate solidarity.[25] As for the independent judiciary, there had long been important officers (such as "incense master," *hsiang-tzu*) which appear to have been lifelong appointments and to have been relatively independent of the *ta-lao* ("great elder," or head). To establish a similar post with purely judicial functions would not have violated traditional Triad practices, but Huang undoubtedly worked hard to ensure that this judiciary did not challenge his own authority. What is being suggested here is that although the rules showed a great deal of American influence, the actual practices of the organization did not. This was also true of the *hui-kuan* and the Six Companies, whose rules were patterned after American models but whose actual functioning was often at variance with the rules.[26]

In addition to helping rewrite the Chih-kung t'ang rules, Sun persuaded Reverend Wu P'an-chao of the *Chung Sai Yat Po* to print eleven thousand copies of Tsou Jung's *Ko-ming chün*. The Chih-kung t'ang undertook primary responsibility for distributing the *Ko-ming chün* in the United States. Sun hoped that the tract would awaken not only Chih-kung t'ang members but also all overseas Chinese everywhere to their "traditional" anti-Manchuism. Like the new Chih-kung t'ang rules, however, the *Ko-ming chün* went considerably beyond anti-Manchuism. It favored some redistribution of wealth in the Chinese countryside and demonstrated a real grasp of the nature of republicanism. Chih-kung t'ang members and other Chinese in the Americas liked it immensely, demonstrating again that radical politics was not limited to the Hsing-Chung hui or Sun Yat-sen.[27]

Surprisingly, Huang San-te claimed, in retrospect, that during all this period he continued to respect K'ang Yu-wei as a scholarly gentleman. This respect supposedly caused him to refuse Sun Yat-sen's request in 1905 that Huang arrange for K'ang's assassination while K'ang was in the United States.[28] Actually, the real reason was probably because Huang did not want to antagonize the Ping-kung t'ang and the Hsieh-sheng t'ang, both of which still supported the Pao-huang hui. Ironically, the cadets in the Pao-huang hui's Western Military Academy, which these two lodges financed, were themselves turning against K'ang, and their American officers had even begun publicly proclaiming that they supported revolution.[29]

The Pao-huang Hui's Entrenchment in the Community

The Founding of the Western Military Academy

The Western Military Academy grew out of the Pao-huang hui drill squad organized by Homer Lea in Los Angeles in 1902. By the summer of 1903, Lea was prepared to expand: he had located a drill master (Ansel O'Banion), the drill master had been initiated into the appropriate Chih-kung t'ang-affiliated lodge, and drill training had begun. In October of 1903, when Liang Ch'i-ch'ao arrived in Los Angeles, Homer Lea was able to meet him at the train station wearing a military uniform of his own design and accompanied by cadets. As we saw earlier, Homer Lea and the cadets were not the only ones to meet Liang. "Many prominent citizens of Los Angeles," a band, and a police escort also awaited his arrival, and a parade was held in his honor, including the local Signal Corps, Los Angeles Mayor Snyder, members of the Los Angeles Chambers of Commerce, the press, and "local Chinese." The presence of the Americans was due primarily to Homer Lea, who had been part of the local Progressive movement before he began dabbling in Chinese politics.[30]

Liang Ch'i-ch'ao was more interested in the Americans than in the Chinese cadets, but Lea was more interested in his cadets. To please Lea, Liang appointed him "Commander-in-Chief of the Chinese Imperial Reform Association Army," a position Lea accepted with alacrity. Liang neglected to mention that he had already bestowed the same title on another person, a Mr. A. R. Falkenburg of the Standard Rock Oil Company in San Francisco. As Mr. Falkenburg kept quiet for the next couple of years, this "commission" did not immediately interfere with Homer Lea's activities.[31]

In late November of 1904, Homer Lea incorporated the cadet training academy with the State of California under the name of the

Western Military Academy (Kan-ch'eng hsüeh-hsiao in Chinese). He asked three Los Angeles-based American businessmen to lend their names as incorporators and directors to make the operation appear legitimate. The cadets requested and received permission to parade in the 1905 Pasadena "Tournament of Roses" parade. Fifty-eight of them participated along with their captain, O'Banion, and their general, Homer Lea. They also marched publicly a few days afterwards in the funeral procession of a leading member of the Chinese community of Los Angeles.[32]

Soon after the incorporation of the academy in Los Angeles, branch academies were set up in Chinese communities across the country. The training consisted of modern drill, troop deployment, and logistics. The cadets drilled with weapons except in the case of some public displays (because of United States neutrality laws), and at least one branch had a Sturn Gatling gun.

When the system reached its greatest extent, training programs operated in twenty-one cities in the continental United States including St. Louis, Chicago, New York, San Francisco, Fresno, and Los Angeles. There were two kinds of training personnel: Chinese, who were volunteers and given the rank of lieutenant, and Americans, who were salaried and given the rank of captain. The Americans were mostly retired men from the United States Army, although a few were active or retired members of the National Guard.[33]

The Commercial Corporation

Of just as much significance as the incorporation and expansion of the Western Military Academy was K'ang Yu-wei's special interest in the Commercial Corporation, an interest he was able to demonstrate when he visited the Americas in 1905. Few details about this trip are known beyond K'ang's entrance problems, his relatively warm reception by American officials, and the meeting he convened to rewrite the Pao-huang hui's rules. The new rules bound the party to unswerving loyalty to the Kuang-hsü Emperor and unalterable opposition to revolution, both aims dear to K'ang's heart.[34] K'ang's journal, as translated and edited by his grandson Dr. Jung-pang Lo,[35] and the interviews K'ang gave to the English-language press show that K'ang was also strengthening the Commercial Corporation and the position of wealthy merchants in the Pao-huang hui. As he said in a speech in Los Angeles, if China became highly developed both commercially and industrially, this would take her far down the road toward the utopian state of *ta-t'ung* (or One World), of which he was so particularly fond.[36] In strengthening the Commercial Corporation, K'ang appealed to the self-interest of wealthy and even middle-class overseas Chinese. He selected many of the wealthy to manage the new enterprises launched between 1905 and 1907 and promised all investors a high return on their capital. Middle-class Chinese as well as the wealthy bought shares in anticipation of the profits. (Ordinary laborers did not, however, since at twenty dollars a share prior to 1908—more than half a laborer's monthy income—they were too expensive.)[37] Expansion of the Commercial Corporation was also of financial benefit to the Pao-huang hui, as a portion of the profits was set aside for party coffers.

The Commercial Corporation established its headquarters in Hong Kong and launched ventures in China, Southeast Asia, and the Americas. Banks and, secondarily, mines were seen as being the key to the corporation's success, both as commercial establishments and as models for China.[38] In Torreón, Mexico, the corporation operated a bank (founded in 1905 or 1906), dealt in real estate, and attempted to construct a streetcar line and to operate a steamship company. In Panama it began work on another streetcar line. The launching of the Mexican and Panamanian ventures led to an increase in the number of Pao-huang hui branches in those countries. By 1908 there were fifteen in Mexico and at least one in Panama. The American division of the Commercial Corporation also purchased three hundred thousand dollars, or about twenty percent, of the stock sold, to enable the construction of the southern section of the Canton-Hankow Railway. Yeh En and Li Fu-chi of Vancouver were heavily involved in these ventures, as were Huang K'uan-cho (also known as Wong Foon-chuck) and others in Torreón.[39]

The Commercial Corporation also helped run some of the English-language schools founded while Liang Ch'i-ch'ao was in North America in 1903. In 1905, the corporation launched a newspaper in Hong Kong and another one in Shanghai, and won over even a third newspaper from prorevolutionaries in Singapore. It operated a hotel, a bank in Shanghai (which had a major branch in New York), and a rice brokerage with headquarters in Penang. It continued running older Pao-huang hui businesses such as the bookstore in Shanghai, and in 1908 it even became involved in a mining scheme in Kwangsi. These several ventures were all financially interrelated and interdependent. One result of this activity was that leaders of branch societies as well as more important leaders became increasingly involved in running business affairs. This diverted their attention from other duties, and after 1905 the Pao-huang hui's four newspapers in the Americas were left without prestigious and highly qualified editors.[40]

The main purpose of the Commercial Corporation was to make a profit. K'ang was sometimes advised in this matter by his friend, the wealthy American Charles Ranlett Flint (the "Father of the Trusts"). His personal acquaintanceship with President Porfirio Díaz of Mexico helped when he launched the Mexican ventures. Even with the help of Flint and Díaz, the Commercial Corporation did not succeed in the way that K'ang had hoped and anticipated, however. But it did enrich some of its managers and major stockholders. A poet stockholder friend of K'ang's who lived in Los Angeles and who was employed by the Commercial Corporation borrowed $160,000 from it which he never returned. Yeh En also borrowed another $129,000, which he refused to return after his business associate Liu Shih-chi was murdered in 1908. Another individual "borrowed" $70,000; the manager of the rice brokerage lost $8,000 of the brokerage's capital in gambling; and so forth. Even K'ang, in spite of all the business reverses suffered by the corporation from 1907–1908, apparently did not lack for traveling funds. He had enough left over to purchase himself a small island in Sweden.[41]

The less wealthy, individual members of the Pao-huang hui and the Pao-huang hui as a political party profited far less than the major leaders. But the Pao-huang hui as a social institution was greatly strengthened by these commercial ventures up until 1908 and 1909. In North America, these ventures contributed to the greater integration of the business community. This, in turn, strengthened the Six Companies and Vancouver's Chung-hua hui-kuan. The Commercial Corporation provided a new outlet for the wealth and talents of the businessmen. Because it encouraged new kinds of ventures (namely, capitalistic ventures and the joint-stock company), it helped blur the distinction between *San-i* and *Szu-i* businessmen: *San-i* could not claim the advantage of greater experience or better contacts. Regional distinctions were further undermined by the fact that the Commercial Corporation's stocks were sold on the open market. And since the ventures often provided handsome returns for the managers and major stockholders, the Commercial Corporation increased the influence of the businessmen over the community as a whole.

Problems with the Western Military Academy

In spite of the successes of the Commercial Corporation, the cadets and backers of the Western Military Academy began to present the Pao-huang hui with serious problems. K'ang did not like Lea, finding him too radical and too independent. (K'ang's biographer notes that many people suspected Lea was a spy for Sun Yat-sen.) The feeling was reciprocated. When K'ang arrived in Los Angeles in 1905, Lea and his supporters were unpleasantly amused to find that K'ang did not know how to review the troops. They were suspicious when K'ang took the money raised by Pao-huang hui chapters but afterwards gave no accounting of it: K'ang's frequent requests for money had long been a source of annoyance to many party members. As far as Lea was concerned, however, the worst offense was that K'ang tried to replace him with Falkenburg, as will be described below. In spite of these differences, the two toured the country together, and Lea even helped secure K'ang an interview with President Theodore Roosevelt. Lea also arranged for the New York branch of the Western Military Academy to put on an especially large public display in their honor, but, for unexplained reasons, when K'ang left New York he left without Lea and the two never met again.[42]

It was earlier while they were still in Los Angeles that K'ang tried to turn the reins over to Falkenburg. He told Falkenburg to exercise the "commission" given him earlier by Liang Ch'i-ch'ao. Falkenburg responded by recruiting National Guardsmen to be the training officers. He also sent a framed photograph of himself to the academy headquarters in Los Angeles, where Lea was supposed to hang it in the central office and salute it as his superior officer. Lea, of course, refused.[43]

Falkenburg then instigated a public investigation of the Western Military Academy, having a friend write to the governor of New

York to say that Lea should not be allowed to continue the training program since it was "contrary to law, as these men [the cadets] are aliens to this country."[44] The investigation grew to involve President Roosevelt, the Secretary of War, and the Governor of California in addition to the Governor of New York. The upshot was that the chief of police of Los Angeles was told to determine once and for all whether or not the academy should be closed down. The chief of police was a man liable to be influenced by Homer Lea since several of Lea's friends held local office in Los Angeles. Captain O'Banion was also an officer on the Los Angeles Police Force. Furthermore, the Governor of California let it be known that he sympathized with Lea's training program, and Theodore Roosevelt is also supposed to have been favorably inclined. The result of the investigation was that Lea and his academy were permitted to continue unchanged, but Falkenburg's recruiting of officers from among National Guardsmen was forced to a halt.[45]

Falkenburg next tried to bring Lea to court and charge him with extortion. Falkenburg claimed that Lea had demanded five thousand dollars on the basis of secret plans that Lea was said to have had, and on the basis of Lea's supposed control of the Los Angeles press. The police, however, refused to permit Falkenburg to file the suit (even though police officers may have witnessed part of the alleged extortion attempt). At this point, Falkenburg turned to T'ang Ch'iung-ch'ang for support. T'ang, however, favored Lea and gave Falkenburg's attempt much adverse publicity in the *Ta-t'ung jih-pao*, thereby causing a number of people to leave the Pao-huang hui. Falkenburg finally withdrew his candidacy for head of the academy, and K'ang publicly announced that Lea was the only commanding officer of the Pao-huang hui's cadets in the United States.[46]

The 1905 Boycott and the Pao-huang Hui

The quarrel over the Western Military Academy had far less impact on Chinese in the Americas than did the 1905 Chinese boycott of American goods. I have noted in chapter 1 that Chinese in the Americas strongly favored revising the treaty between the United States and China which permitted Chinese Exclusion. By 1905, however, most of them preferred to see the matter settled by the Chinese government rather than try to exert pressure themselves. One exception to this was a small group of Christians who urged active community opposition.

But when negotiations between the two governments failed and merchant and student groups in China announced that they would launch a boycott of American goods, Chinese in the Americas had to decide whether or not to join them. They chose to join. Their attempts at organization have been discussed in chapter 1; in the end they were unable to obtain unity of action. K'ang Yu-wei tried independently to use his presumed influence with Theodore Roosevelt to force a change in the treaty. Huang San-te toured the continental United States to speak in favor of the boycott and against K'ang. Chinese merchants in Hawaii, the continental United States, and Canada at first supported the boycott through the antitreaty organization of the Chinese Six Companies, but when Americans responded by boycotting Chinese-owned businesses, the merchants lost interest.

By this time, various factions of reformers and revolutionaries in China had begun accusing each other of selling out or supporting the wrong policy. A principal debate centered on whether to demand that all Chinese be admitted to the United States or to agree that laborers could be excluded but that nonlaborers should be accorded better treatment. Unfortunately, Chinese-language newspapers published in the Americas during this critical period are not available, but the little evidence that remains suggests that the Pao-huang hui leaders were willing to accept the exclusion of laborers, whereas the more radical elements, including many Christians and probably the Chih-kung t'ang, were opposed to this concession.

In any event, by the beginning of 1906 it was evident that the boycott had failed and it became a dead issue in the Americas. The failure probably strengthened the Pao-huang hui since party leaders claimed responsibility for the few improvements that did occur: in response to K'ang's complaint to President Roosevelt, the president ordered some reforms in the administration of the laws. Protests by wealthy Chinese merchants in Chicago produced a few more reforms as well as a public apology. Furthermore, the Pao-huang hui probably blamed the failure of the boycott movement on the radicals. They could note that at the outset, many American businessmen sympathized with the Chinese desire to modify the treaty, but the intransigence of those who refused to accept any limitations on immigration from China to America had led rapidly to the dissipation of this good will.[47]

Evidence of the continued strength of the Pao-huang hui lies in the rapidity with which it was able to raise funds late in 1906 to construct a new headquarters in San Francisco. (The previous building had been destroyed by the great San Francisco earthquake and fire of April 1906.) Party leaders raised the money by selling shares to Pao-huang hui members, shares priced low enough (five dollars each) so as to encourage involvement by a large number of people. By December of 1906, 158 people had purchased shares. Some only bought one or two, but one individual obtained eighty, and there were other people who also purchased sizable blocks. These contributor-stockholders included people from both the *San-i* and the *Szu-i* communities. One was the founder of the newly established Canton Bank (Chin-shan Kwang-tung yin-hang), one of the Chinese community's biggest nonparty-affiliated capitalistic ventures. The bank's headquarters was in San Francisco. Huang Chi-yao, a Ping-kung t'ang leader with extensive gambling interests in Fresno, was another generous contributor; and yet another was a leader of the Hsieh-sheng t'ang.[48]

The contributions of these last two plus the continued loyalty of the Western Military Academy suggest that in 1906, in spite of earlier problems with Homer Lea, the Pao-huang hui still had the support of at least two "fighting tongs." The physical power of the "fighting tongs" combined with the economic power of the merchant/capitalist contingent and the Commercial Corporation made the Pao-huang hui a very powerful organization. Adding to its strength was the relative success of one of its most important political aims: the movement in favor of a constitutional monarchy was gaining support from a large number of Ch'ing officials and even the court. On the local level, the party could point out that the newspapers and schools it had founded or helped support benefited the entire Chinese community. In addition, foreign leaders respected the leaders of the Pao-huang hui. Although the party was becoming increasingly authoritarian and merchant-oriented, in many respects it must have appeared to have had a great deal to offer its members.

The Pao-huang hui in the Americas was so strong at this time that pro-Sun revolutionaries were reduced to attacking it from their newspaper in Hong Kong, the *Chung-kuo jih-pao* (China Daily). In the summer of 1906, Yeh En of Vancouver and K'ang's daughter K'ang T'ung-pi (then attending high school in Hartford, Connecticut) accused the paper of being involved in a Commercial Corporation scheme to defraud overseas Chinese. It also criticized the participation by Yeh En and the Pao-huang hui in the Canton-Hankow Railway Company in Kwangtung. Yeh, then in Hong Kong seeing to the affairs of the Commercial Corporation and the railway, responded by bringing the newspaper to court. He initiated two suits, one which charged the newspaper with libel because of the criticisms of K'ang T'ung-pi and the other which charged defamation of his own character. There is no record as to the judgment in the second case, but in 1910 he won the case involving K'ang T'ung-pi. The resultant damages forced the *Chung-kuo jih-pao* to declare bankruptcy and cease publication.[49]

Towards the end of 1906, the Pao-huang hui underwent a second reorganization and changed its name. This was part of a plan to unify the K'ang-Liang proreform forces in China and overseas. Liang Ch'i-ch'ao and his supporters chose the new name Ti-kuo hsien-cheng tang, or Constitutionalist Association, while K'ang and party representatives (mostly from the United States) drafted the rules.[50] The rules tightened party structure and put it on what should have been a more reliable financial basis. They also show both American and Triad influence.

The ultimate goal of the reorganized Pao-huang hui/Hsien-cheng tang was to bring about a constitutional monarchy based on the English, German, and Japanese model. This constitutional monarchy was to serve the people *(kuo-min);* the "people," according to the party definition, were those who paid land taxes *(tsu-shui)*. Prior to the institution of this constitutional monarchy, the party was to function as an independent nation with its own executive, legislative, and judicial branches. The executive branch (headed by K'ang Yu-wei) had nine subdivisions including a public-speaking division, a charitable works division, a foreign relations division (for dealing with Westerners and other outsiders), a military division (for the party defense forces and the like), and an espionage *(chen-t'an)* division. The party legislature *(i-hui)* was to be selected on three levels according to the principles of democratic centralism. Party members who violated party rules would be subject to discipline by a party "court." Powers not awarded to the central branch of the party would remain the domain of local party branches.[51]

Party members traveling from one place to another would have to obtain a letter of introduction from local party leaders before setting out on the trip. Initiation dues, monthly contributions, and special contributions were required of all members except the most indigent. Opium addicts could not join the party, but students got preferential treatment; some scholarships were even offered. Only party members could buy shares in party businesses (which now included possible land reclamation projects in Manchuria, Brazil, and Argentina). And deceased indigent members could expect to be buried at party expense.[52]

The continued strength of the Pao-huang hui/Hsien-cheng tang combined with the lack of any highly successful revolutionary activity in China also influenced the Chih-kung t'ang. By 1907, it was mixing reform and revolutionary aims to the point of outright contradiction. For example, at one time it called for an anti-Manchu revolution and the establishment of popular rule *(min-chu),* but suggested that the revolution should be achieved through peaceful means *(p'ing-ho shou-tuan)* so as to gain the sympathy of the powers. Elsewhere, it called for the Triads to launch a military campaign in association with local "people's armies" *(min-chün).* The military campaign was to restore freedom to the Chinese, but freedom in this case seems to have meant freedom from the taint of the inferior Manchu culture. All of this was to be achieved by developing a spirit of opposition, promoting education, and encouraging a spirit of cooperation! Throughout this period, the Chih-kung t'ang remained firm in its opposition to the Pao-huang hui,[53] but obviously the ideals of the latter still exercised some influence over it.

The Case of Hawaii

The section above has concentrated on North America, especially the United States. Hawaii presents a different case. Sun Yat-sen always had more success in Hawaii, partly because he had relatives in the Islands, and perhaps also because the Triads there were less centralized. Furthermore, judging by his criticism of Hawaii's Pao-huang hui leaders in 1903, Liang Ch'i-ch'ao was no longer on very good terms with Chinese in the Islands.

Accordingly, although Hawaii's Pao-huang hui raised a considerable sum of money to support the 1905 boycott, when it chose Chung Yü to take this money to Liang Ch'i-ch'ao in Japan, Chung was unenthusiastic about his mission. He refused to give the money to Liang until the latter explained how the earlier money contributed by the Hawaii chapter had been spent, a sum of several thousand dollars, much of which had come from Chung's close friends. Liang gave Chung an answer that Chung considered unsatisfactory, then invited him to dinner and stood him up. Someone in Liang's entourage told Chung that some of the earlier money had been given to Liang Yin-nan, one of Hawaii's early Pao-huang hui leaders who had gone to Shanghai to found a newspaper. This early money was presumably invested in the newspaper. The newspaper, however, was not to Chung's liking and he also claimed that Liang Yin-nan was no longer connected with the Pao-huang hui. Under these circumstances, when he returned to Hawaii in 1906, Chung Yü brought back with him the money raised for the boycott movement. He gave it back to the Pao-huang hui chapter, and refused to attend any more Pao-huang hui meetings. He also gave up his post as head of Hawaii's Chung-hua hui-kuan.[54] As a result, several other wealthy members also withdrew their support from the Pao-huang hui. In 1907, one of these men joined the staff of the Hsing-Chung hui's newspaper. One would presume that this indicated a considerable weakening of the Pao-huang hui in Hawaii.

This was not the only disaster suffered by Hawaii's Pao-huang hui during the period 1906–1907. Early in 1906, before Chung Yü had returned from China, the party's *Hsin Chung-kuo pao* got embroiled in a bitter editorial war with the Hsing-Chung hui's *T'an-shan hsin-pao*. The fight began with an anonymous writer accused the editor of San Francisco's Chih-kung t'ang newspaper of being corrupt, and of secretly being a member of the Hsing-Chung hui. The *Hsin Chung-kuo pao* defended the editor in question; the only problem was that the paper was wrong (at least about his Hsing-Chung hui membership). It took more than a month to find out the truth. In the meantime, the *Hsin Chung-kuo pao* had begun accusing the *T'an-shan hsin-pao* of many "crimes," the most accurate of which was that the revolutionaries favored violent solutions to China's problems. The *T'an-shan hsin-pao* responded by theatening the life of Honolulu's leading Pao-huang hui officers as well as calling for a series of assassinations in China.[55] The combined effect of Chung Yü's abandoning the party, the loss of face related to the newspaper editor in San Francisco, and the threats of the *T'an-shan hsin-pao* was seriously to weaken Hawaii's Pao-huang hui.

In the revolutionary camp, in the late summer of 1907 Hawaii's Hsing-Chung hui split into two factions. One faction then forced Sun's kinsman, the owner-manager of the *T'an-shan hsin-pao,* to retire from the newspaper for "reasons of health." Other of the newspaper's former supporters were also forced out. The newspaper was reorganized and renamed the *Min-sheng pao* (People's Livelihood News) to underline the importance of the "people's livelihood" concept to many Chinese in Hawaii. The same man who had acted as chief editor of the *T'an-shan hsin-pao* remained temporarily as chief editor of the *Min-sheng pao.* The triumphant faction of the Hsing-Chung hui then wrote to Tokyo to ask the central office there for yet another revolutionary editor from China. The man chosen was Lu Hsin, who arrived in Hawaii before the end of the year.[56]

When Lu Hsin arrived, he felt that he was not being given enough freedom to attack the Pao-huang hui in the way he saw fit. Late in 1907, he led a bolt from the *Min-sheng pao* of other disgruntled editors and managers. The rebels then founded the rival *Tzu-yu hsin-pao* (New Freedom News), with Lu Hsin as chief editor. These men were soon joined by at least one former Pao-huang hui leader, Huang Liang of Bishop's Bank. Other important additions to the newspaper included Sun Yat-sen's eldest son, and a Chih-kung t'ang leader from San Francisco (named Wen Hsiung-fei).[57]

Lu Hsin celebrated the founding of the paper and his freedom from the editorial restrictions of the *Min-sheng pao* by writing a series of virulently anti-Manchu editorials. Lu's anti-Manchuism was supposedly part of what had caused the break with the backers of the *Min-sheng pao,* but his ideas went well beyond that. His early *Tzu-yu hsin-pao* editorials also emphasized nationalism and stressed the popular theme that southerners were inherently superior to northerners. He also introduced the idea that youth should be more highly valued in Chinese society,[58] an idea which the T'ung-meng hui's San Francisco newspaper, *Shao-nien Chung-kuo ch'en-pao* (Young China Morning News) (founded in 1911), would later make one of its central themes.

The Christian Problem

It is undoubtedly significant that Chung Yü and Huang Liang, who broke with the Pao-huang hui between 1906 and 1907, were Christian. The Christians in the continental United States, led by the *Chung Sai Yat Po* (and influenced by Huang San-te), had already turned their backs on the Pao-huang hui in late 1904. In Canada, in 1906, the Christian community founded an independent newspaper in Vancouver. Both the chief editor and his assistant had formerly worked in Amoy's Pao-huang hui-affiliated bookstore. The assistant (Ts'ui T'ung-yüeh) had also been the Tokyo correspondent for the Pao-huang hui's Hong Kong newspaper. It may be presumed, then, that the new newspaper in Vancouver represented Christian Pao-huang hui members who were becoming estranged from the reform party. During 1906 and the first half of 1907, Ts'ui in particular helped prevent the development of any feelings of antagonism between the Christian paper and the Pao-huang hui's Vancouver newspaper.[59] Nonetheless, the increasing independence of Christians as a group in Hawaii, the United States, and Canada cannot but have displeased Pao-huang hui leaders.

Most of this did not directly benefit the revolutionaries, however. Attempts to found branches of the T'ung-meng hui in Hawaii and the continental United States in 1907 met with failure, and the revolutionaries did not even dare to try in Canada. They failed in the continental Americas for several reasons. The Chinese Exclusion laws at first thwarted their efforts to send T'ung-meng hui organizers to the United States. In 1907, however, Feng Tzu-yu (of the party's Hong Kong branch) located a prorevolutionary Chinese American, then in Hong Kong, who was planning to return to the United States. This man, named Li Shih-nan, had joined the T'ung-meng hui in 1906 at the urging of one of his kinsmen, a kinsman who was the son of a major Pao-huang hui leader in Canada! Because he was born in the United States, Li Shih-nan could not be denied entrance to the United States, so Feng Tzu-yu asked him to found a branch of the T'ung-meng hui in San Francisco when he arrived there. However, when he attempted to carry out these instructions, he met with stiff opposition from the Chih-kung t'ang and could do nothing until 1909.[60]

In the meantime, in Canada the rift between the Christians and the Pao-huang hui was becoming more acute. Sometime in 1907 or early 1908, Ts'ui wrote a story for Vancouver's Christian newspaper which correctly noted that an official in Kwangtung had publicly declared Pao-huang hui members to be criminals. Pao-huang hui leaders in Vancouver were furious with Ts'ui and the Christian newspaper, and brought suit against the paper, accusing it of slander. Ts'ui turned to Vancouver's Chih-kung t'ang and Hong Kong's revolutionary newspaper, *Chung-kuo jih-pao,* for aid. The former ignored his plea while the latter was evidently too involved in the lawsuits with Yeh En to be of much help. Ts'ui then began publishing prorevolutionary, anti-Manchu editorials in the Christian newspaper. The Pao-huang hui exerted pressure on the proprietors, and toward the end of 1908, the paper was forced to close down. Ts'ui had to flee Canada.[61]

The Development of Political Points of View, 1903–1907

Between Sun's arrival in Hawaii in late 1903 and the close of 1907, Chinese political parties in the Americas became somewhat fragmented as they became more deeply involved in pre-existing social organizations and the local economic structure. On the one hand were the radicals, represented principally by the followers of Sun Yat-sen and Huang San-te, and on the other were the moderates, represented by the leadership of the Pao-huang hui, with the exception of Homer Lea and his associates. Somewhere in between were the independents, sometimes favoring revolution but most often not, a group which included the majority of the Christian community.

The radicals were divided among themselves and were generally weaker than the Pao-huang hui, but they were still a challenge to the latter. They also aired alternative programs and policies, particularly of anti-Manchuism and the need to overthrow the Ch'ing dynasty. In Hawaii, they were led by the Hsing-Chung hui in alliance with certain sublodges of the Triads/Chih-kung t'ang. In addition to advocating revolution and anti-Manchuism, they favored some kind of property redistribution such as would give poor agricultural laborers in Hawaii and their counterparts in China their own land to farm. Under Lu Hsin's influence, by 1907 Hawaii's Hsing-Chung hui also lauded youth and southerners.

In Canada, what radical sentiment existed was kept under control and out of sight by the Pao-huang hui in alliance with the Chih-kung t'ang there. Ts'ui T'ung-yüeh and the Christians who backed him tried to do something about this situation but were quickly suppressed.

In the continental United States, Huang San-te controlled the bulk of the radicals, which included primarily members of the Chih-kung t'ang lodge and other lodges closely associated with it. Sun tried but failed to engineer an alliance with Huang by which the Hsing-Chung hui and Sun would be designated as the vanguard of Huang's organization. Huang's group called for representative democracy, the rule of law, anti-Manchuism, anti-Pao-huang hui-ism, and (usually) violent revolution. In keeping with this spirit, Huang favored the total abolition of Chinese Exclusion rather than agreeing that Chinese laborers could be denied entry to the United States.

Another group of radicals in the continental United States consisted of a handful of Hsing-Chung hui members, all of whom were located in San Francisco and all of whom were Christians. Their Hsing-Chung hui branch apparently had a very brief life, possibly because within six months of founding it, Sun Yat-sen went on to help found and head the T'ung-meng hui. In any case, its members swore the required oath and officially adopted the required rules of the Hsing-Chung hui. Being Christians, they must have considered themselves fairly Westernized, and undoubtedly had a fair grasp of that to which they were subscribing.[62] Beyond this, little is known of them.

Finally, a somewhat larger group of radicals (Homer Lea's cadets) remained loosely affiliated with the Pao-huang hui. They do not seem to have had any aims beyond military preparedness, violent confrontation with the Empress Dowager, and maintaining an ardent nationalism. This group was probably associated with certain factions of the Ping-kung t'ang and the Hsieh-sheng t'ang.

The reformers were far more numerous than all of the radical groups put together. They were strong in the continental United States and dominant in both Canada and Latin America. Represented by the Pao-huang hui, they were better organized and had more money invested in their party. Far earlier than the Hsing-Chung hui, the party had become involved in local affairs and embedded in the social structure. With respect to this social structure, party leaders desired to return to the status quo ante (the pre-1893 situation) with certain modifications. Welcoming both *Szu-i* and *San-i* merchants as community leaders, they sought to establish the fact that the distinction between businessman and laborer was more important than regional differences. In addition, they encouraged middle-class merchants to participate instead of relying exclusively on the very wealthy (although the very wealthy had a greater share of the power). They also felt that the literate, forward-looking businessman/merchant had a fundamental right to participate in government. Some of the confidence shown by the merchants was a reflection of the willingness of K'ang and Liang to rely on them. Another boost came in the formal acknowledgment by the Ch'ing court, through the abolition of the Confucian examination system in 1905, that the traditional educational and social structure was inadequate for the modern age.

Relying on its broad appeal and its entrenchment in local social organizations, between 1903 and 1908 the Pao-huang hui attempted to seize the lead in the overseas communities. It tried to establish a party army (the Western Military Academy) to exercise certain "police powers" (through the "translators' " lodge, Canada's Chih-kung t'ang, and the Ping-kung t'ang and Hsieh-sheng t'ang), to control the economic life of the overseas community (through the Commercial Corporation), and to absorb the local governing apparatus (the Chinese Six Companies). In a word, like the Chih-kung t'ang, the Pao-huang hui was trying to become an *imperium in imperio*.

These pretentions and the growing authoritarianism of the Pao-huang hui led the Chih-kung t'ang in the United States and Christians everywhere in the Americas to split from it. K'ang's feelings

concerning Confucianism were probably a further source of dissatisfaction for the Christians. The latter left the party between 1904 and
1907 and, after leaving, most often espoused an independent political
point of view rather than become too closely involved with either
political party.

As the preceding amply demonstrates, between 1903 and 1908
interest in national (Chinese) politics on the part of Chinese in the
Americas increased significantly. Local concerns were still involved
in this interest, but the 1905 boycott ensured that once immediate,
local problems had been solved, the national commitment would
remain. National concerns were also beginning to have a greater
effect on the local social structure. Some organizations such as the
Chih-kung t'ang had begun using national politics to redefine themselves, while others such as surname and regional associations found
themselves weakened by the national focus of the new politics.

Ironically, the political leaders were dismayed to see that group
distinctions based on political choices were becoming so pro-
nounced.[63] They preferred a one-party system where only one party
and only one political view would be tolerated. Sun's alliance with
the Chih-kung t'ang was definitely only a temporary expediency.
Sun included, the political leaders objected not only to the number
and variety of political groups, but also to the strength of the other
types of organizations in the overseas communities. Calling on Chinese to see themselves as the descendants of the Yellow Emperor,
they asked people to rise above all other affiliations in their nationalism and let their nationalism be directed by the political group. The
Pao-huang hui and the Chih-kung t'ang also tried to define themselves as the governing body of overseas Chinese. They centralized
their organizations. They also tried to increase their appeal by giving a larger proportion of the community a voice in the decision-
making process and a sense that the party "belonged" to them. At
the same time, the political leaders took measures to ensure that
their own influence would not decline. If these several aims came
into conflict, the conflicts were normally resolved in favor of the
existing leaders.

6

THE DENOUEMENT

Between its founding and 1908, the Pao-huang hui/Hsien-cheng tang dominated the political life of Chinese in the Americas. A major element in its success had been the degree to which party and party leaders shared Chinatown's goals. In the context of reformers versus revolutionaries, what was most important was the goal of economic development along capitalistic lines, because this was a goal shared by reformers and America's Chinese but of little interest to Sun Yat-sen and his partisans. In addition, the reformers (whose social prominence already gave them an edge) had shown themselves to be astute political organizers willing to spend considerable amounts of time and money to woo America's Chinese.

In 1908, however, the Pao-huang hui began a long decline which continued until finally, at the end of 1911, it was completely routed. During the same few years, Sun Yat-sen's adherents began to attract substantial support, enough so that by the end of 1911, they had replaced the Chih-kung t'ang as the leading organization of the revolutionaries and had carried the day. The reasons for the reversal are several: overconfident Pao-huang hui leaders increasingly neglected the Americas or antagonized Chinese community leaders with their high-handed methods. The Pao-huang hui's commercial and financial empire, intended as a model of capitalistic development (and as a means of enriching thousands of Pao-huang hui partisans) collapsed between 1908 and 1909. Events in China as well began to play into the hands of the revolutionaries. These events included the death of the Kuang-hsü Emperor in November of 1908, the increasing dissatisfaction of elite groups in China with the court's slow pace in convening a national parliament, the railway rights recovery movement (especially acute in mid-1911), and eventually, ever more frequent and spectacular revolutionary attempts. Finally, in the

Americas as elsewhere, as time passed Sun Yat-sen's partisans became more sophisticated organizers.

As the political parties were changing, American Chinatowns were also changing. A far broader segment of the population of Chinese in America became interested in politics. Nationalism grew at a faster pace than ever before. More and more it served to break down intracommunity barriers and encouraged political activism, as individuals sought ways to help China regain international prestige. With greater political activism came a greater desire for self-determination. This led to revised methods of operation for the *hui-kuan* and to the organization of regular (Chinese) Chambers of Commerce. Nationalism also produced youth factions, anti-opium campaigns, and other movements, many of which reflected developments in China. Most of these changes had long been advocated by the Pao-huang hui, but as they were accomplished they created a more fruitful field for revolutionary organizers. By 1910 and 1911, Sun Yat-sen's partisans had become much better at plowing this field.

Successes and Failures of the Pao-huang Hui, 1908

The year began well for the Pao-huang hui/Hsien-cheng tang. The party had always hoped to force the Ch'ing court to institute a parliament, and as interest in the parliamentary system became more widespread in China, K'ang, Liang Ch'i-ch'ao, and the Pao-huang hui greatly increased their influence. It even began to seem as if Liang could get Yüan Shih-k'ai, their long-time opponent at court, removed from power. Early in the year, K'ang and Liang organized a society in China called the Political Information Club (Cheng-wen she) to complement the (overseas) Pao-huang hui and lead the parliamentary movement. The Ch'ing court was already considering the question of a constitution and a parliament. The function of the Political Information Club was to advance the timetable and ensure that the participation and the rights of citizens would be a part of the effort.[1]

In the meantime, in the spring and summer of 1908, the Pao-huang hui placed itself in the forefront of a movement to boycott Japanese goods. The boycott was supposed to avenge China's humiliation by Japan in an incident (the *Tatsu Maru* affair) involving Japanese smuggling arms into China that Sun had purchased for Chinese revolutionaries.[2] There had been several revolutionary uprisings in the Kwangtung/Kwangsi/Yünnan area in early 1908. Lack of arms, a lack that this shipment was to remedy, had made the attempts short-lived. Paradoxically, the subsequent boycott of Japanese goods was perceived by many as an expression of nationalism, and as such, it engendered real enthusiasm among Chinese in the Americas, even within the supposedly prorevolutionary Chih-kung t'ang in San Francisco.[3]

The boycott's popularity naturally strengthened the Pao-huang hui. Led by that party's San Francisco branch, Chinese from Vancouver to Panama joined in the movement. Hoping to eliminate their dependence on Japanese freighters, a number of the wealthier entrepreneurs even organized a steamship line in San Francisco to compete with the Japanese line and engage in the trans-Pacific trade. Only Chinese were allowed to purchase shares in this company, the China Mail Steamship Line (Chung-kuo yu-ch'uan yu-hsien kung-ssu).[4]

The boycott and the organization of the Political Information Club reemphasized the political aspect of the Pao-huang hui while underlining the relationship between the parliamentary and the nationalist movements. Encouraged by K'ang Yu-wei, at the height of the boycott over two hundred Pao-huang hui chapters in Hong Kong, Southeast Asia, Europe, the Americas, Africa, and Australia gave their official support to a twelve-point petition to the Ch'ing court. This petition demanded the early convening of a parliament, the promulgation of a constitution, the removal of the Empress Dowager from power, transferral of the capital to central or southern China, abolition of the distinction between Manchu and Han, national military conscription, economic reform, the extension of trade, the establishment of chambers of commerce, and the radical reconstruction of China's administrative apparatus. Wholeheartedly supported by the Pao-huang hui in the Americas, the petition was greatly resented by the Ch'ing court. Its presentation, together with the growing influence of the Political Information Club, prompted the court on August 13 to ban that Club permanently and arrest some of its leaders.[5]

In the meantime, Pao-huang hui business ventures also suffered a blow. As the year 1908 opened, most of these had appeared to be doing well. Then, K'ang and Liang were approached by a promoter who wanted the Pao-huang hui to back an even more ambitious project. They readily gave their consent. This was a scheme conceived by Liu Shih-chi, a longtime Pao-huang hui partisan actively involved in educational reform in China and Southeast Asia. He was a native of Kwangtung, and in 1908 was an expectant intendant for the province of Kwangsi. Liu desired to establish a *kuan-tu shang-pan* (government-supervised, merchant-operated) enterprise in Kwangsi to be financed by selling stock in Canada and the United States (including Hawaii) to Chinese whom he intended to approach through the local Pao-huang hui organizations. The enterprise, called the Jun Wah Mining Company (Chen-hua shih-yeh yu-hsien kung-szu) was to include a silver mine in the T'ien-p'ing mountains, a steamboat line, a railway, a bank, and the reclamation of wasteland, all in Kwangsi province. He obtained the support of the governor of Kwangsi, and then of Ou Chü-chia, and through Ou he approached K'ang and Liang, who gave their consent. Yeh En and another officer of Vancouver's Pao-huang hui were then in China and developed an interest in Liu Shih-chi's scheme. They were made sponsors of the company and accompanied Liu Shih-chi to the Americas where the trio toured Chinese communities to raise capital for the venture. By August, they had obtained three hundred thousand dollars.[6]

When the Ch'ing court ordered the dissolution of the Political Information Club, however, the governor of Kwangsi ordered Liu Shih-chi to dissociate himself from the Pao-huang hui organizations. When pressed for an explanation, Liu said people were contributing as individual loyal citizens of China and that his project was supported by the Chinese Minister to Washington, Wu T'ing-fang. Wu denied this, and the authorities in Kwangsi ordered Liu to return to China immediately. Certain Pao-huang hui members began to suspect Liu's motives to the extent that when he arrived in Pittsburgh to solicit funds, the Chinese community there swore out a warrant for his arrest on a charge of fraud. In the face of this opposition, Liu returned to China.[7]

While the Jun Wah Mining scheme was falling under suspicion, other Pao-huang hui ventures suffered from the vicissitudes of American and Mexican finance and politics. A bank panic in the

United States in late 1907 had adversely affected the Pao-huang hui's branch bank in New York. It also lowered land values as far away as Torreón, where the Pao-huang hui had purchased land for a streetcar line and a housing development. Pao-huang hui members in the United States, Canada, and Mexico were heavily involved in the Mexican project. In fact, in 1908 demand for shares caused the project's managers to lower the price per share to five dollars so as to put their purchase within the reach of the less wealthy. Ironically, just as the Pao-huang hui was taking steps to involve more people in the Commercial Corporation, its business ventures were becoming financially dubious. The project in Mexico was further undercut when, in the summer of 1908, the manager of the bank in Torreón began to fight with the manager of the land development scheme for control of the enterprise. As a result, the bank manager refused to release the funds necessary to build the streetcar line. President Díaz of Mexico threatened to withdraw the streetcar concession unless work began immediately, and K'ang sent Li Fu-chi from Vancouver to Mexico to resolve the impasse. Li tried but failed to obtain funds from the now almost insolvent New York bank. Matters remained in this state until the outbreak of the Mexican revolution in 1911, at which time the Mexican authorities solved the problem by appropriating all the land and funds in question.[8]

As the Commercial Corporation's American enterprises began to founder and the problems of its projects in Asia (see chapter 5) became more acute, many people lost confidence in the party. Homer Lea, his supporters, and his cadets, suspicious since 1905 of the way in which funds were handled by Pao-huang hui officials, chose this time to make a permanent break. Under the direction of Yung Wing (a former Pao-huang hui partisan and in 1908 the legal guardian of K'ang's favorite daughter), Lea became a secret agent for Sun Yat-sen. Thus, the "army" went over to the revolutionaries and Lea and Yung began to seek American financial aid for Sun. They approached individual financiers on Sun's behalf, solicited aid from highly placed American officials, and tried to get United States Army officers to agree to work covertly for Sun, either as soldiers of fortune or as supporters of a policy of direct military aid for his revolution.[9]

All of this weakened the Pao-huang hui, but the party still was not mortally wounded. Even the death of the Kuang-hsü Emperor in

November of 1908 was not enough to destroy it. The emperor's death, and the ascent of a new, infant emperor under the regency of conservative Manchu nobles, however, did produce a small upsurge of interest in revolution in areas as disparate as Hawaii and Cuba. Still, in San Francisco, as elsewhere in the Americas, the Pao-huang hui's nationalism, its interest in economic development, and its desire for moderate political reform served to retain for that party the allegiance of most of the *hui-kuan* and the Chinese Six Companies.[10] Through its vigorous promotion of local Chinese schools, which taught Western as well as Chinese subjects, the party also developed a good relationship with many of the young Chinese American students. As a result, the recently organized Chinese American Citizens' Alliance (the T'ung-yüan hui or C.A.C.A.), led by students, also accepted the Pao-huang hui temporarily as a friend and ally.[11]

In 1909, however, internal struggles once again shook the Pao-huang hui. Liu Shih-chi, supported by Yeh En and Ou Chü-chia, launched an attack against Hsü Ch'in, supported by K'ang Yu-wei and Liang Ch'i-ch'ao, over control of the Kwangsi mining venture and disbursal of profits. At the height of this struggle, Liu was assassinated in Hong Kong. One of the nine assassins was a young Pao-huang hui member from Hawaii, a former student of Liang Ch'i-ch'ao. Another was the head of the Triads in Canton. This split the Pao-huang hui in the Americas, for although Liu's assassination certainly pleased Pittsburgh's Chinese community (and the Pao-huang hui in San Francisco),[12] it caused a violent response in the Pao-huang hui in Vancouver and Victoria, both still heavily involved in Liu's scheme through Yeh En, and even from many party members in Hawaii.[13]

Liu's assassination and the news of it generated a tremendous amount of disaffection in Canada. We recall that in 1908, when Ts'ui T'ung-yüeh and Vancouver's Christian newspaper had run into difficulties with the Pao-huang hui, Ts'ui called on the Chih-kung t'ang to come to his aid, but his plea was met with silence. Late in 1909, however, the central headquarters of Canada's Chih-kung t'ang responded to the changing situation by founding a prorevolutionary newspaper. The founders of the newspaper, including Victoria's *ta-lao,* wrote to Feng Tzu-yu in Hong Kong asking him to send them a revolutionary chief editor. Feng responded by going to Canada himself and assuming the editorship.[14]

Liu's murder aided the revolutionary cause in San Francisco as well, enough to permit Li Shih-nan to found a small, pro-Sun Yat-sen revolutionary society called the Youth Study Society (Shao-nien hsüeh-she) in 1909. Most of its members were young laborers, or teachers and students in the local Chinese schools (schools which, it will be recalled, had for the most part been founded by or in association with the Pao-huang hui). At the other end of the continent, someone in New York wrote Feng Tzu-yu to suggest that another visit by Sun Yat-sen to the Americas would be very welcome.[15]

Sun Returns to America

These events, so favorable to Sun's cause when he came to the United States again in late 1908, were in some measure offset by a feud within his own party. The feud split the T'ung-meng hui when the dissenters bolted the party to reestablish an earlier group (the Kuang-fu hui). The dissenters then worked hard to undermine Sun's support in overseas communities, printing leaflets which attacked Sun, accusing him of megalomania, of misusing funds, and of causing revolutionary failures through mismanagement and poor organization. These leaflets were distributed (in part with the Pao-huang hui's help) throughout the Americas, Southeast Asia, and Japan.[16] They were particularly effective in Southeast Asia, but also caused a crisis of confidence in the Americas. Sun found this particularly frustrating since, during the 1909 trip, he saw that America's Pao-huang hui was on the verge of collapse.[17] So seriously did Sun take the threat posed by these attacks that he got one of his supporters to publish letters in his defense in several Hong Kong newspapers. Sun then distributed these newspapers to America's Chinese-language newspaper.[18] Although this was of some help,[19] it took weeks to organize and was of no use to Sun while he was on the East Coast of the United States.

When Sun arrived in New York in October of 1909 he was met at the dock by an old friend who was a merchant and a mid-level leader in the local branch of the Chih-kung t'ang. Sun used this man's store for meetings and, after a few days, managed to find several people (including this friend) willing to let him initiate them into a conspiratorial, prorevolutionary group. Because of the Chih-kung t'ang's antagonism to the T'ung-meng hui, Sun used the name Ko-ming

tang (Revolutionary Party) for this group, and even ordered all
T'ung-meng hui branches in Hong Kong, Southeast Asia, and elsewhere to change their name as well (which most refused to do).[20]
Later than anywhere else in the world, and under an assumed name,
the T'ung-meng hui was thus finally established in the Americas.

Soon afterwards, Sun received a telegram from Feng Tzu-yu and
others in Hong Kong saying that if Sun could raise some twenty
thousand Hong Kong dollars and send it to them immediately, an
uprising could be launched that would utilize elements of the Ch'ing
regime's New Army in Kwangtung. The New Army, developed in
earnest in the years after the Boxer Rebellion, was China's best. At
least partially equipped with modern weapons and partially trained
in modern military tactics, New Army divisions were stationed by
the court in key locations throughout the country after 1908. After
Sun received the telegram, he immediately began pressing people
for funds, relying most heavily on the leaders of the local branches of
the Chih-kung t'ang. In New York, the Chih-kung t'ang branch secretary pledged that his organization would give Sun three thousand
dollars H.K., and Boston's *ta-lao* pledged another five thousand dollars H.K. (although Sun and his partisans in China never actually
received more than one-quarter of this money).[21]

When Sun got to Chicago, he ran into more difficulties. The *ta-lao*
in Chicago was also the head of the Midwestern division of the Pao-
huang hui, and in spite of Sun's assessment of the Pao-huang hui's
weakness, the *ta-lao* was able to prevent Sun from obtaining aid from
Chicago's Chih-kung t'ang. Sun then approached the Chinese
Christian community. Over twenty Christians agreed to form a second branch of the Ko-ming tang, and through them Sun obtained
another three thousand dollars H.K. to send to Hong Kong.[22]

From Chicago, Sun proceeded to the West Coast. He stopped first
in Los Angeles where he assured himself of Homer Lea's support,
then went to San Francisco where he was met by the ten or so members of the Youth Study Society. (One of these members was a student and C.A.C.A. leader who had formerly sympathized with the
Pao-huang hui.)[23]

Once settled in San Francisco, Sun went to call on Huang San-te
to ask for financial assistance. The latter, after consulting with the
other officers of the Chih-kung t'ang, told Sun that it would be difficult to accede to such a request and that it certainly could not be

rushed. Sun then turned to the Youth Study Society, but its members felt themselves too impoverished to be able to give any aid. At this point, Sun received a telegram from Hong Kong announcing that the uprising for which he was raising money, the New Army uprising of 1910, had failed in part for lack of funds.[24]

Ironically, news that the uprising had failed was enough to stimulate contributions (especially from Canada), both because people were impressed with the New Army involvement and because the uprising disproved Sun's critics, who claimed that Sun was misusing funds. Sun was finally able to turn the Youth Study Society into a branch of the Ko-ming tang and to organize a Chicago branch of the latter organization. By this time, the new oath being used was different from the regular T'ung-meng hui oath (although Ko-ming tang members realized that they were actually part of the T'ung-meng hui). Probably the most important difference was the replacement of the phrase "equalize land rights" *(p'ing-chün ti-ch'üan)* with the less specific phrase, "put into effect the principle of People's Livelihood" *(shih-hsing min-sheng chu-i)*. An important bloc of T'ung-meng hui adherents in Asia had objected to the earlier phrase, and the revised oath represented Sun's attempt at an acceptable replacement.[25]

Sun encouraged the new San Francisco chapter of the T'ung-meng hui/Ko-ming tang to establish a propaganda organ. At first, they could only finance a weekly magazine, but in the winter of 1910, they reorganized it into a daily newspaper, *Young China (Shao-nien Chung-kuo ch'en-pao)*. There were four principal editors, one of whom was Li Shih-nan. A second was Huang Po-yao, of the C.A.C.A. and the Chih-kung t'ang. The magazine, and more especially the daily, provided a significant boost to revolutionaries throughout the Americas. The paper, and the magazine before it, circulated in Cuba, Peru, Mexico, Canada, and Hawaii as well as in the continental United States. It introduced many revolutionary sympathizers to the T'ung-meng hui ideology, and it also gave revolutionaries in the Americas a feeling of solidarity with their brethren elsewhere.[26]

Sun also recruited quite a few new members for San Francisco's T'ung-meng hui/Ko-ming tang, including Ts'ui T'ung-yüeh, formerly of Vancouver's Christian newspaper. (Ts'ui had fled to San Francisco when his troubles with Canada's Pao-huang hui grew serious.)[27] A second new member, inspired by Sun's claim that the revo-

lutionaries were going to infiltrate the Ch'ing army and seize power
from within, was able to persuade several friends to join with him.
The same snowball effect was apparent in connection with a third
new member. A high school student, he first persuaded a group of
his classmates to join. Then he interested his father, a man who
owned a general store in California's Sacramento River delta
region. In 1911, the father invited Sun to come to the area to give
speeches. The speeches persuaded the father, who in turn persuaded
thirty to forty percent of the sizable local Hsiang-shan community
(Sun was born in Hsiang-shan) to join Sun's organization. Most of
these were agricultural laborers, fruit farmers, former railroad
workers, and the like.[28] Significantly, almost all were people who
could not expect their voices to be heard in the major Chinatown
social organizations.

In April of 1910, Sun left the mainland of the United States for
Hawaii. Hawaii was well prepared for him: editorship of the T'ung-
meng hui newspaper there had passed from its first, primarily anti-
Manchu, editor to a new man, a fiery writer who was very much
interested in socialism. In Hawaii, Sun began suddenly to experience what appeared to be real success. Thousands came to hear him
speak, and in the space of hardly more than a week he recruited
eight hundred people to the T'ung-meng hui, including the former
Hsing-Chung hui partisans. T'ung-meng hui headquarters was
located in the *Tzu-yu hsin-pao* building, and two separate branches of
the party were organized: a secret one for fearful merchants (including Chung Yü and Huang Liang) and a much larger, public one. Lu
Hsin, the original editor of the *Tzu-yu hsin-pao,* was named secretary
of both branches in order to coordinate their activities.[29] Finally, the
Hsing-Chung hui branches on Maui and Hilo were converted into
T'ung-meng hui branches.[30]

Heady with success, Sun left Hawaii for Tokyo and almost immediately tried to tap the wealth of these new members. In a letter written to Hawaii's T'ung-meng hui in June of 1910, he asked that its
members provide one thousand U.S. dollars each month for a
period of twelve months to be used to further the cause of revolution.[31] Hawaii's T'ung-meng hui members were so taken aback by
this request that they do not seem even to have answered his letter.
This cool reception was partly due to the reservations of the *Tzu-yu
hsin-pao*'s prosocialist editor (who in accordance with Sun's request

was then emphasizing the anti-Manchu theme). This editor may have been disappointed with what he had learned of Sun's ideology. Certainly, he felt suspicious concerning the use to which earlier funds raised in Hawaii had been put. The main problem, as this editor saw it, was that the T'ung-meng hui partisans in China were incompetent, and he communicated his complaint to the major revolutionary contributors in Hawaii. Late in August, Sun wrote again with a modified request: would the T'ung-meng hui in Hawaii simply take responsibility for financing the uprising then being organized (and use any leftover funds to purchase freedom for a certain prominent revolutionary assassin)?[32] These requests for money further dampened revolutionary enthusiasm in Hawaii, and by the end of 1910 the T'ung-meng hui there only had about thirty active members. Their total financial contribution for the years 1910 and 1911 was under one thousand five hundred dollars.[33]

The Rise of the Revolutionary Tide

In spite of Sun's clumsiness on this occasion, continuing strife within the Pao-huang hui worked in his favor. Sometime in 1910, about a year after the assassination of Liu Shih-chi, Liu's son publicly accused the major Pao-huang hui leaders K'ang Yu-wei, Liang Ch'i-ch'ao, Hsü Ch'in, a former editor of the Pao-huang hui's Hawaii newspaper, and the editor of the Pao-huang hui's Vancouver newspaper of being responsible for the death of his father. K'ang's grandson and biographer points out that none of the accused were in China at the time of the assassination. This would not necessarily preclude their having been the instigators, but in any event, whether or not the son's accusation had any basis in fact is less important than the effect it had on the Pao-huang hui.[34]

The Case of Canada

The accusation of Liu's son had immediate and dramatic repercussions on Canada's Pao-huang hui. It aroused Chinese in Canada in the same way that the Railway Rights Recovery Movement of 1911 aroused Chinese in China. Yeh En and his brother had already left the party when Liu was killed. After learning of the accusation, Yeh

En also withdrew his opposition to revolutionary activity, with the result that many revolutionary sympathizers finally dared to air their opinions. K'ang and his supporters tried to stem the tide by branding Yeh En as an embezzler and Ou Chü-chia as a Hakka separatist and prorevolutionary. K'ang sent Hsü Ch'in back to Canada to repair the situation. All of this was to little avail, however. Scores of people left the Pao-huang hui. Canada's Chih-kung t'ang had by this time organized its prorevolutionary newspaper, and in the summer of 1910 Feng Tzu-yu arrived in Canada to assume the editorship. Feng immediately launched an editorial war against Vancouver's Pao-huang hui newspaper (whose editor was one of the accused).[35] In addition, some twenty or so young men asked Feng to initiate them into the T'ung-meng hui. Feng, however, refused, owing to the Chih-kung t'ang's virulent opposition to the existence of what it viewed as a competing prorevolutionary organization. Happily for Sun and Feng, one of these young enthusiasts was on the editorial staff of the Chih-kung t'ang's newspaper.[36] This helped strengthen Feng's control over the newspaper, and gave him more influence over Canada's Chih-kung t'ang.

In the meantime, Sun Yat-sen wrote Huang San-te from Japan and asked him to raise one hundred thousand dollars for Huang Hsing's upcoming Chen-nan kuan uprising in Yünnan.[37] Huang San-te wired Sun seven thousand dollars. After the uprising failed, Sun returned to the Americas. Landing in New York in December 1910, he proceeded to the southern part of the United States, where he met with Huang San-te. Sun and Huang traveled slowly on to San Francisco, raising money along the way. With Huang's help, Sun had obtained a total of two thousand dollars by the time he reached San Francisco, mostly from Chinese in Fresno and Los Angeles. In San Francisco, Sun wrote a few editorials for *Young China,* recruited new members for the T'ung-meng hui, and, more importantly, once again asked Huang to help him get the official endorsement of the Chih-kung t'ang hierarchy. While considering the matter, the Chih-kung t'ang invited Sun to be a guest of honor at their (Chinese) New Year's banquet, which was soon to be held. Sun accepted the invitation.[38]

While Sun was in San Francisco, Feng Tzu-yu was trying to engineer an alliance between Sun and Canada's Chih-kung t'ang. Early in 1911, just prior to the Chinese New Year, Feng wrote asking Sun to come to Canada immediately to consummate a deal that Feng had just worked out. Sun left on the next train, without taking leave of or making his apologies to the Chih-kung t'ang leaders in San Francisco whose banquet (which was scheduled to take place on the same day) he was manifestly not going to be able to attend.[39]

When his train arrived in Vancouver, Sun found a welcoming party at the station to meet him, including over one thousand members of Vancouver's Chih-kung t'ang. The Chih-kung t'ang feted him, and at their suggestion he gave a series of speeches, which were extremely well attended. On four consecutive nights, he had an audience of over one thousand. Pao-huang hui members came, independents came, and, of course, prorevolutionaries came. Feng Tzu-yu, pointing to this evidence of Sun's popularity, suggested that the Chih-kung t'ang in Canada establish an official fund-raising organization for Sun's uprising. The Chih-kung t'ang leaders did so, calling it the Triad Fund-raising Bureau (Hung-men ch'ou-hsiang chü). All of its officers came from the Chih-kung t'ang, but only one of them was closely associated with Sun. The organization's treasurer was also the treasurer of Canada's Chih-kung t'ang and a manager of Vancouver's Chih-kung t'ang newspaper, thereby linking together the three organizations.[40]

Canada's Triad Fund-raising Bureau was highly successful. Vancouver's Chih-kung t'ang inaugurated the fund-raising campaign with a contribution of ten thousand dollars. The young, prorevolutionary supporters of Sun Yat-sen in Vancouver and Victoria developed a plan (along with Feng Tzu-yu) which they thought might help the fund-raising even more. They decided that while the prorevolutionary spirit was at its height, Sun should give a rousing speech at Canada's central Chih-kung t'ang headquarters in Victoria, after which he should excuse himself from the meeting. His supporters would then propose that since Chinese in Canada were mostly poor and yet wanted to help, the Chih-kung t'ang should officially suggest that each headquarters mortgage its building and "lend" the funds raised in this fashion to the Triad Fund-raising Bureau for Sun. Sun agreed to this plan and it worked: Chih-kung t'ang officials were embarrassed to oppose the mortgage plan publicly after having just endorsed Sun and his revolution. The mortgage of Victoria's Chih-kung t'ang building brought in thirty thousand dollars. Three wealthy merchants in Victoria were persuaded

to contribute another twenty thousand. Spurred on by a visit by Sun
Yat-sen, Toronto's Chih-kung t'ang mortgaged its building for
another ten thousand. Montreal contributed several thousand more
through the same means, and smaller communities made smaller
contributions for a grand total of eighty thousand dollars, at least
seventy thousand of which was sent to Hong Kong for Huang
Hsing's Canton uprising of April 1911. This was the bulk of the funds
used for that particular uprising.[41]

This enthusiastic response was due primarily to the influence of
the Liu Shih-chi affair and to Feng Tzu-yu's efforts. Disaffection
occasioned by Liu's assassination was essential to the revolutionaries. Without it, it is even doubtful that Feng Tzu-yu could have
entered Canada in 1910. His passport listed his occupation as one of
the excluded categories of Chinese, but a translator for the Canadian
customs (a wealthy merchant and a former Pao-huang hui stalwart)
noticed this in time and changed Feng's category to guarantee him
entrance.[42] After entering, Feng persuaded several other disaffected
Pao-huang hui leaders to be neutral or even prorevolutionary. These
included the wealthy head of a Pao-huang hui chapter in the Van-
couver/Victoria area and the wealthy treasurer of Victoria's Chih-
kung t'ang.[43] The influence of these new converts and the support
given by the prorevolutionaries on the Chih-kung t'ang's newspaper
was such that prior to Sun's arrival, Feng was made honorary head
of the Chih-kung t'ang in Vancouver.[44] By the time that Sun
arrived, the battle was already more than half won.

Sun, however, not only had to deal with Canada's Chih-kung
t'ang, but he also had to take into account the young enthusiasts
who had wanted Feng Tzu-yu to establish a branch of the T'ung-
meng hui. That they could be of use to him was demonstrated by
their manipulation of the Chih-kung t'ang. Sun agreed with Feng
that it would be inadvisable to organize a branch of the T'ung-meng
hui at that time, in the face of the Chih-kung t'ang's opposition. He
counseled the young enthusiasts to be patient. Not long after Sun
left, in June of 1911, Feng decided that the time was right and
inaugurated a branch with over twenty members. By October of 1911,
the number had increased to over one hundred in Vancouver and
ten or so in Victoria. The existence of this branch was kept secret,
and meetings were held outside Chinatown so as not to arouse the
possible suspicions of the Chih-kung t'ang. Feng Tzu-yu was made

president of this chapter. Other members included one of the staff members of the Chih-kung t'ang newspaper along with several officers of the Triad Fund-raising Bureau.[45]

Triad Fund-raising in the Continental United States

All of this activity undercut the role that Huang San-te was trying to play in the Chih-kung t'ang as a whole and in the revolutionary effort in particular. Worried lest events should pass him by, and hoping to capitalize on Sun's newfound influence, Huang met Sun in April of 1911 when Sun arrived in Chicago from Canada, and the two began another fund-raising tour of the East Coast of the United States. Even before Sun returned to the United States, the Chih-kung t'ang hierarchy in San Francisco had begun calling for people to donate money to Sun. When Sun (with Huang San-te) was enthusiastically received in New York and Chicago, the San Francisco hierarchy agreed to establish a Fund-raising Bureau (Ch'ou-hsiang chü) in San Francisco to tap the wealth of Chinese in the continental United States. This organization, also called the National Salvation Bureau (Kuo-min chiu-chi chü), was founded in June of 1911. It raised money by selling revolutionary bonds called Sun Wen Yin-chih (Sun Yat-sen silver certificates). The bonds were supposedly backed by silver (Huang would have preferred gold) and gave the purchaser part ownership of a nonexistent Chinese Corporation (Chung-hua shih-yeh kung-ssu), to which the postrevolutionary government would supposedly grant a ten-year monopoly on all mining in China.[46] Clearly, Sun was suggesting that to invest in the revolution would be more profitable than to invest in the Pao-huang hui's now discredited Commercial Corporation, and he promised a tenfold return on the bonds. Sun also promised that purchasers/contributors would be made specially privileged citizens of the new republic.[47]

San Francisco's National Salvation Bureau was somewhat different from the Triad Fund-raising Bureau in Canada. It represented a closer alliance between Sun's revolutionaries and the Chih-kung t'ang. At the time of the San Francisco Bureau's founding, the local Chih-kung t'ang and T'ung-meng hui (San Francisco's Ko-ming tang having in 1910 been designated by Sun as the central branch of the T'ung-meng hui in the continental Americas) put out two proc-

lamations which declared that the T'ung-meng hui and the Chih-
kung t'ang would cooperate in helping to further Sun Yat-sen's revolution. In return, all members of the T'ung-meng hui (in San Francisco? in the continental United States?) would be initiated into the
Chih-kung t'ang. For unexplained reasons, their initiation was conducted with a special, abbreviated ritual.[48] Furthermore, seventeen
of the numerous National Salvation Bureau officers were taken from
the ranks of the T'ung-meng hui. These included Li Shih-nan and
two other *Young China* editors, along with the head of the Chinese
American Citizens Association, an organization which formerly
favored the Pao-huang hui.[49]

The money-raising side of San Francisco's National Salvation
Bureau was not as spectacular as the Triad Fund-raising Bureau in
Vancouver/Victoria. This was in part because Huang San-te did not
want to see his organization eclipsed by Sun Yat-sen. In 1910 or 1911,
Sun had promised Huang that after the revolution succeeded, the
Chih-kung t'ang could become a legal political organization in
China, which promise had much to do with Huang's interest in Sun.
As a result, San Francisco's Chih-kung t'ang felt that it need raise
only a modest sum of money. In the two months before the National
Salvation Bureau was founded, the Chih-kung t'ang in San Francisco had sent seven thousand dollars (U.S.) to Hong Kong for what
turned out to be a major revolutionary attempt involving New Army
elements. Organized and led by Huang Hsing, this coup took place
in April of 1911. It failed, a failure which produced the famous "Sev-
enty-two Martyrs." After it failed, the National Salvation Bureau
raised another ten thousand dollars and sent assassins to kill various
people, including the Manchu army commander in Canton. Sun
had little interest in the assassins, however, and found the financial
contribution very disappointing.[50]

Triumph in New York

Although disappointed about the money, Sun was cheered by the
growth of the T'ung-meng hui in the United States. The ability of
Sun's partisans to manipulate other organizations also continued to
improve. In New York, some time between February and April of
1911, pro-Sun revolutionaries left the (Triad) Hsieh-sheng t'ang and
organized a Chih-kung t'ang sublodge called the Chin-lan yü-so.

Chin-lan yü-so leaders included a very wealthy businessman and a notorious gunman nicknamed the "scientific killer." The wealthy businessman subsequently precipitated an open controversy within the local Chung-hua hui-kuan (actually called Chung-hua kung-so in New York). On April 23, the Chung-hua kung-so held a meeting to decide what to do with fourteen thousand dollars it had recently raised for flood relief in Kiangsi and Kiangsu provinces. Most of the community leaders wanted to follow the usual course and send the funds to appropriate Chinese government officials in the affected areas. The wealthy businessman objected vigorously, for such a move implied confidence in the Ch'ing dynasty. After heated debate, the businessman and his supporters persuaded the Chung-hua kung-so to send five thousand dollars of the money to the Red Cross, another one thousand dollars to Shanghai's local relief organization *(shan-t'ang)*, and only eight thousand to government officials.[51] This was a direct affront to the Ch'ing dynasty.

While Sun was in New York in April of 1911, the Chin-lan yü-so feted him repeatedly, solicited contributions for him, and generally acted as a revolutionary front in the Chih-kung t'ang. In order to avoid any misunderstanding with the older organization, the Chin-lan yü-so announced that its aims were the same as those of the regular Chih-kung t'ang branch, and the members cooperated with the Chih-kung t'ang in the attempt to remove the pro-Pao-huang hui president of the Chung-hua kung-so from office. The regular Chih-kung t'ang sublodge was also generous in its aid and praise of Sun, due in part to the presence in New York of Huang San-te.[52]

The public support for Sun on the part of the New York Chih-kung t'ang and Chin-lan yü-so had a powerful effect on local Chinese. Over a thousand people, most of whom had previously shown no interest in revolution and many of whom belonged to the Pao-huang hui, attended and applauded Sun Yat-sen's speeches. A former vice chairman of New York's Pao-huang hui announced that he had decided to join the T'ung-meng hui, and he gave a speech for Sun in which he repeatedly insulted the Pao-huang hui. The audience was ecstatic. In reward, this man was made head of New York's T'ung-meng hui. Through him, other members of the Pao-huang hui were persuaded to express publicly their support for Sun. Chinese students in New York did likewise, including those on government stipend. A New York Chinese-language newspaper which formerly had been independent turned pro-Sun and violently anti-Ch'ing.[53]

Then in late April, the Chih-kung t'ang, Chin-lan yü-so, and T'ung-meng hui invited Sun to give a speech at the Chung-hua kung-so. The chairman of the Chung-hua kung-so was a staunch and influential member of the Pao-huang hui. He and the other officers opposed the idea of Sun giving the speech. They tried to form a living wall consisting of themselves, the Chinese consul, and other loyal reformers in order to prevent Sun from entering the Chung-hua kung-so building. Sun's supporters were so numerous, however, that the reformers retired in temporary defeat.[54]

Sun spoke, and challenged the opposition to a public debate on the spot. Only one person (a Chinese student at Columbia University) dared accept the challenge. The student said revolution was not proper for the country of Confucius and Mencius, and that step-by-step reform would be more appropriate. His argument was promptly refuted by a revolutionary sympathizer, and the audience applauded vigorously. Next, a wealthy reformer who claimed imminent conversion to the revolutionary cause asked Sun to help resolve his remaining uncertainties as to how revolution could succeed. Sun did so to the apparent satisfaction of those present. While the audience was still in an aroused state, someone demanded that the Chung-hua kung-so chairman come to the meeting. A delegation was sent to inform him that his presence was needed, and if he refused, they would interpret his refusal as showing a lack of respect for the audience and the Chih-kung t'ang. He came.[55]

After he arrived, the audience accused him of being a slave of the Ch'ing. More importantly, the new (formerly Pao-huang hui) president of the T'ung-meng hui said that by appealing to the Chinese consul for help without first presenting the matter at a general meeting, the Chung-hua kung-so president had violated the rules of the organization of which he was president. The president had to apologize, but the revolutionaries decided to press their advantage, and force the Chung-hua kung-so president to resign. The meeting ended with a statement to the effect that anyone who did not support the revolution could not serve China or the Chinese community. When the meeting was over, the victorious revolutionaries met to discuss how to raise funds for Sun through the Chung-hua kung-so. In New York, the revolutionaries seemed to have triumphed.[56]

Sun's success in New York had a noticeable effect on his reception in Chicago when he arrived there on April 30. Of the three principal Triad lodges which had branches in Chicago, only one did not send its leader to welcome him at the train station. Even that branch sent a representative, however, and the absence of the leader was more probably due to the "tong war" then in progress in Chicago than to any other reason. Sun's most ardent supporters in Chicago at this time were local merchants and students on government stipend, two groups which had until recently looked askance at him. Chicago seems to have presented little challenge to the revolutionaries after the Pao-huang hui defeat in New York and Canada.[57]

The Fight with the *Sai Gai Yat Po*

The key city of San Francisco presented greater difficulties. For one thing, between the time of Sun's departure from Chicago and his arrival in San Francisco, the failure of Huang Hsing's Canton coup of April 1911 became generally known. Support for Sun and Huang San-te's own prorevolutionary inclinations were enough to permit the founding of the National Salvation Bureau, described earlier. But the Pao-huang hui in San Francisco continued to retain the allegiance of most wealthy merchants, some Triad lodge leaders, and most *hui-kuan* heads.[58] Furthermore, Huang San-te refused to make the Chih-kung t'ang subservient to the T'ung-meng hui or Sun Yat-sen, even if he did accord them greater recognition than did Canada's Chih-kung t'ang.[59]

Under these circumstances, the revolutionaries felt a need to look for more allies. They found one in the *Chung Sai Yat Po* because of a fight that had erupted between that newspaper and the Pao-huang hui in January of 1911. The quarrel began when the *Sai Gai Yat Po* (San Francisco's Pao-huang hui newspaper) took exception to an editorial that appeared in the *Chung Sai Yat Po*. The latter celebrated Christianity and Christian values in what was a rather unusual type of editorial for that newspaper. The Pao-huang hui, through the *Sai Gai Yat Po* and through its New York newspaper, objected to the author's contention that one's duty to God is higher than one's duty to parents and ruler. It accused the *Chung Sai Yat Po* of being anarchistic, but the *Chung Sai Yat Po* vehemently disagreed and castigated the *Sai Gai Yat Po*. One editor of the latter paper was also a recent head of the Ning-yang hui-kuan. For this reason, both the Pao-huang hui and Ning-yang hui-kuan leaders demanded a public apology from the *Chung Sai Yat Po*. They also insisted that the author of the Christian editorial be deprived of two months salary. The *Chung Sai Yat Po* made the apology but would not dock the author's salary. In response, the Pao-huang hui and Ning-yang hui-kuan leaders ordered their members to boycott the *Chung Sai Yat Po*.[60] As almost sixty percent of the Chinese in the continental Americas were from the Ning-yang area, and as both sets of leaders wielded considerable social power, these boycotts were most detrimental to the well-being and solvency of the *Chung Sai Yat Po*.

To counter this attack, the *Chung Sai Yat Po* published a series of editorials denying the charges of the Pao-huang hui. As this did not have the desired effect, near the end of March, the *Chung Sai Yat Po* made a second apology to the Ning-yang hui-kuan, and probably to the Pao-huang hui as well. The apology was not enough to cause either organization to lift its boycott. It was just at this point that the Pao-huang hui in New York was coming under severe attack. Probably for that reason, early in April, two new protagonists began to involve themselves in the quarrel. One of these was the T'ung-meng hui in San Francisco, and the other was a merchant guild in Hong Kong which acted as the Chinese connection for Ning-yang merchants engaged in the import-export business (the Ning-i shang-wu kung-so). The T'ung-meng hui's *Young China* tried to engineer a victory for the *Chung Sai Yat Po* (which would redound to its own credit and that of the larger T'ung-meng hui), whereas the merchant guild in Hong Kong tried to make peace between the warring parties and prevent a Ning-yang hui-kuan (and Pao-huang hui) defeat.[61]

Young China's principal strategy was to capitalize on the increasing weakness of the Pao-huang hui and to encourage Ning-yang people to disagree publicly with the boycott ordered by their leaders. The strategy was a success: first tens, then hundreds of Ning-yang members signed petitions disagreeing with the boycott, and the newspaper published every single name. Most of those willing to sign the petitions lived in areas far removed from San Francisco. One list came from Torreón in Mexico, an indication that the earlier Pao-huang hui dominance in that country was breaking down. In addition, *Young China* printed a series of antiboycott editorials and articles.[62]

In the middle of April, the merchant guild in Hong Kong wrote to *Young China* and to Ning-yang people in the Americas, declaring that peace had been achieved; the boycott then ended. The declaration claimed that those with whom the Ning-yang hui-kuan had been fighting were in relation to the Ning-yang as feet to hands or younger brothers to older brothers (a common Chinese analogy), but *Young China* took offense at the analogy and accused the merchant guild in Hong Kong of using this analogy to oppose freedom and equality. Ning-yang leaders, said *Young China,* felt that the T'ung-meng hui should be appealing to men in authority and in high social position. In reality, it was the little man who mattered. The fight finally ended when, on April 28, the Ning-yang hui-kuan in San Francisco elected a new set of officers, replacing their former president with someone who had not been involved in the quarrel.[63]

In its attempt to end the quarrel, the merchant guild in Hong Kong had even gone so far as to say that the original disagreement had been fomented by the Pao-huang hui. This suggests that Ning-yang leaders were now willing to disassociate themselves to a certain extent from the reform party. *Young China* responded by denying any significant Pao-huang hui involvement, but the revolutionaries then used the weakened position of both the Pao-huang hui and the Ning-yang hui-kuan to attack the Pao-huang hui. *Young China* castigated the Pao-huang hui's New York newspaper for having printed an editorial suggesting that a certain revolutionary patriot/assassin (Wen Sheng-ts'ai) had some connection with the Pao-huang hui and that therefore his exploits added luster to the reform party. More tellingly, starting in late April, *Young China* began giving broad coverage to various scandals involving Pao-huang hui leaders, including the probable involvement of its leaders in extensive gambling operations in Torreón. Another scandal publicized by *Young China* was the involvement of several top officials in New York's Pao-huang hui in an extortion racket. Some of these officials were arrested by the New York police in May of 1911, in part because of information supplied to them by a member of the T'ung-meng hui in that city.[64]

Broadening the attack, on May 20 of 1911, *Young China* castigated both the Pao-huang hui and the members of the new National Assembly in China who were influenced by the Pao-huang hui's Chinese branch, because high office in the latter's Monarchical Constitutional Party depended even more on the size of one's financial contribution to the party than on one's education. In order to join the party, one had to contribute twenty dollars; in order to obtain honor in the party, a two-hundred-dollar contribution was required; and so forth, until finally two thousand dollars would give one the power to start collecting membership dues from others. The *Sai Gai Yat Po* responded by charging that the revolutionaries were destroying the bond between father and son and casting disrespect on the elderly. *Young China* replied that the Pao-huang hui was mainly composed of fathers who were afraid of their sons. These elderly reformers were mice and cattle, unworthy of the slightest attention. Starting on May 24, *Young China* ran an anonymous advertisement calling upon the Chinese Six Companies in San Francisco to expel all members who were associated with the Pao-huang hui.[65]

The Official Ideology of America's T'ung-meng Hui, 1911

Young China's attacks on the Pao-huang hui and its other editorials give a clear indication of what the T'ung-meng hui in the Americas meant when it called for revolution. In its general outlines, the party's ideology was the same as that espoused by Chinese revolutionaries elsewhere. In addition to removing the Manchus from power, the party (in the Americas as well as in China and in other overseas communities) favored democratic government and nationalism, and gave lukewarm support to Sun Yat-sen's version of socialism *(she-hui chu-i)* and "people's livelihood" *(min-sheng chu-i)*. In addition, one faction gave moral and material support to assassination squads, and all were united in their hatred of the Pao-huang hui.

When *Young China* called for democratic government, it meant that the will of the ruled should be determined through the elective process. This usually meant direct democracy and universal suffrage. Appropriately, the T'ung-meng hui in San Francisco chose its officers through elections, although it is not clear whether these officers were elected by the other officers, whether they were voted on by the entire membership, or whether or not it was common to have more than one person nominated for any one office.[66]

In addition to supporting elective government, the editors opposed autocracy. One variation of autocracy, of course, was the rule of the Ch'ing dynastic house; another was the imperial system in general (including that of the Ming). A third variation was rule by the educated and wealthy, which the editors associated with lasciviousness, injustice, and various other socially destructive practices. In contrast to autocracy, *Young China* felt that it and America's T'ung-meng hui stood for the long overlooked and oppressed "little man."[67]

The newspaper did not stop at the "little man." It also celebrated women's rights and, even more vigorously, the rights (and rightness) of youth. The very title of the newspaper shows the concern for youth. Articles in the paper often appealed to "hot-blooded youth" (*jeh-hsüeh ch'ing-nien*). Young T'ung-meng hui members frequently organized fund-raising plays, and, occasionally, free performances were presented for local (Chinese) students. Adopting a point of view later to be seen in China itself during the May Fourth Movement (1919–1921), the quarrel between the Pao-huang hui and the T'ung-meng hui was interpreted in part as a rebellion of the youth against their parents. The newspaper also had several feminist contributors, and the T'ung-meng hui sponsored a set of plays written by women, performed by women, and describing the new role of women as revolutionary heroes. Ch'iu Chin, a famous woman revolutionary in China, was celebrated, and the newspaper proclaimed its support for education for women.[68]

In line with its democratic bent, the newspaper supported the concept of liberty as it was institutionalized in the United States, Great Britain, and France, and insisted that the constitution then being proposed by the Ch'ing government was a sham. A constitution was no good unless it had been fought for. It could not be handed down from above.[69]

Most of these ideas were common to the Chinese revolutionary movement in general. Even the reformers opposed autocracy and the constitution proposed by the Ch'ing court. Ch'iu Chin was a heroine in most radical circles, and education for women had become acceptable even to political moderates in China. Young Chinese students in Southeast Asia and Japan in fact formed the backbone of the revolutionary party there, while Chinese anarchists taught that students by right should be the vanguard of the revolution.

Beyond this, however, *Young China* shows that Chinese revolutionaries in the Americas differed from their counterparts elsewhere in the world in that they attached greater importance to suffrage and the rights of the "little man." In concrete social terms, as the revolutionary tide grew it contributed greatly to a movement to which, ironically, the Pao-huang hui had given birth, a movement for the social reform of America's Chinatowns. The anti-opium campaign then underway in China had an even more effective counterpart in the Americas. The reforming zeal of Chinese in the Americas went even further. Prostitutes, heretofore heavily patronized, fell into disfavor. There was some talk of the evils of gambling. By 1910, girls began to be sent to Chinese schools in large numbers along with boys, outshining even China's treaty ports in this respect. Young Chinese Americans (a few daring women and a fair proportion of the men) registered to vote in American elections.[70]

The T'ung-meng hui in the Americas as well as elsewhere placed at least as much emphasis on nationalism as on liberal and democratic values, however. This nationalism had three main components. It was anti-Manchu, antiforeign, and pro-Han. *Young China* justified its anti-Manchuism by pointing out that the Manchus had bungled foreign affairs and neglected overseas Chinese, leaving the latter at the mercy of their antagonistic host countries. This concern with overseas Chinese was a common theme in almost all overseas Chinese newspapers. *Young China,* like other revolutionary publications, also claimed that the Manchus were foreign thieves who had stolen the homeland of the Han Chinese.[71]

America's T'ung-meng hui gave the anti-Western theme somewhat less emphasis than anti-Manchuism. The former was used primarily to criticize the Pao-huang hui. *Young China* editors claimed that the reform leaders were too pro-West, and hence liable to give in to the demands of the powers rather than to fight. Ironically, in China Sun Yat-sen and his partisans were usually considered the more Western-inclined. Han solidarity, besides its obvious connotations, embodied two additional concepts. In the name of Han solidarity, provincialism was to fade away—but the paramount and rightful role of Cantonese in leading the revolution should never be forgotten.[72]

Young China also called for the institution of socialism and "people's livelihood," but as was generally the case in the Chinese revolutionary camp, these terms were not defined and in fact were referred to very infrequently. The newspaper staff was far more concerned with the task of opposing the Pao-huang hui and other reform parties of K'ang and Liang in China. The reformers were accused of being the kind of educated and wealthy persons who should not rule China (and who were personally corrupt and lascivious). They were also seen as racial traitors. The Pao-huang hui in general was too friendly with the Western powers and too pacifist, and, finally, K'ang and Liang were engaged in traitorous dealings with the Japanese.[73]

One aspect of the T'ung-meng hui that appeared only indirectly in the newspaper was the propensity of some of its members to support or engage in assassination.[74] This was as true of the revolutionaries in the Americas as it was of Chinese revolutionaries elsewhere in the world. As noted earlier, the Chih-kung t'ang sent assassins to Canton to eliminate a local general (Feng-shan), and T'ung-meng hui members in San Francisco seem to have approved of this undertaking. When another assassin managed to kill a different Ch'ing military commander, T'ung-meng hui members voiced their loud approval and publicly rebuked the Pao-huang hui for suggesting that the latter party had some connection with the assassin. Some T'ung-meng hui fund-raising was directed toward supporting assassination squads including the Shanghai "Dare-to-Dies" *(kan-ssu t'uan)*, who began soliciting money and members through *Young China* in May of 1911. Many people contributed money to the latter organization, and a few went to China to participate in the action.[75]

Much of the T'ung-meng hui's ideology as revealed in *Young China* was remarkably similar to Pao-huang hui proposals. Two significant differences, however, were the T'ung-meng hui's anti-Manchuism and its support for the "little man" (and woman). The former was a matter of great concern for Sun Yat-sen, and provided him with a convenient explanation as to why both the Ch'ing government and the Pao-huang hui were doomed to fail. Use of the anti-Manchu theme brought to mind some of the recent Pao-huang hui failures, since these had involved the Manchus, or the Manchu/Ch'ing government. It also pointed to the more general shortcomings of the Ch'ing.

Young China's support for the "little man" (and woman) in part reflected the natural constituency of America's T'ung-meng hui, particularly in light of the recent fight with the Ning-yang hui-kuan.

That fight had antagonized many of the established community leaders, especially *hui-kuan* officials. By the same token, however, it had made the T'ung-meng hui appealing to the heretofore powerless rank-and-file *hui-kuan* member. It had shown *Young China* to be a friend to Chinese Christians, and had demonstrated that Chinese Americans, so long overlooked, could exercise substantial influence in the Chinese community.

The Interplay between Revolutionaries and Other Community Organizations

The substantial success that Sun and his partisans were beginning to enjoy among Chinese in the Americas by mid-1911 was only partly due to astute involvement in grassroots concerns. Simple good luck also played an important role. In Cuba, for example, when the handful of Chinese revolutionaries in Havana launched a demonstration against a Ch'ing naval mission stopping in Cuba, Cuban news reporters mistakenly interpreted the near riot caused by the demonstration as support for the revolutionary cause. Subsequent stories in Cuban newspapers and favorable reactions by Cuban officials lent luster to the Chinese revolutionaries, thereby gaining them new adherents.[76]

As this and many other incidents show, it is important to remember that if Sun's partisans had not been skillful enough to take advantage of the good luck, they would have gained little if anything from it. Canada is an even better case in point. The assassination of Liu Shih-chi (a development totally unrelated to Sun's adherents) led to the disenchantment of the entire Pao-huang hui structure there. Without the efforts of Feng Tzu-yu and others, however, this disenchantment might have led to the development only of a small and ineffective prorevolutionary faction, with the majority of Chinese in Canada simply becoming apathetic. By contrast, in the continental United States, prior to the quarrel between the *Chung Sai Yat Po* and the Ning-yang hui-kuan and Pao-huang hui, Sun's efforts were not really successful: the National Salvation Bureau was established, many of whose officers were Sun's partisans, but the T'ung-meng hui did not acquire much money or many new members. It was the *Chung Sai Yat Po* quarrel (a quarrel not originally related to reform versus revolution) that really began the shift in the balance of power. Once again, if *Young China* had not been able to turn this quarrel to the T'ung-meng hui's advantage, it might have remained an argument between Christians and Confucianists. As for New York, the key elements in the T'ung-meng hui's advances there were the weakening of the Pao-huang hui in Canada and the "conversion" of several key individuals who founded the Chin-lan yü-so. At least one of these (the "scientific killer" tong gunman) became prorevolutionary in part due to rivalry with another gunman.

The upshot of all this was that in 1911, the T'ung-meng hui was presented almost overnight with an audience which, for reasons unrelated to the revolutionaries' efforts, had become far more receptive to their organizational work. It was not only community quarrels that prepared the ground for them. Ideologically speaking, overseas Chinese in the Americas were well prepared by 1911 to accept many of the ideals espoused by the T'ung-meng hui and enunciated in *Young China*. Nationalism had for years been stressed by other influential organizations, including the Pao-huang hui. Fortunately for the T'ung-meng hui, however, the reformers showed less concern for nationalism after 1905, devoting more energy to capital development. The reformers also assigned a smaller role to the average individual, and the changes they desired were less dramatic and awe-inspiring than what the revolutionaries proposed. The Chih-kung t'ang had also based much of its appeal on nationalism, at least since 1905. It was too far removed from the scene in China, however, to direct any major uprisings.

By 1910, nationalism had become a compelling force in the Chinese community. It was strong enough to spark a movement to put an end to the ubiquitous "tong wars," and by 1913, urged on by San Francisco's Chinese consul, "tongs" and some of the regional and surname organizations founded a Ho-p'ing hui—Peace Preservation Society. The direct impetus for this organization was the rising tide of revolutionary enthusiasm and the apparent success of the revolutionary effort. Around the time that the "tong wars" diminished, the frequent practice of permitting the head of a "fighting tong" to become one of the officers of the Chinese Six Companies came to an end.[77]

As nationalism grew, the level of education available to Chinese in the Americas also increased, partly due to the influence of the political parties. The Pao-huang hui provided the foundation, organizing and supporting Chinese schools for many years before the T'ung-meng hui in the Americas came into existence. In 1910 and 1911, however, many of the young teachers in these schools became ardent revolutionaries and T'ung-meng hui members, and as the level of literacy among overseas Chinese began to rise, interest in politics (including radical politics) rose as well. American schools, to which an increasing number of youthful overseas Chinese and young Chinese Americans were being exposed, also contributed to this trend.[78]

Education, as we noted above, meant education for women as well as men. The Pao-huang hui was one of the earliest champions of women's education. On several occasions the *Sai Gai Yat Po* called for education for women, some Pao-huang hui-associated schools accepted female pupils, the Pao-huang hui in Southeast Asia organized at least one school for girls, and K'ang Yu-wei sent his daughter to the United States to get a college education.[79] As time passed, more and more young women sought higher education. Some of these later turned to activism and even to feminism, which went beyond what the reformers had intended: the Pao-huang hui felt that the reason for educating women was to make them better wives and more competent mothers.[80] The revolutionary party, on the other hand, was more willing for women to play an active role in its activities. Hence, the more ardent women tended to be welcomed by the revolutionaries and joined the revolutionary party.

Other major changes taking place in the Chinese communities were not directly related either to the reformers or to the revolutionaries. As they were leading in the direction of greater rationalization of community functions and a greater degree of self-government, however, they were not far removed from the ideals of both parties. Most of these changes surfaced just at the point that the T'ung-meng hui was in the ascendant and subsequently were partially utilized by the revolutionaries, but in fact they were closer in spirit to the Pao-huang hui's program.

One major change was the development of local Chinese Chambers of Commerce. A nationalistic response to Western trade competition and business practices, Chinese Chambers of Commerce during this same period were springing up in the Chinese communities of Southeast Asia and, with court approval, in China itself. In the Americas, by 1910, Honolulu, San Francisco, and Vancouver each had one. Chinatowns elsewhere soon followed suit, but these three cities were first to have Chinese Chambers of Commerce for three principal reasons. Taken together, these cities were the three most important centers for Chinese import-export merchants in the Americas, and all three cities had recently seen an upsurge in political activity of a nationalistic nature. In the name of nationalism, the Chinese Chambers of Commerce normally absorbed the early merchant guilds such as San Francisco's Shao-i kung-so and K'o-shang hui-kuan.

Another important change was the surfacing of the movement for social reform noted above. Finally, the method of selecting *hui-kuan* presidents underwent significant change, at least in San Francisco. Since the 1850s, the *hui-kuan* had preferred to import local notables from China. Between 1910 and about 1913, however, one after another abandoned this practice, and began to select their president from among the local merchants. Home rule had triumphed.[81]

Home rule meant that instead of having traditionally educated men unacquainted with the American scene, *hui-kuan* presidents as well as their other officers would be people influenced by the American environment and accountable to local pressure. By mid-1911, one element in this pressure was the rising tide of revolutionary sentiment. Developments in China eased the T'ung-meng hui's organizational efforts even further. Revolutionaries in China were greatly discouraged by the failure of Huang Hsing's uprising of April 1911 (Chung Yü even reports that Sun came to Hawaii late in the summer of 1911 and talked of giving up revolution in favor of medicine),[82] but Chinese in the Americas were very impressed by the scope of the operation. Furthermore, it was now obvious that elements of the Ch'ing New Army were willing to work with the T'ung-meng hui, and enthusiasm for revolution grew. News that the Ch'ing court, in the name of centralization, was negotiating with the powers for a huge loan to finance railway development and had nationalized privately held railway concessions to this end also helped the revolutionary cause because it seemed to put the court in the role of traitor to the nation. Virulent opposition in Szechuan province to the loan and railway policy in the summer and fall of 1911 also served to highlight the weakness of the central government. Inspired by all of these developments, new branches of the T'ung-meng hui sprang up in communities as distant as Cuba, Peru, and Mexico.[83] When in

October of 1911 the first uncertain news concerning the Wu-ch'ang revolution began to filter back to the Americas, in all the communities except in Hawaii, T'ung-meng hui members became emboldened and vigorously pressed the attack.

The T'ung-meng Hui Triumphs

Since the late summer and early fall of 1911, San Francisco's T'ung-meng hui had been sending members to raise funds throughout the United States. When Sun Yat-sen reentered the United States in the fall of 1911, he joined them, but the results were disappointing until the situation changed in China in late October. Then, the revolutionaries managed to gain control of Red Cross funds and solicited revolutionary contributions through the Red Cross. They also established more branches of their own fund-raising organizations and increased their activity in the National Salvation Bureau in San Francisco. Money began to pour in. Now that revolution seemed to be on the rise in China, the names of all the contributors were published in *Young China* as a public acknowledgment of thanks, and contributions came in from as far away as Mexico.[84]

In addition to fund-raising, the revolutionaries organized congratulatory parades (including one in Hawaii), held banquets in honor of the new republic, set up military schools for youths who wanted to participate in the fighting, and in Cuba and Peru, T'ung-meng hui newspapers were finally established. In the meantime, Sun Yat-sen was traveling with (General) Homer Lea to various Western capitals soliciting funds and support from the governments of the powers. Chinese in the Americas and elsewhere were led to believe that this effort was achieving success, which increased their enthusiasm for revolution and for Sun. Overnight, Homer Lea's cadets became an elite branch of Sun's revolutionary army. Some are said to have been smuggled back into China prior to the success at Wu-ch'ang. When the question arose as to who would be the first provisional president of the new Republic of China, Huang San-te arranged for thirty telegrams a day to be sent to Shanghai in support of Sun's candidacy,[85] and this helped win the election for Sun.

Attacks on the Pao-huang hui grew more vigorous. In Seattle, local revolutionaries were able to defeat the pro-Pao-huang hui consul when he tried to appoint someone as a teacher in a local (Chinese) school. Various former officers of the Pao-huang hui changed party, and their shift in allegiance was well publicized by *Young China*. The T'ung-meng hui in San Francisco raised the flag of the Republic of China, although at first the Pao-huang hui countered by raising its own flag. This led to a campaign to force all businesses and organizations in San Francisco to raise the flag of the republic, and to force all Pao-huang hui members in the Chinese Chamber of Commerce to renounce their party ties. According to *Young China*, by November 25 the campaign had succeeded, and everyone was flying the republican flag. The last organization to give in had been the Ning-yang hui-kuan.[86]

In Vancouver, the T'ung-meng hui packed the annual elections of the local Chung-hua hui-kuan. It was able to do this because most Chinese there simply did not vote. Therefore, all the T'ung-meng hui members got their relatives to attend the election and, in the name of family solidarity, vote as directed. The end result was that twelve members of the T'ung-meng hui were elected to office as opposed to four non-T'ung-meng hui members of the Chih-kung t'ang, three independents (including one lukewarm revolutionary supporter), and one Pao-huang hui member. This gave the T'ung-meng hui temporary ascendancy in the Chinese community in Vancouver, although it turned out that in the long run their tactics alienated much of the community.[87]

Finally, in San Francisco the T'ung-meng hui refused to accept any new members, declaring instead that all were now citizens of the Republic of China. The party established a new organization, the Nationalist Chinese Association (Chung-hua kuo-min kung-hui) to manage fund-raising activities, assume the functions of the Chinese consul and minister, and act as representative of the revolutionary army. Late in December of 1911, the Pao-huang hui publicly acquiesced to Sun's election to the provisional presidency, and the T'ung-meng hui, now in control of Chinese in the Americas, had triumphed.[88]

CONCLUSION

The organization and activities of Chinese political parties made Chinese in the Americas feel for the first time that they could have a hand in directing China's fate. This, they hoped, would not only revive their native land but also improve their own lot. Participation in the political parties and the development of an active interest in Chinese national politics led to social change, especially in the Chinatowns of North America and Hawaii. Equally important, this study has revealed much about the political parties themselves, including the early strength of the Pao-huang hui and the depth of that party's interest in revolution. Finally, in terms of both social change and the development of political parties, the Americas reflected and to a certain extent anticipated events in China. In addition to their value as financial contributors to change in China, then, the study of political developments among America's Chinese offers up a mirror—albeit somewhat distorted—of what was taking place in their motherland.

Different as they were in aims, functioning, and criteria for membership than any preexisting Chinatown organizations, the fact that the political parties could put down roots in the Americas was in itself significant. The parties owed their strength to several causes. Changing economic and social factors had strained Chinatown society close to the breaking point. The political parties and their principle of nationalism offered a real way around the impasse. Evidence that substantive change was under way in China led Chinese in the Americas to hope to influence that change; the political parties were the best available means for them to do so. The determination of the United States to renew Chinese Exclusion in 1905 produced a crisis atmosphere. Ordinary Chinese, long accustomed to leaving political and governmental decisions to others, found that they were no longer willing to keep silent. Finally, the North American version of political democracy based on a small number of political parties with at least some grass-roots participation must surely have influenced the Chinese political leaders in their own organizational drives.

Experiments in grass-roots participation were certainly very important among Americans in California at this time, as demonstrated by the activities of the Workingman's Party and even, to a certain extent, by the Progressives. Grass-roots politics was also an important component of the Chinese political parties. In the case of the Pao-huang hui, grass-roots participation at its extreme took an economic form, as in the purchasing of shares in the Commercial Corporation. It can also be seen in the recruiting for the Western Military Academy. On the side of the T'ung-meng hui, grass-roots participation was more evident in the politically motivated revolt against the *hui-kuan* in 1911.

It is interesting to compare this 1911 revolt against the *hui-kuan* with the 1893 revolt against the Chinese Six Companies that occurred after the Geary Act fiasco. In 1893, when the Six Companies backed the failed policy of legal resistance to the Geary Act and ordered all Chinese in the United States to continue this resistance, tong wars broke out. These tong wars were the means whereby those out of power opposed those in power. In 1911, when the Ning-yang hui-kuan ordered its thousands of members in the Americas to support groups which traditionally exercised community control and to oppose those seen as friendly to the revolutionary cause, the result was public revolt by hundreds of members acting as individuals. It was no longer a case of one type of social organization opposing another. Instead, it was individuals insisting upon their right to make political decisions. In truth, not only had Chinatown organizations become politicized, but individual Chinese in the Americas had as well.

Along with grass-roots participation and politicization, the political ferment of these years helped bring greater rationalization to America's Chinatowns. The older organizations had sought to satisfy practically the entire range of their individual members' social needs: religious, economic, commercial, familial, legal, cultural, political, and even recreational. Between 1894 and 1911, however, politics, economics, and commerce were partially removed from the preserve of the *hui-kuan* and surname associations. At the same time, new organizations with only one principal function—the political parties, the Chinese Chambers of Commerce, even the new capitalistic ventures—sprang up. The earlier, regionally orientated merchant guilds disappeared and the Chih-kung t'ang shifted its emphasis to national politics. And along with greater rationalization came increased local autonomy: no more imported notables with their direct ties to the Ch'ing dynasty.

A related change for which the political parties were largely responsible was the inculcating of nationalism in Chinese communities throughout the Americas. Nationalism meant increased awareness and concern with the motherland's fate. The concern was strongest with respect to Kwangtung, the province from which most of America's Chinese had emigrated. But by 1911, concern with China as a whole had become both deep and widespread. It also was enduring: witness the striking contribution America's Chinese were to make to China's national air force between 1912 and 1945, to say nothing of money sent, rallies attended, and demonstrations participated in on China's behalf up until at least 1949.[1]

As of 1911, however, none of these changes was complete. For one thing, the political parties tended to become bogged down in local community issues. They also became inextricably intertwined with the older community organizations. This was probably inevitable, for the political parties had to involve themselves in immediate community issues in order to become part of community life. Entanglement in local issues and with the older organizations was made more complete because of the relative ease with which small groups of partisans could obtain control of the political parties. This, in turn, was a result of the varying rates at which the community became politicized, and was also a carry-over from the older types of social organizations. Still, by 1911 those exercising control were only able to do so as long as they publicly shared the broader political goals that their party represented. It was not a question, for example, of powerful reformers enforcing the unwilling allegiance of relatively powerless, would-be revolutionaries—or vice versa.

A more important weakness was the failure of the ideal of a loyal opposition to develop. Liew, Fairbank, Bodde, and others have already mentioned this problem in connection with the development of Chinese political parties elsewhere in the world.[2] Here, I will only note that the example of the multiparty systems in the United States and Canada along with the advantage of developing in relatively open societies still failed to produce a spirit of political tolerance among the Chinese.[3] The cause of this failure probably lay in the newness of political parties and political consciousness to the Chinese.

In addition to what this study has taught us about the effect of the political parties on American Chinatowns, it has revealed much about the political parties themselves. It has been shown here, for example, that the enthusiasm with which Sun Yat-sen was received has generally been exaggerated. On comparing the Pao-huang hui/ Hsien-cheng tang in the Americas with the Hsing-Chung hui, the T'ung-meng hui, and possibly the Ko-ming tang, one cannot fail to be struck by the vigor and strength of the former. The Hsing-Chung hui in the Americas was never really a sustained organization. It was, instead, a series of small cells pretty much unconnected with each other that arose when Sun traveled through a given community. With the exception of Hawaii, these cells disappeared within a few months of Sun's departure. Even the exception, namely, the Hsing-Chung hui of Hawaii of 1903–1910, was characterized by frequent schisms. The fact that it was able to endure at all was due to the skill of the revolutionary organizers that Feng Tzu-yu, in Sun's name, was able to send to it, organizers who had been students in Japan. The T'ung-meng hui in the Americas was much more coherent and better organized than the Hsing-Chung hui had been, but it was founded very late, and by the middle of the summer of 1911 it was still very small. With the exception of Hawaii, it did not draw its membership from the old Hsing-Chung hui organizations, and it was slow to win the acceptance of the older community organizations.

The Pao-huang hui did not face these kinds of problems. In spite of the early, virulent opposition of Ch'ing officials in the Americas (as well as elsewhere overseas and in China), it enrolled more than fifteen percent of the Chinese in North America and practically all those in Hawaii by April of 1900. Later, membership grew even more dramatically. Although the party developed more slowly in Latin America, prior to 1911 it was significantly stronger than the revolutionary parties. Mexico had numerous Pao-huang hui branches and adherents as early as 1905. Since good evidence exists that this pattern was repeated among Chinese in Southeast Asia (along with those in Japan and in China itself), it is regrettable that so little scholarly attention has heretofore been devoted to this party.[4]

The social status of K'ang and Liang, combined with the sense of urgency that Chinese in the Americas had begun to feel by 1899 concerning China's fate, helped give the Pao-huang hui its firm foundation. Furthermore, K'ang at first refrained from interfering with the power and prerogatives of the local Chih-kung t'ang leaders. As a result, activists from the latter organization in particular flocked to his party. The majority of these men either favored an armed uprising (or revolution) in China, or wanted to use the Pao-huang hui to promote China's reform and commercialization and to increase the role of businessmen *(Szu-i* as well as *San-i)* in the overseas Chinese communities.

Even after the failure of T'ang Ts'ai-ch'ang's coup, the Pao-huang hui retained a significant number of active members, members who as before were either determined revolutionaries or people determined to use the party as a new vehicle for directing the inevitable evolution of their community. It was the latter who favored the greater rationalization of community functions, along with the development of a more self-sufficient economic base, a lessening of the barriers of region and surname, and more local control over local affairs. The Pao-huang hui was clearly a more suitable organization through which to work for these changes than were the various local Chung-hua hui-kuan, surname, and regional associations. The older organizations encompassed too many die-hard conservatives, along with a passive majority. Furthermore, they were too closely associated with regionalism and surname divisions, and, because of the practice of importing notables from China, were not clearly committed to local autonomy.

Once both prorevolutionaries and "progressives" (or moderates) had seen in the Pao-huang hui an adequate vehicle for achieving their respective aims, the party secured a permanent place in the Americas.[5] As the two factions struggled for control, the fight grew to involve other community organizations, and began to affect the internal structure of these organizations as well as the major class divisions of the overseas communities. As we know, the revolutionaries and Chih-kung t'ang lost out in the immediate struggle. The losers began to flirt with the idea of forming an alliance with Sun Yat-sen, although they were anxious to keep Sun's own political-revolutionary parties an insignificant force.

Then in 1908, Homer Lea broke publicly with the Pao-huang hui and led his (largely Triad) cadets into Sun's camp. Even this did not seriously compromise the dominant position of the Pao-huang hui. What finally enabled Sun to triumph in 1911 was not Homer Lea's move but the greed of the principals of the Commercial Corporation and their vituperative quarrels. (Significantly, Rhoads, Hwang, and others have shown that the same greed and quarrels helped weaken the Pao-huang hui in Southeast Asia and even in Kwangtung province.)[6] The Pao-huang hui, in other words, destroyed itself. Just as it was doing so, T'ung-meng hui exploits in China were attaining new heights. This led, late in 1911, to mass support for Sun Yat-sen and the T'ung-meng hui effort by Chinese in the Americas.

One final element helped account for the Pao-huang hui's early success and long dominance: Pao-huang hui leaders, from K'ang Yu-wei on down, seem to have understood the mechanics of organization much better than did Sun Yat-sen and his associates. The role of the peripatetic organizer was particularly important. Between 1899 and 1905, K'ang sent out a whole series of such organizers and made two trips himself. Those that he sent to the Americas inevitably joined the Chih-kung t'ang shortly after their arrival. They were usually men of high social standing with some prior experience in political movements or political agitation. They were invariably either eloquent speakers or eloquent writers. After 1905, the need for such peripatetic organizers declined, and to the extent that it was felt, it was usually filled by American Pao-huang hui leaders like Yeh En, who had by that time become highly respected in Chinese communities throughout the Americas. In this regard, it is significant that although K'ang came to the Americas several times between 1906 and 1908, he did not feel called upon to devote these trips to organizational drives. The pattern, then, was one of dedicated outside notables joining a local social organization (in this case the Chih-kung t'ang) and using it to appeal to the overseas Chinese while being careful (at first) to avoid interfering with the workings of the preexisting organization. Through this means, they were able to lay a firm foundation for their own organization, the Pao-huang hui. Once the latter had become established, its organizational reins were turned over to local leaders.

Sun Yat-sen was slow in learning these lessons. He did not join the Chih-kung t'ang (or any other American organization) until late in 1903, and it is not clear that he ever saw the value of sending over

organizers likely to be respected by the local community. Feng Tzu-
yu and the Chih-kung t'ang did: the former sent people over and
finally went himself; the latter requested that such be sent. Sun's
method was to attempt to convert local figures and rely on them.
These local men, however, often lacked political experience. Furthermore, they might back Sun only temporarily, their influence in
the Americas might be very restricted, and so forth. For this reason
and others, when Sun Yat-sen's party in China began to falter in the
middle of 1912, the T'ung-meng hui members in the Americas were
ousted from their controlling positions. Organizations like the Chih-
kung t'ang became Sun's mortal enemies, and the Pao-huang hui
was able partially to revive itself in spite of the fact that the imperial
system had been destroyed.

Although the political expertise of the Pao-huang hui/Hsien-
cheng tang leaders was far greater than that of Sun's partisans, in
terms of internal organization and the personal backgrounds of the
members there was more of a similarity. Even here, however, important differences remained. The Hsing-Chung hui of the continental
Americas was so small as to have been insignificant. Hawaii's
Hsing-Chung hui drew its membership from among merchants,
Christians, and secret society members. The much larger Pao-
huang hui in the Americas relied on much the same groups, along
with the occasional foreign adventurer. Evidently, these groups were
among those most likely to be involved in the new political movements. They were not, as has sometimes been suggested, the exclu-
sive preserve of the revolutionaries.

Members of the T'ung-meng hui in the Americas, however (prior
to the late 1911 rush into that party), present a slightly different picture. This is because most were new recruits and because the Chih-
kung t'ang was a competing prorevolutionary organization. With
the exception of Hawaii, most of the T'ung-meng hui's members
were either Chinese Americans, grammar and high school students,
teachers in the local Chinese schools, or small and middle-level merchants. In Hawaii, the T'ung-meng hui's substantial membership
and the broad social base from which it was drawn (resembling
Southeast Asia) was counterbalanced by the fact that after 1910, the
chapters were relatively inactive.

Ideologically speaking, the Pao-huang hui/Hsien-cheng tang and
the Hsing-Chung hui/T'ung-meng hui agreed on the principle of a

single party system for China, and they agreed that China should be regenerated through partial Westernization. They both favored creation of a party army. What they disagreed on was whether or not this latter goal should be achieved by working through the existing dynastic system or by overthrowing it: after 1903, the Pao-huang hui supported the Ch'ing, although it wanted to reform it. Furthermore, the parties' definitions of "Westernization" and "regeneration" differed increasingly as time passed, with America's T'ung-meng hui venturing in 1911 into a realm of radicalism (including a concern for the "little man") never reached by the Pao-huang hui, except possibly in late 1902 and early 1903.

There were other areas in which the aims of the several parties and, indeed, the ideals of Chinese in the Americas in general coincided. They valued constitutionalism and the right of the citizenry to participate in politics. They supported the efforts to reform the Ch'ing court and the penal system. They particularly applauded Wu T'ing-fang's efforts in this direction.[7] Chinese in the Americas were ardently provincial as well, and enthusiastically supported Cantonese nationalism, so both the Pao-huang hui and the revolutionaries directed their greatest energies and attention to Kwangtung in spite of their attempts to speak for, and to, all of China. Yet as time passed, Chinese in the Americas started to become nationalistic in the broader sense, and could be counted upon to keep national issues alive. They even let their nationalism change their community structure. Finally, Chinese in the Americas were committed to commercialism and the changes that capitalism was supposed to introduce gradually into a society. Hence, for example, the great interest in the various commercial and industrial projects of the Pao-huang hui/Hsien-cheng tang, along with the willingness to purchase Sun Yat-sen's "revolutionary bonds."

Almost all of what we have said here of Chinese in the Americas and their political development applies to China as well, to a greater or lesser extent. The parallel is closest when we examine "returned students" (Chinese students who had studied abroad), "treaty-port Chinese," new-style merchant-industrialists, and the progressive, activist segment of the literati-gentry. Among these groups, nationalism, the imperialist threat, and even the challenge of Western thought were suggesting the need for a substantive change which would include a broadening of the political base and a revised economy. The largest and, for most of the period up to 1911, the most influential of these groups pressing for substantive changes came to agree on the immediate need for a parliament and a constitutional monarchy. Significantly influenced by K'ang, Liang, and their followers, this group also desired to recapture China's economic rights as evidenced in particular by the Railway Rights Recovery Movement of 1910–1911, whereby China's merchants and gentry would redeem from the powers the right to build China's railways and would finance these through joint stock companies in which shares— and hence participation—would be available to anyone who could afford them, regardless of social class or other criteria. Another important point of similarity between China and Chinese in the Americas was the reaction to Chinese Exclusion in 1905, and the spread of politicization and radicalization that occurred in the wake of the failure of the boycott of American goods.

Rather than point to further parallels between political developments in China and in the Americas, it would be well here to examine two of the ideals noted earlier which deserve special note. They deserve this attention because they were to have such great influence in the later history of China. One is the party army. Embraced in 1923 by Sun Yat-sen (for reasons largely unrelated to his experience in the Americas, however), the party army became a source of real strength to him and was also later a principal source of power for figures as disparate as Chiang Kai-shek and Mao Tse-tung. The concept in the Americas of a party army seems to have been born of a combination of the Chih-kung t'ang's traditions and Homer Lea's ambitions. A lesser but contributing factor was the difficult situation in which Chinese found themselves with respect to the American population. The party army surfaced first in the Pao-huang hui in 1900, pointing up the intimate connection between the early Pao-huang hui and Chinese secret societies. But the party army was not simply to be a collection of fighting braves; it was also to be a national force trained in modern military techniques with a unified command. The commander, in turn, was subordinate to the political leaders of the party he served. The principal difference between this system and the Ch'ing military apparatus with its bannermen was that the Manchus were a tribe, not a political organization, and they were loyal to the idea of their tribal triumph, not indoctrinated in (or convinced of) any very specific political goals.

The second set of ideas that is especially noteworthy relates to the concept of the rights and the values of the "little man" and its complement, feminism. In China, these ideas did not really become important until the May Fourth Movement of 1919. In the Americas, they began to become especially prominent in the six months directly preceding the Wu-ch'ang uprising, although even then, only a minority of the revolutionaries espoused them. Earlier, an undercurrent of interest in the plight of the "little man" had been evident from time to time in the Christian community (as revealed in certain editorials in the *Chung Sai Yat Po*). It was present in certain portions of the text of Ou Chü-chia's *Hsin Kwangtung* and was also to some degree inherent in the organization of the Chih-kung t'ang federation. The "little man" in Triad terms meant those people who would normally find themselves at or near the bottom of the social scale. In the Americas, it generally signified laborers, the unemployed, certain of the most financially insecure merchants, and the various spokesmen for these groups.

As the Chih-kung t'ang became increasingly involved in politics, some lodges began to think more coherently about this kind of social division (as during the 1905 boycott of American goods; see also the later suggestion that wealthy Pao-huang hui merchant leaders were absconding with the hard-earned money of their less fortunate compatriots). But it was left to a number of the T'ung-meng hui members in San Francisco in 1911 to suggest that youth, women, younger brothers, and ordinary people deserved the same social and political rights as their elders and social superiors, and that China should not be divided into rulers and ruled, but that real equality and democracy should prevail.

By 1911, then, Chinese in the Americas as in China still had not fully articulated their political concerns, and as a consequence they had difficulty realizing their ostensible political goals. But the political ferment of the fifteen or so years prior to the revolution had left a permanent mark on their communities. A major byproduct of this ferment was the development of a political consciousness. As a result, even after it became clear that the 1911 revolution had failed to achieve most of its objectives, Chinese political parties continued to operate in the Americas, and the nationalism and politicization encouraged by these parties became permanently rooted.

APPENDIX A

PRINCIPAL SURNAME ASSOCIATIONS

IN NORTH AMERICA, 1903

SIMPLE SURNAME ASSOCIATIONS	SURNAME
Yin-ch'uan t'ang　穎川堂	Ch'en　陳
Jung-yang t'ang　榮陽堂	Tseng　鄭
K'en-ch'in kung-so　懇親公所	Li　李
Ma-chia kung-so　馬家公所	Ma　馬
Chiang-hsia t'ang　江夏堂	Huang　黃
Hsi-ho t'ang　西河堂	Lin　林
Chung-hsiao t'ang　忠孝堂	Liang　梁
Pei-kuo t'ang　沛國堂	Chu　朱
Lu-chiang t'ang　廬江堂	Ho　何
Hsü-shan t'ang　胥山堂	Wu　伍
Feng-ts'ai t'ang　風采堂	Yü　余
Ch'ing-pai t'ang　清白堂	Yang　楊
P'eng-ch'eng t'ang　彭城堂	Liu　劉
Wu-lu t'ang　武陸堂	Kung　龔
T'ien-shui t'ang　天水堂	Chao　趙
Kao-mi t'ang　高密堂	Teng　鄧
Ch'ing-ho t'ang　清河堂	Chang　張
Nan-yang t'ang　南陽堂	Yeh　葉
Lung-hsi t'ang　隴西堂	Kuan　關
Ai-lien t'ang　愛蓮堂	Chou　周
Kuang-yü t'ang　光裕堂	T'an　譚
An-ting t'ang　安定堂	Hu　胡
San-sheng t'ang　三省堂	Tseng　曾
Pao-shu t'ang　寶樹堂	Hsieh　謝

MULTIPLE SURNAME ASSOCIATIONS	**SURNAMES**
Lung-kang ch'in-i kung-so　龍岡親義公所	Liu, Kuan, Chang, Chao　劉, 關, 張, 趙
Chih-te t'ang　至德堂	Wu, Chou, Ts'ai　吳, 周, 蔡
So-yüan t'ang　遡源堂	Lei, Fang, K'uang　雷, 方, 鄺
Tu-ch'in kung-so　篤親公所	Ch'en, Hu　陳, 胡
Shao-lun kung-so　昭倫公所	T'an, T'an, Hsü, Hsieh　譚, 談, 許, 謝
Lin-te t'ang　鄰德堂	Lu, Lo, Lau　盧, 羅, 勞
Shih-tse t'ang　世澤堂	Teng, Ch'en, Yeh, Pai　鄧, 岑, 葉, 白
Feng-lun t'ang　鳳倫堂	Ssu-t'u, Hsieh　司徒, 薛
Chung-shan t'ang　中山堂	T'an, T'ang　甄, 湯

SOURCES: Liang Ch'i-ch'ao, *Hsin-ta-lu*, pp. 391–393; interview with Charles Mah, June 1979; and *Shih-chieh jih-pao*, 19 and 21 August 1978.

APPENDIX B

TRIAD LODGES IN THE AMERICAS, 1893–1911

CHIH-KUNG T'ANG FEDERATION

Continental North America:
Chih-kung t'ang　致公堂
Pao-an t'ang　保安堂
Chü-liang t'ang　聚良堂
Ping-kung t'ang　秉公堂
Ping-an t'ang　秉安堂
An-i t'ang　安益堂
Jui-tuan t'ang　瑞端堂
Ch'ün-hsien t'ang　群賢堂
Chün-ying t'ang　俊英堂
Hsieh-ying t'ang　協英堂
Chao-i t'ang　昭義堂
I-ying t'ang　儀英堂
Hsieh-sheng t'ang　協勝堂
Pao-shan t'ang　保善堂
Hsieh-shan t'ang　協善堂
Ho-sheng t'ang　合勝堂
Hsi-an she　西安社
Tun-mu t'ang　敦睦堂

Ts'ui-sheng t'ang　萃勝堂
Sung-shih shan-fang　松石山房
An-p'ing kung-so　安平公所
Tsu-ying t'ang　卒英堂
Hua-t'ing shan-fang　華亭山房
Yang-wen cheng-wu szu　洋文政務司
Pao-liang t'ang　保良堂
Chu-lin shan-fang　竹林山房
Chin-kung t'ang　進公堂
An-liang t'ang　安良堂
Ch'in-i t'ang　親義堂
Chin-lan yü-so　金蘭寓所

In Hawaii:
Pao-liang she　保良社
Ho-an hui-kuan　和安會舘

In Latin America:
No information

NOT ADHERENTS OF CHIH-KUNG T'ANG FEDERATION PRIOR TO 1911

Hawaii's Kuo-an hui-kuan　國安會舘
　(Ket On Society)*
Most if not all of Latin America's
　lodges*

SOURCES: Liang Ch'i-ch'ao, *Hsin-ta-lu*, pp. 395–396; Loretta O. Q. Pang, "The Chinese Revolution"; *Sai Gai Yat Po*; *Chung Sai Yat Po*; and Eng and Grant, *Tong War!*
*Some of these joined the federation around 1919.

NOTES

INTRODUCTION

1. Two recent books whose titles suggest that they might cover the same topics as the ones I am addressing here are *The Overseas Chinese and the 1911 Revolution,* by Ching Hwang Yen, and *Americans and Chinese Reform and Revolution, 1898–1922: The Role of Private Citizens in Diplomacy,* by Key Ray Chong. In fact, however, the first is concerned almost exclusively with Chinese in Southeast Asia while the second is primarily focused on attempts by Chinese political leaders to borrow money from Americans.

CHAPTER I

Parts of this chapter have appeared in a different form in L. Eve Armentrout, "Conflict and Contact Between the Chinese and Indigenous Communities in San Francisco, 1900–1911" (1976), pp. 55–70; and L. Eve Armentrout Ma, "The Social Organization of Chinatowns in North America and Hawaii in the 1890s" (1988).

1. Most American countries denied Chinese the right to citizenship. Hawaii was an exception, granting Chinese the right to naturalization until 1898, when it became part of the United States. The United States itself permitted a few Chinese to become naturalized between the 1850s and 1870s, but rejected (on the basis of race) more than it accepted. (See *Daily Alta,* 22, 23, and 24 December 1852 for an early instance of rejection.) In 1882, this semi-de facto prohibition was embodied in laws buttressed by a treaty between China and the United States; from then until 1943, Chinese were denied the right to naturalization in the United States.

2. For more on Chinese Exclusion, United States-China relations, and the impact of United States-China relations on Chinese immigrants during this period, see Michael H. Hunt, *The Making of a Special Relationship: The United States and China to 1914* (1983); Daniel M. Crane and Thomas A. Breslin, *An Ordinary Relationship: American Opposition to Republican Revolution in China* (1986); Shih-shan Henry Tsai, *China and the Overseas Chinese in the United States, 1868–1911* (1983); and Charles McClain, "The Chinese Struggle for Civil Rights in Nineteenth Century America: The First Phase, 1850–1870" (1984). A volume of articles edited by Sucheng Chan devoted exclusively to the effect on Chinese of Chinese Exclusion is currently in the final stages of preparation.

3. *Chung Sai Yat Po (Chung-hsi jih-pao),* 19 November 1901; and Liang Ch'i-ch'ao, *Hsin-ta-lu yu-chi,* p. 287. For a translation of the section of Liang's *Hsin-ta-lu yu-chi* which deals with his travels in Canada, see L. Eve Armentrout Ma, "A Chinese Statesman in Canada, 1903: Translation from the Travel Journal of Liang Ch'i-ch'ao" (1983).

4. *Chung Sai Yat Po,* 24 July 1901.

5. Liang Ch'i-ch'ao, *Hsin-ta-lu,* pp. 377–380.

6. Ibid., pp. 226–227. Anthony B. Chan, in *Gold Mountain* (1983), pp. 68–73, suggests significantly lower population figures for Chinese in Canada at that time. His figures, however, are based on recent books, articles, and interviews rather than on turn-of-the-century sources.

7. *Chung Sai Yat Po,* 21 November 1900; and Jung-pang Lo, *K'ang Yu-wei: A Biography and a Symposium* (1967), pp. 200–203. In 1900, a newspaper article reported that the Mexican government had asked a certain Chinese merchant to bring in ten thousand Chinese to work the silver mines. Other Chinese arrived both earlier and later, especially prior to the Mexican revolution of 1911.

8. Ch'en K'uang-min, *Mei-chou hua-ch'iao t'ung-chien* (1950), pp. 632, 637, 672, and 766; and Huang Chia-mo, "Mi-lu hua-ch'iao te ai-kuo huo-tung" (1971), p. 1. Chinese were forbidden to enter Cuba after 1902.

9. William Hoy, *The Chinese Six Companies* (1942), pp. 10–17; Lung Doo Benevolent Society, *Lung Doo Benevolent Society Diamond Jubilee Edition;* and Chang Dai Chow, ed., *Ket On Society 100th Anniversary August 17, 1969.* Hsiang-shan district is now called Chung-shan.

10. Liang Ch'i-ch'ao, *Hsin-ta-lu,* p. 289.

11. Ibid.; Ch'en K'uang-min, *Mei-chou,* pp. 45, 672; Huang Chia-mo, "Mi-lu," p. 1; and Loretta O. Q. Pang, "The Chinese Revolution: Its Activities and Meaning in Hawaii" (1963), Preface, p. i.

12. In the year 1855, for example, about 3,300 Chinese arrived in the United States, whereas some 3,400 left. In 1873, 17,000 arrived and about 7,000 left. See Thomas W. Chinn, H. Mark Lai, and Philip P. Choy, *A History of the Chinese in California: A Syllabus* (1973), pp. 18–19.

13. American labor unions and anti-Chinese sentiment largely prevented the use of Chinese as skilled laborers.

14. In the United States, for example, "foreign-born Chinese" were forbidden to support themselves by engaging in manual labor, a ruling often interpreted in the spirit of the following quote from the Chinese Inspector in San Francisco: "Under the laws and regulations, a Chinese person (whether or not a merchant) is classed as a laborer if he owns or works in a restaurant, laundry, barber shop or lodging house; or if he is employed as a miner, fisherman, huckster, or peddler, etc." (James R. Dunn to the Postmaster of Sanderson, Texas, 24 October 1899, in Immigration and Naturalization Service, Chinese E Files, National Archives, Washington, D.C.).

15. Liang Ch'i-ch'ao, *Hsin-ta-lu,* pp. 226–234. Opium smoking became illegal in the United States in 1881 and in Canada in 1903.

16. Ibid., pp. 287–289, 366, 380–382. For a general account of the situation in Hawaii, see Chung Kun Ai, *My Seventy-Nine Years in Hawaii* (1960).

17. *Chung Sai Yat Po,* 20 July 1901; Ch'en K'uang-min, *Mei-chou,* p. 496; and Lo, *K'ang Yu-wei,* pp. 201–204.

18. Ch'en K'uang-min, *Mei-chou,* pp. 632–637.

19. Hoy, *Chinese Six Companies,* pp. 1–26. For more on these and the other major Chinatown social organizations, see L. Eve Armentrout-Ma, "Urban Chinese at the Sinitic Frontier: Social Organizations in United States Chinatowns, 1849–1898" (1983); and Ma, "The Social Organization of Chinatowns."

20. Existing shipping routes forced most Chinese who wished to return to China from North America to use the port of San Francisco. They could not board a ship in San Francisco without a certificate of approval from the Chinese Six Companies. This was a legal requirement up until 1876, and then it became extralegal (but still effectively enforced) up until 1949. The Six Companies would not issue the certificate to any Chinese who had not first joined a *hui-kuan* and had his name inscribed on the registry of the Chinese Six Companies. See William J. Courtney, *San Francisco's Anti-Chinese Ordinances, 1850–1900* (1971), p. 34; Hoy, *Chinese Six Companies,* pp. 23–25; Mary Roberts Coolidge, *Chinese Immigration* (1909), p. 410; Rev. O. Gibson, *The Chinese in America* (1877), pp. 340–345; and Senate of the State of California, *Chinese Immigration: The Social, Moral, and Political Effect: Testimony (1876),* p. 26. The person planning to return had to pay an exit fee to the Six Companies and the appropriate *hui-kuan* in addition to the membership requirement. More information on extralegal means of enforcing these requirements came from the author's interview with Charles Mah, September 1977, and with Lee Jit-sing, August 1977. (Both were officers in Chinatown organizations and members of the Six Companies.)

21. L. Eve Armentrout Ma, "Fellow-Regional Associations in the Ch'ing Dynasty: Organizations in Flux for Mobile People. A Preliminary Survey" (1984).

22. Armentrout-Ma, "Chinese at the Sinitic Frontier."

23. Ibid.; Chinn, Lai, and Choy, *Chinese in California;* and Edgar Wickberg et al., *From China to Canada: A History of the Chinese Communities in Canada* (1982), p. 36.

24. Ibid.; and Ma, "Chinese at the Sinitic Frontier."

25. Ibid. (both of the above); Lo Hsiang-lin, *K'o-chia shih-liao hui-p'ien* (1965), pp. 33–34, 41–43, 387; Hsieh Shu-hsin, ed., *K'o-chia yüan-liu* (1967), pp. 26–50; and Pang, "Chinese Revolution," pp. 13–14, 25, 43, and Appendix A (the latter notes that Sun joined the Hakka Triad lodge in Hawaii).

26. Yuk Ow, Him Mark Lai, and P. Choy, eds., *Lü-Mei San-i Tsung Hui-kuan chien-shih* (1975) (hereafter cited as *Sam Yup*), p. 152. The Six Companies somewhat resembled the traditional Chinese system of administration, with the Six Companies representing the provincial government and the *hui-kuan* representing the districts. There is even a parallel between the importing of notables and the law of avoidance practiced by the Ch'ing administration.

27. Linda Pomerantz, "The Chinese Bourgeoisie and the Anti-Chinese Movement in the United States, 1850–1905" (1984), pp. 18–19, 22; and Renqiu Yu, "Chinese American Contributions to the Educational Development of Toisan 1910–1940" (1983), pp. 55, 60. Late Ch'ing efforts to raise capital from overseas Chinese, including those in Hawaii and the Americas, were none too successful. For a discussion of this issue, see Ching-hwang Yen, "The Overseas Chinese and Late Ch'ing Economic Modernization" (1982).

28. For more on the labor-contract and credit-ticket systems, see Gunther Barth, *Bitter Strength,* pp. 50–108, and Sing-wu Wang, *The Organization of Chinese Immigration, 1848-1888* (1978). In the 1850s, Kapitan China commissioned and even purchased ships to bring immigrants from China. However, Ow, Lai, and Choy, *Sam Yup* (pp. 58–59) and Chinn, Lai, and Choy (*Chinese in California,* pp. 15–16) indicate that from the mid-1870s on, instead of a Kapitan China the creditor was often a relative (clan member) of the borrower.

29. Chinese had other means of financing the trip to the Americas. Many of those sent to Latin America were kidnapped and sold into slavery; the slavers paid their passage. In the case of North America and Hawaii, some could afford to pay their own passage and others borrowed from close relatives. Still others obtained a loan from American employers such as the Central Pacific Railway of the United States (see Coolidge, *Chinese Immigration,* p. 52). Kapitan China, however, remained an important source of credit and employment in the overseas communities.

30. Coolidge, *Chinese Immigration,* p. 52; L. Eve Armentrout-Ma, "Big and Medium Businesses of Chinese Immigrants to the United States, 1850–1890: An Outline" (1978); *Chung Sai Yat Po;* and Hoy, *Chinese Six Companies,* pp. 1–28.

31. Charles Caldwell Dobie, *San Francisco's Chinatown* (1936), p. 125. Dobie tells us that up through the 1880s, only merchants could vote in the *hui-kuan.* See also Hoy, *Chinese Six Companies,* pp. 1–28; and Ow, Lai, and Choy, *Sam Yup,* p. 58.

32. Armentrout-Ma, "Big and Medium Businesses," pp. 2–4; and L. Eve Armentrout Ma, "The Big Business Ventures of Chinese in North America, 1850–1930" (1984). The trade between the United States and China that was handled by Chinese in the Americas amounted to more than three million dollars annually at its high point in the 1880s.

33. Hoy, *Chinese Six Companies;* and Ow, Lai, and Choy, *Sam Yup,* p. 58. Part of the change in the pattern of business in San Francisco reflected and had required a change in the Canton-Hong Kong area: *Szu-i* businessmen in America developed import-export contacts in China around the turn of the century because their fellow regionals had begun opening shops in Canton by that time. Major *Szu-i* businesses in the Americas as of 1900 included two large canneries located near San Francisco.

34. Hoy, *Chinese Six Companies;* and Liang Ch'i-ch'ao, *Hsin-ta-lu,* p. 400.

35. Ibid. (both of the above).

36. *Chung Sai Yat Po,* 26 March 1903.

37. Hoy, *Chinese Six Companies.*

38. Liang Ch'i-ch'ao, *Hsin-ta-lu,* pp. 388–390, 400.

39. Canada's Chung-hua hui-kuan dates its founding as 1885. See "Yü-to-li Chung-hua hui-kuan kuei-t'iao," in the author's collection.

40. Hoy, *Chinese Six Companies,* pp. 1–28; *Shao-nien Chung-kuo,* 13 and 20 May 1911; *Chung Sai Yat Po,* 16 February and 21 March 1900, and 19 June 1901; Ch'en K'uang-min, *Mei-chou,* pp. 75–79; and Him Mark Lai, "Mei-kuo hua-ch'iao chien-shih" (1980).

41. *So-yüan chi-k'an* 6 (December 1974): 2.

42. *Shih-chieh jih-pao,* 19 and 21 August 1978; Eng Ying Gong and Bruce Grant, *Tong War!* (1930), pp. 126, 141, 149; and interview with Charles Mah, June 1979.

43. Liang Ch'i-ch'ao, *Hsin-ta-lu,* p. 392. Liang also listed no association for the

surname T'ang, the surname of T'ang Ch'iung-ch'ang, a prominent man we will encounter again later. Clearly, strong surname ties could be helpful, but were not a necessity.

44. *Shih-chieh jih-pao,* 19 and 21 August 1978.

45. Liang Ch'i-ch'ao, *Hsin-ta-lu,* pp. 394–395. For a complete list of the surname associations and the surnames they represented, see Appendix A.

46. Pardee Lowe, *Father and Glorious Descendant* (1943), pp. 85–86; interview with William Fong (former president of the So-yüan t'ang), August 1977; and Liang Ch'i-ch'ao, *Hsin-ta-lu,* pp. 392–394.

47. *Chung Sai Yat Po,* 30 and 31 December 1901.

48. Feng Tzu-yu, *Hua-ch'iao ko-ming k'ai-kuo shih* (1953), pp. 34–36, 66–68; and Feng Ai-ch'un, *Hua-ch'iao pao-yeh shih* (1967), pp. 117–131.

49. *Chung Sai Yat Po,* 25 February 1901.

50. Wickberg et al., *From China to Canada,* pp. 34–37.

51. Ow, Lai, and Choy, *Sam Yup,* p. 589; Barth, *Bitter Strength,* pp. 87–88; and Liu Po-chi, *Mei-kuo hua-ch'iao shih* (1976), p. 215.

52. Examples of this are scattered throughout Chung Kun Ai's *My Seventy-Nine Years in Hawaii.* See also the benevolent activities of the Chinese Six Companies, most of which were directed toward Kwangtung province; and interview with Irwin Chew (officer of the Chinese American Citizens Alliance), June 1976.

53. Feng Tzu-yu, *Hua-ch'iao,* pp. 54–55; and Liang Ch'i-ch'ao, *Hsin-ta-lu,* p. 396. Other, similarly high, estimates can be found in Barth, *Bitter Strength,* p. 102; and *San Francisco Examiner and Chronicle,* 26 August 1973, section B, which contains an interview with Taam Wu, then head of the organization. See also Loretta Pang, "Chinese Revolution," pp. 11–13 and Appendix C. In the late nineteenth and early twentieth centuries, only about ten percent of the Chinese in the Americas were women and children. As women and particularly children were not normally members of the Triad organization, their small numbers meant a proportionally larger number of Triads in the Americas. In addition, community conflict in the continental United States had greatly strengthened the Triads in that area by the 1890s. See Armentrout-Ma, "Chinese at the Sinitic Frontier." Studies on the Triads in the Americas, including the Chih-kung T'ang, include Richard Dillon, *The Hatchet Men: San Francisco's Chinatown in the Days of the Tong Wars, 1880–1906* (1962); Eng and Grant, *Tong War!;* and C. Y. Lee, *Days of the Tong Wars* (1974).

54. For example, the Reverend Wu P'an-chao of San Francisco's Chinese Presbyterian Church was a member (interview with Taam Wu, head of the Chih-kung t'ang, November 1975).

55. *Sai Gai Yat Po,* 20 November 1909.

56. Huang San-te, *Hung-men ko-ming shih* (1925), pp. 2–4, 37, 45–46; Pang, "Chinese Revolution," pp. 11–13 and Appendix C; and Liang Ch'i-ch'ao, *Hsin-ta-lu,* pp. 395–397. For a list of all the Triad lodges in the Americas, see Appendix B.

57. Pang, "Chinese Revolution," pp. 11–13 and Appendixes A, B, and C.

58. From 1919 on, the Chih-kung t'ang began enlisting Latin American Triad lodges into the federation, and Huang San-te even founded a lodge in Jamaica. See Huang San-te, *Hung-men,* pp. 35–38, 45–47.

59. *Tsung-ku t'e-k'an* 6 (November 1961): 3, and no. 8 (January 1962): 15; and *Sai*

Gai Yat Po, 20 November 1909. The *Tsung-ku t'e-k'an* is the official organ of the Chih-kung t'ang international headquarters in San Francisco.

60. Liu Po-chi, *Mei-kuo hua-ch'iao,* p. 226; Stewart Cullin, *The Gambling Games of the Chinese in America* (1972), pp. 13–14; *Tsung-ku t'e-k'an* 6 (November 1961): 3; and Liang Ch'i-ch'ao, *Hsin-ta-lu,* pp. 396–397. For more on the early history of the Chih-kung t'ang, see Armentrout-Ma, "Chinese at the Sinitic Frontier."

61. *Tsung-ku t'e-k'an* 6 (November 1961): 3, and no. 8 (January 1962): 15; Liang Ch'i-ch'ao, *Hsin-ta-lu,* pp. 395–397; and Eng and Grant, *Tong War!,* pp. 23–34.

62. Armentrout-Ma, "Chinese at the Sinitic Frontier."

63. Eng and Grant, *Tong War!,* pp. 30–35, 56, and 102.

64. *Tsung-ku t'e-k'an* 4 (September 1961): 17; Pang, "Chinese Revolution," pp. 11–13 and Appendixes A, B, and C; and Stanford M. Lyman, W. E. Willmott, and Berching Ho, "Rules of a Chinese Secret Society in British Columbia" (1964), pp. 530–539. The hierarchy in Canada had certainly been established by 1903. It probably began in the 1890s, as suggested by the reaction of Chih-kung t'ang lodges in Vancouver and Victoria to the founding of the Pao-huang Hui in 1899. A lodge in the Vancouver/Victoria area was founded in 1886.

65. For the usual pattern in China, see Jean Chesneaux, *Les sociétés secrètes en Chine* (1965); G. William Skinner, "Marketing and Social Structure in Rural China," part 1 (1964); and Frederic Wakeman, Jr., *Strangers at the Gate: Social Disorder in South China, 1839–1861* (1966) (esp. chap. 11: "The Secret Societies of South China"), and "Les sociétés secrètes du Guangdong (1800–1856)" (1970).

66. Armentrout-Ma, "Chinese at the Sinitic Frontier."

67. Liang Ch'i-ch'ao, after spending a year in North America in 1903, estimated that one-third of the Chinese population in the continental United States was involved in the not very remunerative laundry business, and another ten percent was unemployed. See Liang Ch'i-ch'ao, *Hsin-ta-lu,* pp. 392–393.

68. Chinn, Lai, and Choy, *Chinese in California,* pp. 22–26.

69. Liang Ch'i-ch'ao, *Hsin-ta-lu,* pp. 233–234; and interview with Charles Mah (officer in the Mah Family Association and Bing Kong Tong, and representative on the councils of the Chinese Six Companies), June 1978.

70. Liang Ch'i-ch'ao, *Hsin-ta-lu,* pp. 233–234. In the United States, those lodges most deeply involved in criminal activities were also the ones most prone to violence, but this was not the case in Canada. There was a great deal of gambling in Canada's Chinese communities; certain Chinese "merchants" there specialized in smuggling opium, while others smuggled Chinese, into the United States. However, these activities did not produce much violence in Canada, probably because of the greater degree of social control due to the fact that Canada was seen as a way station on the way to the United States. For remarks on the gambling and opium, see Liang Ch'i-ch'ao, *Hsin-ta-lu,* pp. 229–230.

71. Good descriptions of "tong wars" can be found in C. Y. Lee, *Days of the Tong Wars,* pp. 24–32 and 97–105.

72. Eng and Grant, *Tong War!,* pp. 14, 57–60, and 94–101.

73. Ibid.; C. Y. Lee, *Days of the Tong Wars;* and Liang Ch'i-ch'ao, *Hsin-ta-lu,* pp. 233–240.

74. Ibid., pp. 14, 194–202; *Chung Sai Yat Po,* 1 October and 26 November 1900, 15

January and 1 March 1901, and 9 August 1904; *Sai Gai Yat Po,* 8 September 1910; and interview with Howard Ah-Tye (grandson of the founder of the Ts'ui-sheng t'ang), February 1978.

75. Chung Kun Ai, *My Seventy-Nine Years,* gives numerous examples of greater assimilation, and the friendly relations between the various ethnic communities. In 1901, Chinese who had resided long in the Islands were given the option of becoming naturalized United States citizens. The acting Governor of Hawaii in 1903 characterized the Chinese community there as being peaceful and full of responsible, respected, and wealthy individuals who led the community. See Acting Governor Ernest Cooper to Secretary of State John Hay, 20 April 1902; and United States Department of State, *Papers Relating to the Foreign Relations of the United States, 1902,* pp. 244–248.

76. Liang Ch'i-ch'ao, *Hsin-ta-lu,* pp. 391, 396; Chinn, Lai, and Choy, *Chinese in California,* pp. 49–50, 52–55; and Eng and Grant, *Tong War!,* pp. 94–101, 195. There were other occupational organizations which were not affiliated with the Triads. These were usually associated with the *hui-kuan,* and developed most often when all those employed in a given profession came from the same region.

77. Prior to the 1880s, a few *hui-kuan* had branches in rural areas, but from the 1880s on, such as existed began to die out (Armentrout-Ma, "Chinese at the Sinitic Frontier").

78. Ch'en Ju-chou, *Mei-chou hua-ch'iao nien-chien* (1946), pp. 409–646, shows that it is still true that the only social organization in most of the smaller Chinese communities is usually a Triad sublodge.

79. Lyman, Wilmott, and Ho, "Rules of a Chinese Society," pp. 530–539.

80. Ow, Lai, and Choy, *Sam Yup,* p. 152; and Dillon, *Hatchet Men,* pp. 196–200.

81. Ibid. (all of the above); and Ow, Lai, and Choy, *Sam Yup,* pp. 17–18 of the English version and pp. 60–61, 105, and 152–153 of the Chinese version.

82. Ibid. (all of the above).

83. Ibid. (all of the above). During the course of these "tong wars," the infamous "Little Pete" (Feng Cheng-ch'u, or Feng Ching) was assassinated. "Little Pete" had been a leading member of the *San-i* community, a Triad lodge leader, a wealthy proprietor of a shoe-manufacturing business, and a man heavily involved in gambling operations in San Francisco.

84. Dillon, *Hatchet Men,* pp. 196–200; and Ow, Lai, and Choy, *Sam Yup,* pp. 17–18 of the English version and pp. 60–61, 105, and 152–153 of the Chinese version.

85. Liang Ch'i-ch'ao, "Hsia-wei-i yu-chi" (n.d.), chüan 37, pp. 183–196; and Pang, "Chinese Revolution," p. 33.

86. *Chung Sai Yat Po,* 1, 2, 6, and 16 June 1900; *San Francisco Morning Call,* 6 June 1900; *San Francisco Examiner,* 31 May 1900; and Joan B. Trauner, "The Chinese as Medical Scapegoats in San Francisco, 1870–1905" (1978), p. 78.

87. *Chung Sai Yat Po,* 6 June 1900; and *San Francisco Morning Call,* 6 June 1900.

88. *Chung Sai Yat Po,* 1 and 2 June 1900.

89. *Chung Sai Yat Po,* 14, 19, and 22 June 1900; and *San Francisco Examiner,* 30 May and 16 June 1900. The lawyer hired by the Chinese Six Companies was Samuel M. Shortridge.

90. Pomerantz, "Chinese Bourgeoisie," pp. 20–23. This article maintains that

the United States policy of Chinese Exclusion was a major stumbling block to China's development of modern commerce and industry.

91. For a detailed account of the movement, see Chang Ts'un-wu, *Chung-Mei kung-yüeh feng-ch'iao* (1966).

92. *Chung Sai Yat Po,* 12 and 26 June 1900; 4 March, 16 and 19 August, 2 and 17 September, and 8 November 1901.

93. Ibid., 26 November 1901.

94. Ibid., 25 December 1901; 14 January, 7 March, 23 April, 1 May, and 14 August 1902; 4 and 28 March 1903.

95. Ibid., 30 October 1903.

96. Ibid., 2 November 1903; Liang Ch'i-ch'ao, *Hsin-ta-lu,* pp. 469–471, 478, 488; and Chang Ts'un-wu, *Chung-Mei kung-yüeh,* pp. 25–33. The governor-general in question was the one for Liang Kwang.

97. *Chung Sai Yat Po,* 26 March and 4 April 1904; 27 April and 1 May 1905.

98. Ibid., 3 May 1905.

99. Ibid., 11 and 12 May; 5, 6, 7, and 30 June 1905; Chang Ts'un-wu, *Chung-Mei kung-yüeh,* pp. 134–141; and Tsai, *China and the Overseas Chinese,* p. 115.

100. *Chung Sai Yat Po,* 7, 9, 15, and 20 June 1905; *Ta-tung jih-pao (Tai Tung Yat Po),* 1 July 1905; *Shao-nien Chung-kuo,* 11 March 1911; and Chang Ts'un-wu, *Chung-Mei kung-yüeh,* pp. 57–61, 134–141, 218–220. During Reverend Wu's 1905 tour, he was granted an interview with President Theodore Roosevelt. Reverend Wu felt that it was because of this interview that Chinese newspaper editors and religious ministers were shortly afterwards reclassified as "educators" (rather than "laborers"), thereby qualifying them for entry into the United States. See "Special Magazine/ Book to Commemorate the Fortieth Anniversary of the *Chung Sai Yat Po*" (1940). K'ang's interview with Roosevelt produced a promise that, henceforth, the exclusion provisions would be executed more evenhandedly and with less malice.

101. *Chung Sai Yat Po,* 7, 9, 15, and 20 June 1905. The split between the Pao-huang hui and other proboycott organizations was also related to a quarrel between the reformers and revolutionaries in Canton (Chang Ts'un-wu, *Chung-Mei kung-yüeh,* pp. 218–220).

102. *Chung Sai Yat Po,* 7 and 23 September 1907; and Him Mark Lai, "Mei-kuo hua-ch'iao."

103. Between 1854 and 1870, for example, Chinese were forbidden by law to testify against a white person (Corinne K. Hoexter, *From Canton to California: The Epic of Chinese Immigration* [1976], pp. 42–44; and Courtney, *San Francisco's Anti-Chinese Ordinances,* p. 9). After 1894, Chinese desiring to enter the United States found it increasingly difficult to obtain the right of habeas corpus when petitioning for admission (Vincente Tang, "Chinese Women Immigrants and the Two Edge Sword of Habeas Corpus," pp. 48–54); and Lucy Salyer, "Captives of Law: Judicial Enforcement of the Chinese Exclusion Laws, 1891–1924," in a volume of articles on Chinese exclusion edited by Sucheng Chan, forthcoming. Many constitutional issues were ruled in favor of Chinese, however. In 1864, an 1860 law levying a special tax on Chinese fishermen in California was found unconstitutional. In 1870, the law denying Chinese the right to testify against whites was found unconstitutional. In 1872, the 1852 law requiring a five hundred-dollar bond for every Chinese landing in

California was overturned. A series of laws directed against Chinese laundrymen and against Chinese living in crowded conditions were also found unconstitutional, and so forth. In many cases, Chinese launched test cases so as to overturn these laws (Courtney, *San Francisco's Anti-Chinese Ordinances*).

104. See Alexander Saxton, *The Indispensable Enemy: Labor and the Anti-Chinese Movement in California* (1971), pp. 271–284; and also Theodore Roosevelt, *African and European Addresses* (1910)—in particular, "Biological Analogies in History" (pp. 175–240) and "The World Movement" (pp. 99–142).

105. For one version of this view, see Homer Lea, *The Valor of Ignorance* (1909), pp. 124–126.

106. Feng Tzu-yu, *Ko-ming i-shih* (1947), p. 231.

107. *Chung Sai Yat Po*, 14 August 1902; and *Shao-nien Chung-kuo*, 12 and 15 April 1911, provide three examples of expressions of these sentiments.

108. K'ang was received by Premier Laurier of Canada and President Theodore Roosevelt of the United States, and was befriended by President Porfirio Díaz of Mexico. K'ang first met Díaz in 1905 (Lo, *K'ang Yu-wei*, p. 201). Liang Ch'i-ch'ao was granted an interview with Roosevelt in 1903, and with Secretary of State John Hay as well. The head of San Francisco's branch of the Pao-huang hui was given an interview with Roosevelt in 1904, and other United States officials gave other Pao-huang hui leaders special recognition (*Chung Sai Yat Po*, 17 March 1904; and L. Eve Armentrout, "American Involvement in Chinese Revolutionary Activities, 1898–1913" [1972], chaps. 2 and 3).

CHAPTER 2

1. The organization of this, Sun's first, uprising has been thoroughly covered in Harold Z. Schiffrin, *Sun Yat-sen and the Origins of the Chinese Revolution* (1968); see especially chapter 4, pp. 57–97.

2. Chung Kun Ai, *My Seventy-Nine Years*, pp. 108–111, 278–279; and Feng Tzu-yu, *Ko-ming i-shih*, vol. 2, pp. 1–2.

3. Feng Tzu-yu, *Ko-ming i-shih*, vol. 3, pp. 8–16.

4. Chung Kun Ai, *My Seventy-Nine Years*, pp. 1–89, 284–285, 309–312. In addition to antagonism toward the Ch'ing, much of the populace of Kwangtung viewed all government officials with uneasiness. Opium smuggling operated through Chung's native village, a traffic in which part of his family seems to have been involved.

5. Schiffrin, *Sun Yat-sen* (1968), p. 41; Fu Ch'i-hsüeh, *Kuo-fu Sun Chung-shan hsien-sheng chüan* (1968), pp. 41–43.

6. Feng Tzu-yu, *Ko-ming i-shih*, vol. 4, pp. 5–6.

7. Fu Ch'i-hsüeh, *Kuo-fu*, p. 42; and Feng Tzu-yu, *Hua-ch'iao*, pp. 25–33.

8. Schiffrin, *Sun Yat-sen* (1968), p. 45; and Feng Tzu-yu, *Ko-ming i-shih*, vol. 1, p. 43.

9. Schiffrin, *Sun Yat-sen* (1968), p. 43. Shelley Cheng, "A History of the T'ung-meng Hui (1905–1912)" (1961), chap. 2, pp. 10–12, holds that Chinese in Hawaii thought that the Hsing-Chung hui was some kind of self-strengthening organization, but both Schiffrin and Feng Tzu-yu disagree, saying Sun never hid his revolutionary intentions. See Feng Tzu-yu, *Hua-ch'iao*, pp. 25–33.

10. This latter reason is how Feng Tzu-yu explains Sun's meager success in 1894. See Feng Tzu-yu, *Ko-ming i-shih*, vol. 1, p. 41.

11. Huang San-te, *Hung-men*, p. 2; and Feng Tzu-yu, *Ko-ming i-shih*, vol. 1, pp. 138, 148. Sun Mei was one of those who thought Sun Yat-sen should join the Triads in Hawaii.

12. Ting Wen-chiang, *Liang Jen-kung hsien-sheng nien-p'u ch'ang-p'ien ch'u-kao* (1958), vol. 1, p. 102.

13. Pang, "Chinese Revolution," Appendix D; and Feng Tzu-yu, *Hua-ch'iao*, pp. 25–33.

14. Fu Ch'i-hsüeh, *Kuo-fu*, pp. 41–42.

15. Chung Kun Ai, *My Seventy-Nine Years*, pp. 1–19; Schiffrin, *Sun Yat-sen* (1968), pp. 41, 44; Feng Tzu-yu, *Ko-ming i-shih*, vol. 3, pp. 3–17; and letter from Acting Governor of Hawaii, Henry Ernest Cooper, to the Secretary of State, 29 April 1902; and Meeting of the Executive Council of the Government of Hawaii, 12 April 1900 (the latter two in Hawaii State Archives).

16. Ibid. (all of the above), and Chung Kun Ai, *My Seventy-Nine Years*, p. 187.

17. Many Chinese in Hawaii had adapted themselves to the Hawaiian environment by marrying Hawaiians, learning to speak Hawaiian, or establishing ties with the Hawaiian monarchy. When the monarchy was overthrown in 1893, they found that they could experience problems with Americans. In 1904, for example, Sun Mei lost the lease of his land in Maui, land originally leased from the Hawaiian crown but taken from him by the American government (Feng Tzu-yu, *Ko-ming i-shih*, vol. 2, pp. 6–7).

18. Feng Tzu-yu, *Ko-ming i-shih*, vol. 1, pp. 43–44, 148; Schiffrin, *Sun Yat-sen* (1968), p. 45; Chung Kun Ai, *My Seventy-Nine Years*, pp. 1–34; and L. Eve Armentrout, "The Canton Rising of 1902–1903: Reformers, Revolutionaries, and the Second Taiping" (1976), p. 95. Sung Chü-jen was one of the Triad members who joined at this time. He returned to China with Sun in 1894, and later helped solicit Triad braves for uprisings in Kwangtung in 1898, 1900, and 1903.

19. Feng Tzu-yu, *Hua-ch'iao*, pp. 25–33; and Schiffrin, *Sun Yat-sen* (1968), p. 97.

20. Feng Tzu-yu and Ch'en Shao-pai, *Chung-hua Min-kuo k'ai-kuo-ch'ien ko-ming shih* (1971), p. 36.

21. Wickberg et al., *From China to Canada*, pp. 73–74; and Feng Tzu-yu, *Hua-ch'iao*, p. 55. Feng Tzu-yu, in his *Ko-ming i-shih* (vol. 1, p. 138), also claims that T'ang Ch'iung-ch'ang and one other Chih-kung t'ang leader joined the Hsing-Chung hui at this time, but this seems unlikely in view of later events.

22. Lo, *K'ang Yu-wei*, pp. 127, 134, 139, 142, 178–180, 186.

23. Ibid., pp. 496, 512.

24. Ibid., p. 179. Yeh En was a relative of or the same person as the extremely wealthy and influential Yip Sang, a merchant, labor contractor, and the like who owned Victoria's Wing Sang Company (Letter from Edgar Wickberg to the author, 8 December 1977).

25. Edgar Wickberg et al., *From China to Canada*, p. 35.

26. Shanghai Shih Wen-wu Pao-kuan Wei-yüan Hui, ed., *K'ang Yu-wei yü Pao-huang hui* (1982), p. 3 (petition from the Chinese in British territories to the Ch'ing

Empress Dowager); Lo, *K'ang Yu-wei,* p. 128; and Feng Tzu-yu, *Ko-ming i-shih,* vol. 1, p. 138.

27. Lo, *K'ang Yu-wei,* pp. 179–182; *Chung Sai Yat Po,* 21 August 1900; Schiffrin, *Sun Yat-sen* (1968), pp. 157–158; and letter from Lo Fêng-luh to British Foreign Office, 7 February 1900; and letter from Lo Fêng-luh of the Chinese Legation to Lord Salisbury, 7 February 1900 (both letters in British Foreign Office, pp. 153–154).

28. Shanghai Shih, ed., *K'ang Yu-wei,* p. 92 (K'ang's announcement to the Pao-huang hui branches, 1899).

29. Lo, *K'ang Yu-wei,* pp. 180, 256.

30. Ibid. The man who proposed the title of Pao-huang hui was named Huang Hsüan-lin.

31. Feng Tzu-yu, *Hua-ch'iao,* p. 55; and Huang Fu-luan, *Hua-ch'iao yü Chung-kuo ko-ming* (1954), pp. 99, 109–110.

32. Joan E. Smythe, "The Tzu-li Hui: Some Chinese and their Rebellion" (1958), pp. 51–68.

33. Letters from Li Fuk Ki (Li Fu-chi) to K'ang Yu-wei, 9 and 11 September 1900; and letter from Tom Chue Phom (Tom Chhui Pak) to K'ang Yu-wei, 8 August 1900 (in British Foreign Office, pp. 414–421).

34. It is worth remembering that K'ang, like Sun, found no large organizations of his surname in the Americas, nor did K'ang have any relatives there in 1899.

35. Three of the known *Szu-i* men were from Hsin-ning and two from Hsin-hui; the *San-i* man was from P'an-yü. See Lo, *K'ang Yu-wei,* pp. 180, 488, 491, 499, and 512.

36. *Chung Sai Yat Po,* 10 October 1900.

37. Ow, Lai, and Choy, *Sam Yup,* pp. 60–61, 105, and 152–153; and Dillon, *Hatchet Men,* pp. 196–200.

38. Lo, *K'ang Yu-wei,* pp. 128–131, 139–142, and 178–180; and letter to the author, with enclosures, from National Archives, received 25 June 1971.

39. Articles of Incorporation of the Chinese Empire Reform Association, 31 October 1899, p. 4, in California State Archives.

40. Feng Ai-ch'un, *Hua-ch'iao,* pp. 117–131.

41. Letter from Wu T'ing-fang, Minister to the United States, to the United States Secretary of State, 31 January 1900; and letter, with enclosure, from Joshua K. Brown, Chinese Inspector Honolulu, to Secretary of the Treasury, 19 February 1900 (both of these enclosures in letter to the author, National Archives, 25 June 1971).

42. Letter from Lee Fuk Ki (Li Fu-chi) to K'ang Yu-wei, 11 September 1900, in British Foreign Office, pp. 419–421; and Shanghai Shih, ed., *K'ang Yu-wei,* p. 169 (letter from K'ang Yu-wei to K'ang T'ung-wei and K'ang T'ung-pi, 19 May 1900).

43. *New York Tribune,* 1 August 1900.

44. Letter from Lin (Sin?) to K'ang Yu-wei, 24 October 1900; letter from Li Fuk Ki to K'ang Yu-wei, 11 September 1900; and letter from Lo Fêng-luh to Lord Salisbury, 7 February 1900 (all of the above in British Foreign Office, pp. 253–254, 419–422); *Chung Sai Yat Po,* 3 May, 3 September, and 10 October 1900; letter to Secretary of State John Hay from C. K. Ai (Chung Yü), Ho Fon (Ho K'uan), Wong Leong

(Huang Liang), K. F. Li, M.D. (Dr. Li Ch'i-hui), et al., 26 February 1902; letter to Secretary of State John Hay from Wong Leong (Huang Liang), 4 March 1902 (the latter two items in Hawaii State Archives); letter from J. P. Jackson, Collector of the Customs, San Francisco, to Commissioner-General of Immigration, 12 September 1900, in Chinese E Files; and *Chung Sai Yat Po,* 18 June 1901.

45. *Chung Sai Yat Po,* 22 August 1900.

46. Letter from Deputy Attorney General E. P. Dole to the Executive Council of the Republic of Hawaii, 9 March 1900; letter from Yang Wei-pin, Chinese Consul, to E. A. Mott Smith, Minister for Foreign Affairs, 17 March 1900; letter from William A. Henshall, lawyer for Bow Wong Progressive Association, to the President of the Republic of Hawaii, 5 April 1900; statement by Joseph Goo Kim (with enclosure) submitted to Executive Council of the Republic of Hawaii, 5 April 1900; meeting of the Executive Council of the Republic of Hawaii, 12 April 1900; and letter from Henry Ernest Cooper, acting Governor of Hawaii, to the United States Secretary of State, 29 April 1902, p. 3 (all of the above in Hawaii State Archives).

47. *San Francisco Examiner,* 8 June 1900; *Chung Sai Yat Po,* 23 April, 3 May, and 22 August 1900; and letter from Li Fuk Ki to K'ang Yu-wei, 11 September 1900, in British Foreign Office, pp. 419–421.

48. *Chung Sai Yat Po,* 6 August 1900, p. 2.

49. Letter from Tom Chue Phom to K'ang Yu-wei, 8 August 1900, in British Foreign Office, pp. 414–415.

50. Letters from Li Fuk Ki to K'ang Yu-wei, 9 and 11 September 1900, in British Foreign Office, pp. 418–421.

51. Ibid.

52. Shanghai Shih, ed., *K'ang Yu-wei,* pp. 244–263 (Pao-huang hui rules, 1900).

53. Feng Tzu-yu, *Ko-ming i-shih,* vol. 1, p. 122, and vol. 4, p. 136; Lo, *K'ang Yu-wei,* p. 185; and Huang San-te, *Hung-men,* pp. 1–55.

54. *Chung Sai Yat Po,* 21 August 1900; and Lo, *K'ang Yu-wei,* p. 193.

55. Mei-shu T'an-hsiang-shan pao Kuang-hsü Huang-ti hui chih li, p. 1, an enclosure in Joseph Goo Kim, 5 April 1900; and Brief Translation of the Rules and Regulations of the Bow Wong Progressive Association (Royal Protective Union) of the Hawaiian Islands, 17 March 1900, pp. 2–3 (both in Hawaii State Archives).

56. Shanghai Shih, ed., *K'ang Yu-wei,* pp. 244–263 (Pao-huang hui rules, 1900), and pp. 264–265 (Outline of Pao-huang hui aims and organization, 1900).

57. Articles of Incorporation of the Chinese Empire Reform Association (San Francisco branch), 2 November 1899, pp. 1–2, in California State Archives.

58. Lo, *K'ang Yu-wei,* p. 185; *Chung Sai Yat Po,* 23 April, 9 July, and 9 August, 1900; *New York Tribune,* 1 August 1900; and letter from Li Fuk Ki to K'ang Yu-wei, 11 September 1900, in British Foreign Office, pp. 419–421.

59. Lo, *K'ang Yu-wei,* pp. 195, 269 n.

60. "Special Magazine/Book to Commemorate the Fortieth Anniversary of *Chung Sai Yat Po*" (1940) (in Chinese). After the paper moved to San Francisco, Teng I-yün became first editor of the *Chung Sai Yat Po.* Reverend Wu P'an-chao was one of the managers as well as the English-language translator, and Wu Yü-yen was the reporter.

61. *Chung Sai Yat Po,* 16 February 1900.

62. Frederick Chapin, "Homer Lea," pp. 15–19.

63. L. Eve Armentrout, "American Involvement in Chinese Revolutionary Activities, 1898–1913" (1972), pp. 30–32, 34; and *Chung Sai Yat Po,* 23 April 1900.

64. Huang Fu-luan, *Hua-ch'iao,* pp. 109–110; and Feng Ai-ch'un, *Hua-ch'iao,* pp. 118–119, 125–126.

65. Pang, "Chinese Revolution," Appendix D; and Feng Tzu-yu, *Ko-ming i-shih,* vol. 3, pp. 1–23.

66. Ibid., and Feng Tzu-yu and Ch'en Hsiao-pai, *Chung-hua Min-kuo k'ai-kuo-ch'ien ko-ming shih* (1971), pp. 47–50.

67. Schiffrin, *Sun Yat-sen* (1986), pp. 164, 182–189, and 313–314. When Liang went to Australia later that same year, he told Chinese in Australia that the Pao-huang hui sought to restore the Kuang-hsü Emperor in a republican revolution; the emperor would presumably become the first president of the republic. This is probably what he told Chinese in Hawaii, as well (*Chung Sai Yat Po,* 1 December 1900).

68. Pang, "Chinese Revolution," pp. 42, 47–51; Ting Wen-chiang, *Liang Jen-kung,* vol. 1, p. 102; Anonymous, *Chung-kuo pang-hui shih* (1969), pp. 116–118; and Chung Kun Ai, *My Seventy-Nine Years,* pp. 301–302. Chung Shui-yang later was Sun Yat-sen's guarantor when Sun was initiated into the Chih-kung t'ang.

69. *Chung Sai Yat Po,* 29 June, 6 August, 3 September, and 10 October 1900.

CHAPTER 3

1. *Chung Sai Yat Po,* 31 August, 10 and 13 October, 7 and 26 November, and 8 December 1900; and 30 March 1901.

2. Ibid., 11, 12, and 17 October 1900.

3. Ibid., 31 July 1900.

4. Ibid., 31 July and 7 December 1900; and *New York Tribune,* 26 December 1900. The Pao-huang hui leader in question was Wen Chin-ya (W. A. Cumrow).

5. *Chung Sai Yat Po,* 26 and 29 November 1900.

6. The Reverend Wu P'an-chao, for example, was both one of the critics and a Triad member.

7. *Chung Sai Yat Po,* 7 December 1900. The rules of the Chih-kung t'ang lodge (in Lyman, Willmott, and Ho, "Rules of a Chinese Society," pp. 530–539) contained the required phrase, *"fan-Ch'ing, fu-Ming"* (overthrow the Ch'ing, restore the Ming), but evidently it was no longer taken seriously.

8. *Chung Sai Yat Po,* 9 July and 1 August 1900.

9. Chinn, Lai, and Choy, *Chinese in California,* pp. 70–71.

10. *Chung Sai Yat Po,* 4 December 1900; 5 January and 5 and 8 April 1901.

11. Ibid., 1 December 1900.

12. Feng Ai-ch'un, *Hua-ch'iao,* p. 135; and *Chung Sai Yat Po,* 1 December 1900 and 15 January 1901. In Australia, Liang founded a newspaper dedicated to the union of the Pao-huang hui and the Hsing-Chung hui. Its editor was T'ang Ts'ai-chih, brother of the 1900 uprising leader T'ang Ts'ai-ch'ang.

13. *Chung Sai Yat Po,* 4, 5, and 16 January 1901.

14. Ibid., 18, and 22 October 1900.

15. Ibid., 22 October 1900.

16. Ibid.

17. Liang Ch'i-ch'ao, *Hsin-ta-lu,* pp. 226–234.

18. Ibid., p. 397.

19. *Chung Sai Yat Po,* 29 October 1900.

20. Literally, "Chin-shan ta-pu Chung-hua tsung hui-kuan ko shen-shih tung-shih."

21. *Chung Sai Yat Po,* 18 October 1900, and 20 March 1902.

22. After T'ang Ts'ai-ch'ang's rising failed, K'ang Yu-wei decided against using an army to help him achieve his political aims. Other reform leaders (including Liang Ch'i-ch'ao) continued to favor revolution, especially during the years 1901 and 1902. Adding to the confusion, Chinese in the Americas were frequently misinformed as to the whereabouts and activities of the various political leaders. See Don C. Price, *Russia and the Roots of the Chinese Revolution, 1896–1911* (1974), pp. 104–130; and *Chung Sai Yat Po,* 14 June 1901 and 25 February 1902.

23. *Chung Sai Yat Po,* 1 March and 12 August 1901; and Lo, *K'ang Yu-wei,* p. 180.

24. *Chung Sai Yat Po,* 27 August and 10 October 1900. One of those whom Liang Ch'i-t'ien removed from office was the ardent Chih-kung t'ang leader, T'ang Ch'iung-ch'ang.

25. *Chung Sai Yat Po,* March 1, 1901. The "peach garden oaths" were intended to follow in the tradition of the three famous *San-kuo yen-i* heroes (Liu Pang, Chang Fei, and Kuan Yü) who swore an oath of brotherhood and loyalty in a peach garden.

26. *Chung Sai Yat Po,* 4 April 1901. In this article, Liang is referred to by his *tzu,* "Mao-ts'ai."

27. Ibid., 1 March 1901.

28. Ibid., 13 May 1901.

29. Between March and November of 1901, Liang Ch'i-ch'ao changed from being antirevolutionary to being prorevolutionary. K'ang violently disagreed with Liang's new prorevolutionary sympathies and ordered Liang (and Chinese in the Americas) to cease discussing revolution (Lo, *K'ang Yu-wei,* pp. 190–192; Price, *Russia and the Roots,* pp. 109–117; and Chang P'eng-yüan, *Liang Ch'i-ch'ao yü Ch'ing-chi ko-ming* (1964).

30. *Chung Sai Yat Po,* 10 and 12 August 1901.

31. Ibid., 12 August 1901.

32. Ibid.

33. Ibid., and Shanghai Shih, ed., *K'ang Yu-wei,* pp. 205–206 (letter from Hsü Ch'in to Pao-huang hui chapters, 16 October 1902).

34. Shanghai Shih, ed., *K'ang Yu-wei,* p. 204 (letter to K'ang from Hsü Wei-ching and Li Fu-chi, 2 August 1902); and Chinese Empire Reform Association proclamation, 1904.

35. *Chung Sai Yat Po,* 12 August and 3 December 1901; and Lo, *K'ang Yu-wei,* p. 258 n. 8. It is unclear why Hsü Ch'in avoided Hawaii.

36. Lo, *K'ang Yu-wei,* p. 258 n. 8; and Huang Ting-chih, "Ku-pa te San-min yüeh-shu pao-she," in Chung-kuo she-hui (CASS) (eds.), *Hua-ch'iao yü hsin-hai leoming,* pp. 312–313.

37. Liang Ch'i-ch'ao's renewed interest in revolution in 1902 must have encouraged the activities.

38. Lo, *K'ang Yu-wei*, pp. 195, 269n; Chapin, "Homer Lea," pp. 40–45; L. Eve Armentrout, "The Canton Rising of 1902–1903: Reformers, Revolutionaries, and the Second Taiping" (1976), pp. 552–553, 561; and Ting Wen-chiang, *Liang Jen-kung,* p. 186.

39. Lo, *K'ang Yu-wei,* pp. 195, 269n.

40. Ibid., pp. 195, 204, 208, 210, 269n, 273n, 275n, and 275–276 n. 53.

CHAPTER 4

1. The first branch of the Hsing-Chung hui in the continental Americas, founded in San Francisco in 1896, became defunct well before the founding of the Pao-huang hui. It was not until the reestablishment of the Hsing-Chung hui in San Francisco in 1904 that the Pao-huang hui was challenged by a rival political party in the continental Americas (Ow, Lai, and Choy, *Sam Yup,* pp. 190–191).

2. *Chung Sai Yat Po,* 19 November 1901.

3. Ou Chü-chia, *Hsin Kuangtung* (1950), pp. 46–91; and Armentrout, "Canton Rising," pp. 83–105.

4. Armentrout, "Canton Rising," pp. 83–105.

5. British Public Records Office, "Report submitted by Lo Shang (Captain of left wing of Kwangtung army) on Hung Ch'un-fuk's uprising," pp. 558–560. The rich California resident in question was "Chan Tin Shao." H. Mark Lai of the Chinese Historical Society believes "Chan Tin Shao" was Ch'en T'ien-shen, a powerful man in the Americas, a gambler, and the proprietor of gambling houses (interview with H. Mark Lai, 4 April 1976).

6. Shanghai Shih, ed., *K'ang Yu-wei,* pp. 211–212 (letter from Ho T'ing-kuang to Yeh Hui-po [Yeh En] and Li Fu-chi, 14 February 1903).

7. Ting Wen-chiang, *Liang Jen-kung,* vol. 1, p. 175.

8. *Chung Sai Yat Po,* 8–14, 21, 23–25 April, 9–10, 15, 22–29 May, 2–3, 11–13, 24–25, 28, 30 June, 1–3 July 1902, and so forth.

9. Huang Fu-luan, *Hua-ch'iao,* p. 99; Li Shao-ling, ed., *Ou Chü-chia hsien-sheng chuan* (1950), pp. 1–31; and *Chung Sai Yat Po,* December 1900, 15 January and 25 and 29 April 1901, and so forth. In 1900, the *Chung Sai Yat Po* even suggested that the capital should be moved to the south so that southerners, who were inherently superior to northerners, would have a larger voice in the government.

10. Ibid. (all of the above); and Edgar Wickberg et al., *From China to Canada,* pp. 74–76.

11. *Chung Sai Yat Po,* 12 and 16 April, 1–3, 6, 17, 20, 30 May, 10, 19–21 June, and 14 August 1902, and others.

12. Feng Tzu-yu characterizes T'ang as one of the most ardent prorevolutionaries in San Francisco (Feng Tzu-yu, *Ko-ming i-shih,* vol. 2, pp. 112–114).

13. Li Shao-ling, *Ou Chü-chia,* pp. 13–31; Huang Fu-luan, *Hua-ch'iao,* p. 99; and Feng Tzu-yu, *Hua-ch'iao,* pp. 62–63.

14. Armentrout, "Canton Rising." See also *Chung Sai Yat Po,* 17, 27, and 28 May 1903; and Shanghai Shih, ed., *K'ang Yu-wei,* p. 168 (letter from K'ang Yu-wei to Li Fu-chi et al., 1 June 1903).

15. *Chung Sai Yat Po,* 27 March 1903.

16. *Chung Sai Yat Po,* editorial (p. 1), 6 July 1903. The newspaper based its circula-

tion figures on the number of pounds of newsprint it sent through the mails as opposed to the other newspapers.

17. Ting Wen-chiang, *Liang Jen-kung,* vol. 1, pp. 175, 181–182.

18. Li Shao-ling, *Ou Chü-chia,* pp. 13–31.

19. *Chung Sai Yat Po,* editorials (p. 1), 22 April and 5 and 9 May 1903.

20. *Chung Sai Yat Po,* 9 July 1903.

21. Ibid., 6, 9, and 11 July 1903. The fight between the *Chung Sai Yat Po* and the *Wen-hsing pao* began several days before it first appeared in the *Chung Sai Yat Po.*

22. A good account of this trip which emphasizes Liang's reception by American officials is Joseph R. Levenson, *Liang Ch'i-ch'ao and the Mind of Modern China* (1959), pp. 69–74. See also Armentrout, "American Involvement," pp. 43–45; Wickberg et al., *From China to Canada,* pp. 74–76; and Key Ray Chong, *Americans and Chinese Reform and Revolution, 1898–1922: The Role of Private Citizens in Diplomacy* (1984). Minister Wu T'ing-fang had tried to prevent Liang's trip, even persuading the Six Companies to tell Liang he might be assassinated if he came to San Francisco. Liang responded that he was prepared to die for his cause. See Liu Po-chi, *Mei-kuo hua-ch'iao,* pp. 449–453.

23. Ting Wen-chiang, *Liang Jen-kung,* vol. 1, p. 176. See also Price, *Russia and the Roots,* pp. 119–130; and Hao Chang, *Liang Ch'i-ch'ao and Intellectual Transition in China, 1890–1907* (1971), p. 238.

24. Ting Wen-chiang, *Liang Jen-kung,* vol. 1, pp. 175, 181–182; and Shanghai Shih, ed., *K'ang Yu-wei,* pp. 203–204 (letter from Hsü Wei-ching and Li Fu-chi to "whom it may concern," 2 August 1902), and pp. 242–243 (letter from Liang Ch'i-ch'ao to K'ang Yu-wei, 19 December 1903).

25. Ibid., pp. 175–176, 182.

26. The *Chung Sai Yat Po,* for example, employed the term *"shen-shang"* from the very beginning of its existance, in 1900.

27. Armentrout, "American Involvement," pp. 46–48; Wickberg et al., *From China to Canada,* p. 75; and Chung-kuo shang-wu kung-szu chiao-ku chien-ming chang-ch'eng.

28. Ting Wen-chiang, *Liang Jen-kung,* vol. 1, p. 192; and Armentrout, "American Involvement," pp. 48–49.

29. On April 17, the *Chung Sai Yat Po* published an announcement by the Chih-kung t'ang saying that the latter was organizing the *Ta-t'ung jih-pao.*

30. Huang Fu-luan, *Hua-ch'iao,* p. 99; *San Francisco Examiner,* 26 August 1973, section B, p. 6; and *Chung Sai Yat Po,* editorial, 20 July 1904.

31. *Chung Sai Yat Po,* 14 July 1904. Ch'en Min-sheng was head of San Francisco's Pao-huang hui in 1903–1904 (*Chung Sai Yat Po,* 25 September 1903).

32. Liang Ch'i-ch'ao, *Hsin-ta-lu,* p. 397; and Eng and Grant, *Tong War!,* pp. 34–36, 94–101. As the Chih-kung t'ang's official translator, T'ang Ch'iung-ch'ang would also have been a member of the "translators' " lodge, but he seems to have been at odds with its directors.

33. Ting Wen-chiang, *Liang Jen-kung,* vol. 1, pp. 183, 186.

34. Ibid.

35. *Chung Sai Yat Po,* 25–26 and 28–29 September, and 1 and 6 October 1903.

36. Liang Ch'i-ch'ao, *Hsin-ta-lu,* p. 401; and *Chung Sai Yat Po,* 7 November 1903.

37. Ting Wen-chiang, *Liang Jen-kung,* vol. 1, pp. 184–192; and *Chung Sai Yat Po,* 15 October 1903. All of the funds collected in the western United States went to the Pao-huang hui's Ta-t'ung hsüeh-hsiao school, partly because two Pao-huang hui leaders (T'an Shu-pin and one other) had gained control of the funds. Liang ordered these two to send the monies to the school rather than divide the funds up and "dissipate" them on other projects (as others evidently desired) (Ting Wen-chiang, *Liang Jen-kung,* vol. 1, p. 184). Liang also felt that wealthy Chinese in the Americas were not contributing enough. He suspected that they felt the Pao-huang hui to be incompetent. His solution was to establish a large school in Kwangtung. Wealthy Chinese in the Americas were more interested in Kwangtung than in China generally. They might also prefer a school since it could operate in the open, thereby enabling them to demonstrate publicly their financial largesse (without endangering their families in China).

38. Armentrout, "American Involvement," pp. 52–55.

39. *Chung Sai Yat Po,* 11 November 1903.

40. Ting Wen-chiang, *Liang Jen-kung,* vol. 1, p. 86; Tsai, *China and the Overseas Chinese,* pp. 130–140; and *Chung Sai Yat Po,* 26 November 1901, and 30 October and 2 November 1903.

41. Ting Wen-chiang, *Liang Jen-kung,* vol. 1, pp. 187–188.

42. Ibid., p. 187; and Liang Ch'i-ch'ao, *Hsin-ta-lu,* pp. 397–406.

43. *Chung Sai Yat Po,* 14 July 1904. T'an Chin-yung (Tom Kim-yung) was a Ch'ing military attaché in Boston. In 1903, the Boston police beat and humiliated him, and T'an responded by committing suicide. See Tsai, *China and the Overseas Chinese,* p. 106.

44. *Wei-shin pao,* 10 March–6 October 1904.

45. Ibid., 24 March 1904.

46. I have translated a small portion of his travel journal, covering his stay in Canada, in Ma, "A Chinese Statesman."

47. *Chung Sai Yat Po,* 18 and 20 July 1904.

48. Ibid., 23 March 1904; Huang San-te, *Hung-men,* pp. 3–4; Li Shao-ling, *Ou Chü-chia,* pp. 13–31; and Armentrout, "American Involvement," pp. 56–63.

49. Ibid. (all of the above); and *San Francisco Examiner,* 26 April 1973, section B, p. 6.

50. Feng Tzu-yu, *Hua-ch'iao,* pp. 56–60; and Huang Fu-luan, *Hua-ch'iao,* pp. 99–101. The first editor that Feng sent was not suitable (Feng Tzu-yu, *Ko-ming i-shih,* vol. 1, pp. 153–154). The second, Liu Ch'eng-yü, was found to be suitable. Liu had had close connections with the reformers before he started publishing prorevolutionary editorials in the *Ta-t'ung jih-pao.* Before leaving China for the United States late in 1904, Liu got the editor of the reformers' Shanghai newspaper and others to write letters of introduction to San Francisco's Pao-huang hui. The reformers believed Liu was going to the United States to study. Without the letters of introduction, Liu felt he might have had difficulty landing in San Francisco (Lo, *K'ang Yu-wei,* p. 270n).

51. *Chung Sai Yat Po,* 23 March, 7 April, and 3, 9, and 16 May 1904; *San Francisco Examiner,* 26 April 1904, section B, p. 6; Huang Fu-luan, *Hua-ch'iao,* pp. 99–108; and Feng Tzu-yu, *Ko-ming i-shih,* vol. 3, pp. 154, 158.

52. Huang Fu-luan, *Hua-ch'iao,* pp. 99–101.

53. This is because in 1902, various Pao-huang hui leaders in Hawaii (including Chung Yü) persuaded the United States government to protect the families in China of Hawaii's Pao-huang hui members. United States Secretary of State John Hay had been particularly sympathetic to the Pao-huang hui (Special Report to Washington by Henry Ernest Cooper, Acting Governor of Hawaii, 29 April 1902).

54. *Chung Sai Yat Po,* 27 May 1904.

55. An interesting variation on this situation existed in Southeast Asia, where Yu Lieh, a member of the Hsing-Chung hui and a Triad leader, was organizing pro-revolutionary Triad lodges, which competed quite successfully with Sun's party. In 1909, however, British authorities expelled Yu Lieh from its colonies and then suppressed the Triad lodges that he had founded (Ching Hwang Yen, *The Overseas Chinese and the 1911 Revolution* [1976], pp. 94, 131n; and Png Poh Seng, "The Kuomintang in Malaya" [1961], pp. 2–3).

56. *Chung Sai Yat Po,* 14 July 1904.

57. Ibid., 17 May, and 22 and 30 June 1904. One point that helped turn the editors against the Ch'ing was the court's evident disinterest in the plight of Chinese in the Americas at a time when revision of the treaty which permitted Chinese Exclusion was supposedly taking place (*Chung Sai Yat Po,* 16 December 1904).

58. *Chung Sai Yat Po,* 1 and 9 August 1904.

59. Armentrout, "American Involvement," pp. 67–73.

CHAPTER 5

1. In spite of repeated attempts, the first branch of the T'ung-meng hui in the Americas was not established until 1908, when serious dissatisfaction with the Pao-huang hui had developed.

2. The young radical in question was Sung Chü-jen. See Chung-hua Min-kuo K'ai-kuo Wu-shih-nien Wen-hsien Pien-tsuan Wei-yüan Hui, eds., *Chung-hua Min-kuo k'ai-kuo wu-shih-nien wen-hsien,* ser. 1, part 9 (vol. 2 of *Ko-ming shih ch'ang-tao yü fa-chan* [Hsing-Chung hui] [1964], pp. 462–466). In 1902, two of the leaders of this coup (Yung Wing and Hsieh Tsuan-t'ai) urged Sun Yat-sen to join the Triads, but he refused and subsequently was only minimally involved in the coup.

3. Feng Tzu-yu, *Hua-ch'iao,* pp. 33–34.

4. Feng Tzu-yu, *Ko-ming i-shih,* vol. 2, pp. 6–7.

5. Ibid., vol. 1, p. 43. The preacher, Reverend Mao Wen-ming, had participated in this uprising along with Sung Chü-jen and Teng Yin-nan, who had lived in Hawaii, and Shih Chien-ju.

6. Ibid., vol. 2, pp. 102–104; and Feng Tzu-yu, *Hua-ch'iao,* pp. 33–34. The *Chung Sai Yat Po* in San Francisco reported that both Chinese and Americans went to pay their respects to Sun. His speeches had a capacity audience and were well received (*Chung Sai Yat Po,* 25 December 1903).

7. Feng Tzu-yu, *Hua-ch'iao,* pp. 33–34.

8. Ibid. This is the first time the phrase was made part of the Hsing-Chung hui oath. Sun may have used it one month earlier as an oath required of students in a military school he tried to found in Yokohama (Schiffrin, *Sun Yat-sen,* p. 308).

9. "Equalization of land rights" was a traditional Chinese rebel slogan (see the T'ang dynasty and, later, Li Tzu-ch'eng). A recent head of the Kuo-an hui-kuan (Ket On Society) has said that around the turn of the century, his organization's membership consisted largely of agricultural laborers (Pang, "Chinese Revolution," Appendix C).

10. Feng Tzu-yu, *Ko-ming i-shih*, vol. 2, pp. 102–104; and Feng Tzu-yu, *Hua ch'iao*, pp. 33–34.

11. Feng Tzu-yu, *Ko-ming i-shih*, vol. 3, p. 141; and Feng Tzu-yu, *Hua-ch'iao*, pp. 33–34. This "second choice" editor was Chang Tzu-li.

12. No copies of the *Hsin Chung-kuo pao* attacks remain.

13. Feng Tzu-yu, *Hua-ch'iao*, pp. 33–34. The *Hsin Chung-kuo pao* editor who wrote these attacks was Ch'en I-k'an, a student of K'ang Yu-wei and the man who, earlier in 1903, had proposed a boycott of American goods and gone to continental North America to persuade Chinese there to adopt that tactic (see chapter 1). He was a former reporter for the Pao-huang hui's Macao newspaper and was the man who notified San Francisco's Pao-huang hui of Sun's travel plans in late 1903 so as to enable them to deny entry to Sun in San Francisco (Feng Tzu-yu, *Ko-ming i-shih*, vol. 1, p. 148, and vol. 2, p. 102). Perhaps because his attacks on Sun were not entirely successful, by mid-December of 1903, the *Hsin Chung-kuo jih-pao*'s chief editor was Dr. Li Ch'i-hui, who in 1900 had helped found Hawaii's Pao-huang hui (*Hsin Chung-kuo pao*, 10 December 1903).

14. At this time in both the West and the East, the questions of majority and minority races and inborn racial characteristics were important ones. It would be incorrect to attribute Sun's racial preferences entirely to Chinese sources. The idea that a nation could not be strong unless the majority race ruled was a popular one at that time among many Westerners as well. Sun's later allies in California, Homer Lea and Ansel O'Banion, certainly shared this view. Many Chinese reformers also employed racial arguments. K'ang Yu-wei believed that there was an intimate connection between a temperate climate, skin color, and intelligence. One means he favored to improve the standing of the Chinese race was to move large numbers to favorable climates where, theoretically, over the centuries their skin would lighten and their native intelligence would grow (L. G. Thompson, trans., *Ta T'ung Shu: The One World Philosophy of K'ang Yu Wei* [1958], pp. 139–148).

15. Overseas Chinese Penman's Club, eds., *The Chinese of Hawaii*, pp. 18–21, contains the complete text of the two most important of these editorials.

16. Ibid.

17. Pang, "Chinese Revolution," Appendix D.

18. Anonymous, *Chung-kuo pang-hui shih*, pp. 116–118 and Chung-hua Min-kuo, eds., *Chung-hua Min-kuo*, vol. 1, part 10, p. 262.

19. Anonymous, *Chung-kuo pang-hui shih*, pp. 116–118; and Huang San-te, *Hung-men*, pp. 2–3. Huang reports that in his correspondence with Sun at this time, Sun did not speak of revolution (*ko-ming*) but of rebellion (*tso-fan*), although while Sun was in Hawaii in 1903, the *Chung Sai Yat Po* noted that he was the leader of the revolutionary (*ko-ming*) party. See *Chung Sai Yat Po*, 15 October and 25 December 1903.

20. Huang San-te, *Hung-men*, pp. 6–12. Huang says that the Chih-kung t'ang (through Huang) paid all of Sun's bills while in the United States, and raised one

thousand dollars for his traveling expenses when he left for Europe. Huang also says that many people were too afraid of the Pao-huang hui to come to Sun's speeches, and those that did come left early, also because of their fear.

21. "Chih-kung t'ang hsin chang," in Chung-hua Min-kuo, eds., *Chung-hua Min-kuo,* vol. 1, part 10, p. 258.

22. Ibid., pp. 256–258.

23. Ibid., pp. 259–260.

24. Ibid.

25. Each of the various lodges and sublodges already had an "office" that roughly seems to have corresponded with the new rules' office of the "legislators" (*i-yüan*), and that was the *shu-fu* (Huang San-te, *Hung-men,* pp. 5–6, etc.).

26. Liang Ch'i-ch'ao, *Hsin-ta-lu,* p. 400.

27. Ch'en K'uang-min, *Mei-chou,* pp. 154, 158; and Huang Fu-luan, *Hua-ch'iao,* pp. 99–108.

28. Huang San-te, *Hung-men,* pp. 13–15.

29. Lo, *K'ang Yu-wei,* pp. 271–272 n. 34; Carl Glick, *Double Ten: Captain O'Banion's Story of the Chinese Revolution* (1945), pp. 36, 47–52, 91–100, 277; Armentrout, "American Involvement," pp. 63, 104, and 110–137; and Huang San-te, *Hung-men,* pp. 13–15.

30. Glick, *Double Ten,* pp. 47–105, 277; and *Los Angeles Times,* 23 October 1903. Lea and O'Banion claim that United States Army Chief of Staff Major General Adna R. Chaffee, in response to a request from Lea, recommended O'Banion to Lea (Glick, *Double Ten,* pp. 21–26). Documentation to substantiate this is lacking. For more on the Western Military Academy and Homer Lea, see Chong, *Americans and Chinese.*

31. Joseph R. Levenson, *Liang Ch'i-ch'ao,* pp. 74–75n. Mr. Falkenburg was given this honor to recompense him for having written a letter to President McKinley in 1900 suggesting that the United States use its troops in China to restore power to the Kuang-hsü Emperor (Chapin, "Homer Lea," pp. 55 and 80–86).

32. Letter to the author from Edmund G. Brown, Jr., Secretary of State, California, 10 March 1971; Glick, *Double Ten,* pp. 58–67 and 88–89; and *Los Angeles Times,* 3 January 1905.

33. Glick, *Double Ten,* pp. 58–67, 75; and letter from Major George W. Gibbs to General Homer Lea, 6 January 1905; and "Petition to Charter a Chinese-American Educational Association" of 2 February 1905 (both in the Powers Collection). See also Pao-huang hui Kan-ch'eng hsüeh-hsiao hsiao-shih.

34. Pao-huang hui kung-i kai-ting hsin-chang.

35. Lo, *K'ang Yu-wei,* pp. 197–204. See also Robert Worden, "A Chinese Reformer in Exile: The North American Phase of the Travels of K'ang Yu-wei, 1899–1909" (1971).

36. Lo, *K'ang Yu-wei,* pp. 197–204.

37. Chung-kuo shang-wu kung-szu chiao-ku chien-ming chang-ch'eng; *Sai Gai Yat Po,* 16 April 1908; "Mei-kuo cheng-pu Ti-kuo Hsien-cheng hui chien-lou ku-fen-pu"; and interview with H. Mark Lai, January 1976. Lo, *K'ang Yu-wei,* p. 200, also notes that "Leaders of the local branches [in Montana, Idaho, Washington, and Oregon, among other places] of the Society to Save the Emperor (China Reform Association [Pao-huang hui/Hsien-cheng tang]) enthusiastically supported K'ang's

promotion of commercial ventures through the Commercial Corporation." See also Lo, *K'ang Yu-wei,* pp. 269–272 (footnotes).

38. Shanghai Shih, ed., *K'ang Yu-wei,* pp. 266–286 (Commercial Corporation rules, 1903) and pp. 287–293 (revised rules of the Commercial Corporation, June 1906). The Ch'ing court was also trying to tap the wealth and entrepreneural expertise of overseas Chinese at this period. As part of its campaign, the court offered to sell aristocratic titles and official ranks. The dynasty hoped to persuade overseas Chinese to invest in state-sponsored enterprises, and/or simply to increase their investments in China. This campaign was not very successful, partly because of (Chinese) official mismanagement and interference at the local level. See Yen, "Overseas Chinese."

39. Lo, *K'ang Yu-wei,* pp. 200–202; and *Sai Gai Yat Po,* 16 April 1908.

40. Lo, *K'ang Yu-wei,* pp. 200–202.

41. Ibid., pp. 204, 210, and 275n. At least $431,000 seems to have been lost through peculation by managers and other Pao-huang hui officials. Its assets (before the peculation) in the year 1908 were on the order of $1,200,000.

42. Armentrout, "American Involvement," pp. 73–92.

43. Ibid.; and Feng Tzu-yu, *Ko-ming i-shih,* vol. I, pp. 155–156.

44. Letter from William H. Eckley to Governor Frank W. Higgins, 25 May 1905, an enclosure in letter to the author from Elmer O. Parker, National Archives, 12 March 1971.

45. Armentrout, "American Involvement," pp. 76–86. Falkenburg had some influential supporters including a Colonel A. B. Hotchkiss (U.S.A., Ret.), but Lea had more powerful ones, such as California Governor Pardee and, to a lesser extent, President Theodore Roosevelt and Army Chief of Staff Adna R. Chaffee. The investigations were initiated while Lea and K'ang were still in Los Angeles. They did not end until after the two had parted company in New York.

46. Armentrout, "American Involvement," pp. 78–79.

47. Ibid., pp. 92–100, describes various attempts that K'ang made to produce a change in the exclusion laws. Other minor improvements were produced through the efforts of the Reverend Wu P'an-chao, who was in part responsible for newspaper personnel (editors and managers) being reclassified as educators.

48. Interview with H. Mark Lai, January 1976; and "Mei-kuo cheng-pu Ti-kuo hsien-cheng hui chien-lou ku-fen-pu." In 1906 San Francisco suffered a major earthquake, which destroyed most of Chinatown. This forced both the *Chung Sai Yat Po* and the *Sai Gai Yat Po* to stop publication for a time. The *Chung Sai Yat Po* then moved to Oakland, and the *Sai Gai Yat Po* to Los Angeles. In 1907, the *Chung Sai Yat Po* and in 1908 the *Sai Gai Yat Po* returned to San Francisco. The effect of the earthquake on the *Ta-t'ung jih-pao* is not known. The buildings of the Pao-huang hui, Chih-kung t'ang, *Chung Sai Yat Po,* and Chinese Six Companies were all destroyed by the earthquake, but they were all rebuilt by 1908.

49. Lo, *K'ang Yu-wei,* pp. 272–273 nn. 37 and 38.

50. Lo, *K'ang Yu-wei,* p. 273 nn. 40 and 42, and p. 277 n. 58; Wu Hsien-tzu, *Chung-kuo min-chu hsien-cheng tang tang-shih* (1952), pp. 46–47; and Shanghai Shih, ed., *K'ang Yu-wei,* pp. 487–495 (Hsien-cheng tang rites as decided by official delegates, 23 March 1907).

51. Shanghai Shih, ed., *K'ang Yu-wei*, pp. 371–373 (letter from Tseng T'ing-hui instructing partisans in Hawaii on how to change their Pao-huang hui branch into a Hsien-cheng tang branch, 1907), and pp. 487–495 (Hsien-cheng tang rules as decided by official delegates, 23 March 1907).

52. Ibid.

53. "Mei-kuo hua-ch'iao Chih-kung t'ang hsüen-yen shu," in Chung-hua Min-kuo, eds., *Chung-hua Min-kuo*, vol. 1, part 10, pp. 260–261.

54. Chung Kun Ai, *My Seventy-Nine Years*, pp. 284–285, 274.

55. *Hsin Chung-kuo pao*, 3, 6, 8, 10, 13, and 22 February 1906; and Lo, *K'ang Yu-wei*, pp. 270, 498.

56. Feng Tzu-yu, *Ko-ming i-shih*, vol. 4, pp. 135–137; Feng Tzu-yu, *Hua-ch'iao*, pp. 142–143; and Feng Ai-ch'un, *Hua-ch'iao*, pp. 118–119.

57. Ibid. (all of the above); Wen Hsiung-fei, "Hsin-hai-ch'ien wo tsai T'an-hsiang-shan T'ung-meng hui han *Tzu-yu hsin-pao* kung-tso te hui-i," in Chung-kuo she-hui (CASS), eds., *Hua-ch'iao yü hsin-hai ko-ming*, pp. 226–227, and Appendix C, pp. 1–3. Just as the Pao-huang hui in San Francisco had used its members who worked for the customs office to try to keep Sun Yat-sen out of the continental United States, so the Pao-huang hui in Hawaii tried to keep Lu Hsin out. Because of the revised rules for administering the exclusion laws that Roosevelt issued in 1905, however, it was decided that a newspaper editor was an educator and Lu was admitted. Since the Pao-huang hui so actively tried to keep Lu out in 1907, it may be presumed that they were involved in the United States authorities' denying entrance to the pro-Sun editor sent over in 1903. See Feng Tzu-yu, *Ko-ming i-shih*, vol. 4, p. 137.

58. Overseas Chinese Penman's Club, *Chinese of Hawaii*, p. 22.

59. Huang Chen-wu, *Hua-ch'iao yü Chung-kuo ko-ming* (1963), pp. 88–89.

60. Huang Fu-luan, *Hua-ch'iao*, pp. 99–108; and Feng Tzu-yu, *Ko-ming i-shih*, vol. 2, p. 272, and vol. 4, p. 176.

61. Huang Chen-wu, *Hua-ch'iao*, pp. 88–89. A letter from Sun Yat-sen to Wu Chih-hui in November 1908 indicates that the *Hua-ying jih-pao* was then still in existence. It must have gone under shortly afterwards. See Chang Ch'i-yün, ed., *Kuo-fu ch'üan-shu*, pp. 419–420.

62. The chairman of the chapter was then an instructor of oriental languages at the University of California, Berkeley (Feng Tzu-yu, *Kuo-ming i-shih*, vol. 4, p. 22; and *Chung Sai Yat Po*, 27 November 1900).

63. The Christians did not object to there being a variety of political groupings, and permitted a multiplicity of views within their own ranks. However, this liberalism prevented them from being a true political group, as they had no consistent ideology (or "party line").

CHAPTER 6

1. Ting Wen-chiang, *Liang Jen-kung*, vol. 1, pp. 287–288; Wu Hsien-tzu, *Chung-kuo Min-chu*, pp. 55–57; and Lo, *K'ang Yu-wei*, p. 209.

2. Edward J. M. Rhoads, *China's Republican Revolution: The Case of Kwangtung,*

1895–1913 (1975), pp. 135–141, 181–182; and Lo, *K'ang Yu-wei*, p. 274 n. 42. In February of 1908, a Japanese ship called the *Daini Tatsu Maru* was found to be shipping arms to Sun Yat-sen's adherents. The Chinese government seized the ship, and the reformers spearheaded a boycott of Japanese goods to protest Japan's interference in China's affairs. Sun's partisans, having ordered the arms to begin with, did not support the boycott. One of the Pao-huang hui leaders who was very active in the boycott was Hsü Ch'in.

3. *Chung Sai Yat Po*, 10 and 24 February 1908; *Ta-t'ung jih-pao*, 18 April 1908; and *Kwok Won Yat Po*, 22 April 1908.

4. *Sai Gai Yat Po*, 2 and 16 April 1908; and Ma, "Big Business Ventures." There was also talk of founding a second line to go from Mexico to China, but it never materialized.

5. Ting Wen-chiang, *Liang Jen-kung*, vol. 1, pp. 187–188; and Wu Hsien-tzu, *Chung-kuo Min-chu*, pp. 55–57. The banning of the Political Information Club was not the end of the reformers' agitation on behalf of a parliament. Liang Ch'i-ch'ao and others formed a secret society to continue the agitation. This secret organization had two representatives from the overseas Chinese. Three times between 1909 and 1911 these two presented petitions or memorials to the court on the question of a constitution and a parliament.

6. Lo, *K'ang Yu-wei*, pp. 275–276 n. 53, and p. 212; and Yen, *Overseas Chinese*, p. 157.

7. Lo, *K'ang Yu-wei*, p. 276 n. 53.

8. Ibid., pp. 211, 215.

9. They approached former Army Chief of Staff General Adna R. Chaffee, Harrison Gray Otis, a New York financier named W. W. Allen, a retired banker named Charles Beech Boothe, and, in 1911, Senator Elihu Root, Senator Philander Knox, President Taft, and so forth. See Armentrout, "American Involvement," pp. 110–143; and Chong, *Americans and Chinese*.

10. *Sai Gai Yat Po*, 2, 17, 18, and 22 April 1908; *Kwok Won Yat Po*, 22 April 1908.

11. *Sai Gai Yat Po*, 2, 16–18, and 21–23 April, 20 and 27 May, and 1 and 9 June 1908; Huang Ting-shih, "Ku-pa te San-min," pp. 312–313; and Wen Hsiung-fei, "Hsin-hai-ch'ien wo tsai T'an-hsiang-shan T'ung-meng hui han *Tzu-yu hsin-pao* kung-tso te hui-i," pp. 223–226. The situation with respect to the Chinese schools and Chinese American students was in contrast to the situation in Southeast Asia, where many of the schools organized by overseas Chinese had already become fronts for pro-Sun enthusiasts. Incidentally, the head of the C.A.C.A. at that time was Huang Po-yao.

12. In 1909, the San Francisco chapter of the Pao-huang hui repeatedly attacked Liu Shih-chi's policies and declared that K'ang, Liang Ch'i-ch'ao, Hsü Ch'in, and the Pao-huang hui in general had had nothing to do with Liu's assassination (*Sai Gai Yat Po*, 12, 18, and 19 November 1909).

13. Lo, *K'ang Yu-wei*, pp. 276–277 n. 53; and Huang Fu-luan, *Hua-ch'iao*, pp. 109–114. For more on the quarrels over money and investments, see K'ang Yu-wei chih Chang Pin-ya tzu-pien han; Chien chiao yin-hang t'ieh-lu ku-yu ke fei-ch'ang t'e-li chang-ch'eng; and especially Yün-kao-hua pu hsien-cheng hui pu-kao shu.

14. Huang Chen-wu, *Hua-ch'iao*, p. 52. Prior to Feng's arrival, Chang Tzu-li (former editor of the Hsing-Chung hui's *T'an-shan hsin-pao* and *Min-sheng pao*) was editor. The Chih-kung t'ang newspaper in Vancouver was called the *Ta-Han pao (Greater Han-Chinese Newspaper).*

15. Ch'en Kuang-min, *Mei-chou*, pp. 55–56; Huang Fu-luan, *Hua-ch'iao*, p. 106; and Feng Tzu-yu, *Ko-ming i-shih*, vol. 4, pp. 172–173.

16. Jeffery Garrigus Barlow, "Vietnam and the Chinese Revolution of 1911" (1973), pp. 193, 208, 212–213; and letters from Sun Yat-sen to Wu Chih-hui, 12 November, and 4, 13, and 16 December 1909; and letter from Sun to Wang Tzu-kuang, 29 October 1909 (all of these letters in Chang Ch'i-yün, ed., *Kuo-fu ch'üan-shu*, pp. 419–421); Yen, *Overseas Chinese*, pp. 215–216; and Huang Chen-wu, *Hua-ch'iao*, p. 157.

17. Letter from Sun Yat-sen to Belgium's T'ung-meng hui, 26 November 1909, in Chang Ch'i-yün, ed., *Kuo-fu ch'üan-shu*, p. 417.

18. Letters from Sun to Wu Chih-hui, 12 and 25 November, and 4, 13, and 16 December 1909, and 3 January 1910, in Chang Ch'i-yün, ed., *Kuo-fu ch'üan-shu*, pp. 419–421.

19. Letter from Sun to Wu Chih-hui, 3 January 1910, in Chang Ch'i-yün, ed., *Kuo-fu ch'üan-shu*, p. 421.

20. Barlow, "Vietnam and the Chinese Revolution," p. 223. As early as 1904, Chinese in the Americas had sometimes referred to Sun as the head of the Ko-ming tang.

21. Feng Tzu-yu, *Ko-ming i-shih*, vol. 4, pp. 173–174; and letters from Sun to Chao Kung-pi, 7 and 20 January 1910, in Chang Ch'i-yün, ed., *Kuo-fu ch'üan-shu*, p. 422.

22. Feng Tzu-yu, *Ko-ming i-shih*, vol. 4, pp. 173–174.

23. Ibid.; and Ch'en K'uang-min, *Mei-chou*, pp. 55–56.

24. Feng Tzu-yu, *Ko-ming i-shih*, vol. 4, pp. 173–175.

25. Ibid.; Michael Gasster, *Chinese Intellectuals and the Revolution of 1911: The Birth of Modern Chinese Radicalism* (1969), pp. 148–149; and letters from Sun to Wu Chih-hui, 12 February and 10 March 1910, and letter from Sun to Chao Kung-pi, 20 January 1910, in Chang Ch'i-yün, ed., *Kuo-fu ch'üan-shu*, p. 423. Barlow, in "Vietnam and the Chinese Revolution," states (p. 223) that in the summer of 1910, after Sun had left the Americas and was in Southeast Asia, he ordered all branches of the T'ung-meng hui to change their name to Ko-ming tang to facilitate an alliance with the Triads in America. Many branches refused to do so. To the extent that this name was used earlier in the Americas, it may be presumed to have been a ploy to keep from antagonizing the Chih-kung t'ang.

26. Feng Tzu-yu, *Ko-ming i-shih*, vol. 3, pp. 144, 150; vol. 4, p. 175; Huang Ting-shih, "Ku-pa te San-min," pp. 313–314; and Wen Hsiung-fei, "Hui-i Hsin-hai-ko-ming ch'ien Chung-kuo T'ung-meng hui tsai Mei ch'eng-li te kuo-ch'eng," in Chung-kuo she-hui (CASS), eds., *Hua-ch'iao yü hsin-hai ko-ming*, pp. 179–192. The three other principal editors were Huang Yün-su, Huang Ch'ao-wu, and Wen Hsiung-fei.

27. Feng Tzu-yu, *Ko-ming i-shih*, vol. 4, p. 175; and Victor G. and Brett de Bary Nee, *Longtime Californ': a Documentary Study of an American Chinatown* (1972), pp. 73–79.

28. Nee, *Longtime Californ'*, pp. 108–109.

29. Feng Tzu-yu, *Ko-ming i-shih*, vol. 4, pp. 176–177; letter from Sun to New York's T'ung-meng hui, April 1910, in Chang Ch'i-yün, ed., *Kuo-fu ch'üan-shu*, p. 424; and Wen Hsiung-fei, "Hsin-hai-ch'ien wo tsai T'an-hsiang-shan T'ung-meng hui han *Tzu-yu hsin-pao* kung-tso te hui-i," pp. 228–251.

30. Ibid.

31. Sun to Hawaii's T'ung-meng hui, June 1910, in Chang Ch'i-yün, ed., *Kuo-fu ch'üan-shu*, p. 426.

32. Sun to Hawaii's T'ung-meng hui, 20 August 1910, in Chang Ch'i-yün, ed., *Kuo-fu ch'üan-shu*, pp. 429–430; and Wen Hsiung-fei, "T'an-hsiang-shan," pp. 228–251. The assassin in question was Wang Ching-wei, later president of the Chinese government under the Japanese.

33. Feng Tzu-yu, *Ko-ming i-shih*, vol. 4, pp. 176–177; and Wen Hsiung-fei, "T'an-hsiang-shan," pp. 228–251.

34. Lo, *K'ang Yu-wei*, pp. 276–277 n. 53.

35. Ibid.; and Sun to America's Chih-kung t'ang, November 1910, in Chang Ch'i-yün, ed., *Kuo-fu ch'üan-shu*, p. 431.

36. Huang Chen-wu, *Hua-ch'iao*, pp. 52–53. Feng claims that most of the younger members of the *Ta-Han pao*'s staff came under his influence and wanted to join the T'ung-meng hui. See Feng Tzu-yu, *Ko-ming i-shih*, vol. 4, p. 178.

37. Huang San-te, *Hung-men*, p. 15.

38. Ibid., pp. 15–16; and Feng Tzu-yu, *Ko-ming i-shih*, vol. 4, p. 178.

39. Huang Chen-wu, *Hua-ch'iao*, pp. 52–53; and Huang Fu-luan, *Hua-ch'iao*, pp. 108–114.

40. Huang Fu-luan, *Hua-ch'iao*, pp. 109–114; *Young China*, 14 April 1911; and Feng Tzu-yu, *Ko-ming i-shih*, vol. 4, p. 176. There is some question as to whether the money raised through mortgaging the buildings was seen as a loan or as a gift. In any case, Sun never paid back any of the money, nor of course did he honor the debts on his revolutionary bonds with the exception of those bought by Chung Yü. For more on Sun's fund-raising travels in Canada in early 1911, see *Young China*, 29 March and 10, 14, 16, and 26 April 1911.

41. Feng Tzu-yu, *Ko-ming i-shih*, vol. 1, pp. 230–232.

42. Ibid.

43. Ibid.

44. Ibid., p. 232.

45. Huang Chen-wu, *Hua-ch'iao*, pp. 52–53; and Huang Fu-luan, *Hua-ch'iao*, pp. 109–114. One of these thirty or so who gave the dinner for Sun was evidently a man of some wealth, as he had founded a textile mill. See Feng Tzu-yu, *Ko-ming i-shih*, vol. 4, p. 178.

46. Sun to Hsieh Chiu, 7 May 1911, in Chang Ch'i-yün, ed., *Kuo-fu ch'üan-shu*, pp. 434–435.

47. Ch'en K'uang-min, *Mei-chou*, pp. 55–56; Huang San-te, *Hung-men*, pp. 20–21; *Young China*, 8, 12, 23, and 30 April and 2–3 May 1911; and Sun to Shao Han-wei, 15 April 1911, in Chang Ch'i-yün, ed., *Kuo-fu ch'üan-shu*, p. 434. This suggested relationship between revolution and personal wealth was turned into a slogan by Feng

Tzu-yu, who declared: "The wealth of the people is constitutional government; if we have constitutional government, the people will be wealthy" *(min-ts'ai hsien-cheng, hsien-cheng min-ts'ai),* where *hsien-cheng* referred to the true constitutionalism that was a product only of revolution (*Young China*, 16 April 1911).

48. The contents and significance of this abbreviated ritual are unclear. Perhaps it did not require them to swear supreme loyalty to Huang San-te. See also *Young China,* 23 and 26 April and 3 and 15 May 1911.

49. Huang Fu-luan, *Hua-ch'iao,* pp. 99–108.

50. Ibid.; Huang Chen-wu, *Hua-ch'iao,* pp. 217–219; *Young China,* 4 and 20 May 1911; Huang San-te, *Hung-men,* p. 23; and Feng Tzu-yu, *Ko-ming i-shih,* vol. 4, p. 177. One account claims that prior to the Wu-ch'ang revolution, Sun promised Huang that after the revolution, he would make Huang governor of Kwangtung province. See *Tsung-ku t'e-k'an* 4 (October? 1961): 8–9.

51. *Young China,* 23 April and 15 May 1911; and Eng and Grant, *Tong War!,* pp. 203–205.

52. Ibid. (all of the above); and *Young China,* 26 April and 3 May 1911.

53. *Young China,* 25, 27, and 30 April, and 2, 4, and 24 May 1911. The independent newspaper in question was the *Wen-jung pao.*

54. *Young China,* 4 May 1911.

55. Ibid.

56. Ibid.

57. *Young China,* 30 April and 2, 3, 8, and 11 May 1911. The three Triad lodges were the Chih-kung t'ang, the An-liang t'ang, and the Hsieh-sheng t'ang (*Young China,* 2 May 1911).

58. Lo, *K'ang Yu-wei,* pp. 275–276; and Feng Tzu-yu, *Ko-ming i-shih,* vol. 4, pp. 175–179. See also *Sai Gai Yat Po,* 14 February and 26 December 1910, and 1 February 1911.

59. *Young China,* 5 May 1911.

60. *Chung Sai Yat Po,* 2 and 6 January and 6 February 1911; and *Sai Gai Yat Po,* 2, 18, and 26 January 1911. Pao-huang hui and Ning-yang leaders repeatedly stressed that they were using "civilized" *(wen-ming)* means of conducting the fight, as if other means were also available to them.

61. *Sai Gai Yat Po,* March 1911; and *Chung Sai Yat Po,* 26 March 1911. The importance of a merchant connection in China has been referred to in chapter 1.

62. *Chung Sai Yat Po,* 6 February 1911; and *Young China,* 29 March and 15 and 21 April 1911.

63. *Young China,* 1, 15, and 21–28 April 1911.

64. Ibid.; and *Young China,* 13 and 21 May 1911, and 12 January 1912. Huei Kin, in *Reminiscences,* pp. 51–55, seems to refer to some of this. His dates, incidentally, are not correct.

65. *Sai Gai Yat Po,* 21 May 1911; and *Young China,* 20–25 May 1911. Even if the anonymous advertisement had been written by the *Young China* editors, several months earlier they would hardly have dared print it.

66. *Young China,* 8, 16, 18, and 27 April, and 2, 13, 17, and 24 May 1911. Local Pao-huang hui branches in the Americas, or at least its Hawaiian branch, as early as 1903 often nominated at least two candidates for every party office, and gave each

party member one vote in the subsequent elections. See *Hsin Chung-kuo pao,* 10 December 1903.

67. *Young China,* 12 and 15–20 April, and 5, 12, 13, and 24 May 1911.

68. *Young China,* 19 March, 10, 23, and 26 April, and 4, 13, 14, 21, and 24 May 1911.

69. Ibid.

70. Lowe, *Father and Glorious Descendant,* pp. 86–120; interview with Mrs. Charles Lee; and Mei-chou Chung-hua Ti-kuo Hsien-cheng hui pin.

71. *Young China,* 12–16 April and 3, 5, 12, 13, 20, and 24 May 1911. One editor in particular, Huang Yün-su, emphasized the anti-Manchu theme.

72. *Young China,* 19 March, 17 April, and 4, 22, and 23 May 1911.

73. Ibid.

74. This interest may have indicated that younger members of certain "fighting tongs" were beginning to join the T'ung-meng hui.

75. *Young China,* 19 March, 25 April, and 2, 3, 20, 23, and 24 May 1911. The T'ung-meng hui member in San Francisco most directly involved in recruiting "Dare-to-Dies" was Huang Po-yao. Revolutionary assassins in San Francisco tried, but failed, to kill a Ch'ing prince on his official visit to the United States early in 1911 (Ch'en K'uang-min, *Mei-chou,* pp. 55–56).

76. Huang Ting-chih, "Ku-pa te San-min," pp. 315–330.

77. Hoy, *Chinese Six Companies,* pp. 1–28; Eng and Grant, *Tong War!,* p. 210; and "Ho-p'ing hui chih li," in author's collection.

78. Information on schools founded by the Pao-huang hui or through its encouragement can be found in Lo, *K'ang Yu-wei,* pp. 181, 193, and 259 n. 9; and in the *Sai Gai Yat Po* editorials. See also Renqiu Yu, "Chinese American Contributions." At least one T'ung-meng hui member in San Francisco established a school to solicit prorevolutionary youth (Feng Tzu-yu, *Ko-ming i-shih,* vol. 2, p. 273). In Hawaii, the Pao-huang hui and T'ung-meng hui established rival schools in February of 1911 (Pang, "Chinese Revolution," pp. 54–55).

79. *Sai Gai Yat Po,* 13 December 1909; Lo, *K'ang Yu-wei,* pp. 193, 196, 205, 271 n. 34, and 272 n. 37; and Yen, "Overseas Chinese," p. 43.

80. *Sai Gai Yat Po,* 13 December 1909 and 15 December 1910.

81. Hoy, *Chinese Six Companies,* pp. 1–28; Ch'en K'uang-min, *Mei-chou,* pp. 77, 84, 284, and 643; and *Young China,* 24 November 1911. Because the Confucian exams were abolished in China in 1905, the *hui-kuan* also had more trouble finding suitable notables to import. Besides, overseas Chinese merchants were rising in social status.

82. Chung Kun Ai, *My Seventy-Nine Years,* pp. 110–111.

83. Feng Tzu-yu, *Ko-ming i-shih,* vol. 4, p. 141; Ch'en K'uang-min, *Mei-chou,* pp. 4–5, 672, and 766; and Huang Ting-chih, "Ku-pa te San-min," pp. 312–330.

84. *Hsin Chung-kuo pao,* 13 October 1908; and *Young China,* 21, 23, 24, and 26–28 November 1911.

85. *Young China,* 24–26 and 28–29 November, and 29 December 1911; Barlow, "Vietnam and the Chinese Revolution," pp. 452–453; Feng Tzu-yu, *Ko-ming i-shih,* vol. 4, p. 142; Huang San-te, *Hung-men,* pp. 22–23; Glick, *Double Ten,* pp. 223–233; and letter from "X" to "My Dear Sir," 25 September 1910, in Joshua B. Powers Collection, Hoover Institution, Stanford, California.

86. *Young China,* 21 November (p. 5), and 22–26 and 28–29 November 1911. The Fresno branch of the Pao-huang hui was loyal to the end (*Young China,* 22 November 1911).

87. Huang Fu-luan, *Hua-ch'iao,* p. 114.

88. *Young China,* 27 and 29 November, and 31 December 1911.

CONCLUSION

1. Beginning in 1912, Chinese in the Americas provided important support for China's air force. This included pilots and airplanes. In fact, the revolutionaries' air force in 1912 consisted of a pioneer aviator who had flown his first self-built airplane in Oakland in 1907. Much later, during World War II, the Chih-kung t'ang trained pilots and purchased and sent airplanes to China for the war against Japan. In the intervening years, Chinese in the Americas made other significant contributions along these lines. See Him Mark Lai, "Growing Wings on the Dragon" (1977); L. Eve Armentrout Ma, "Short Biography of Mr. Taam Wu, Head of the Chee Kong Tong" (1984); and interviews with Charles Mah and Dr. Jung-pang Lo. More information on demonstrations by Chinese in the Americas in favor of China, came from the author's interview with Gee Guey, 1978; and the author's interviews with Ira C. Lee, 1976–1978. During World War II, the China War Relief Association, which operated throughout North America and Hawaii, channeled the energies and money of Chinese in support of their homeland.

2. See, for example, Derk Bodde, *China's Cultural Tradition* (1957), pp. 65–66 and 83–85; K. S. Liew, *Struggle for Democracy: Sung Chiao-jen and the 1911 Chinese Revolution* (1971), pp. 198 and 200–201; and John King Fairbank, *The United States and China,* 3d ed. (1972), pp. 181–186, 197–198, 207–208, 242–253, and 403–411, in which Fairbank discusses the development of liberalism and monolithic political parties in China.

3. I should qualify this statement by noting that in 1908, the Christian *Chung Sai Yat Po* did call for a multiparty system. However, the newspaper did not represent a political party, and its call was ignored by both the Pao-huang hui/Hsien-cheng tang and the T'ung-meng hui (*Chung Sai Yat Po,* 6–24 February 1908).

4. There are a number of works devoted to the lives and thoughts of the leaders of the Pao-huang hui, particularly K'ang Yu-wei and Liang Ch'i-ch'ao. Some attention has also been devoted to the influence of the reformers on very late Ch'ing provincial politics (see P'eng-yuan Chang, "The Constitutionalists," pp. 143–184 in Mary Clabaugh Wright, ed., *China in Revolution: the First Phase, 1900–1913* [1971]). However, not even Ching Hwang Yen, *The Overseas Chinese and the 1911 Revolution,* devotes serious attention to the Pao-huang hui/Hsien-cheng tang as a party.

5. The Pao-huang hui under its more modern name of Chung-kuo min-tzu hsien-cheng tang still exists in the Americas.

6. Liu Shih-chi had loyal supporters in both Kwangtung and Southeast Asia. Furthermore, several prominent members of Southeast Asia's Pao-huang hui left the party between 1901 and 1905 because of their disappointment with the way K'ang Yu-wei was handling money. Several fortuitous events also weakened the reformers and strengthened the revolutionaries in Southeast Asia. For example, an early influential reformer in Sarawak turned to the revolutionaries in 1902 largely because

the British took away his opium concession. And a powerful reformer in Malaya died shortly prior to June 1906, greatly facilitating Sun's organizational task in Ipoh. See Yen, *Overseas Chinese,* pp. 55–56, 63, 84 n. 175; and Png Poh Sung, "Kuomintang in Malaya," p. 5. For the situation in Kwangtung province, see Edward J. M. Rhoads, *China's Republican Revolution.*

7. This interest probably owed something to their own use of the United States court system to overturn prejudicial legislation and counteract prejudicial practices by Americans.

GLOSSARY

An-i t'ang　安益堂
Bow Wong　保皇
Chang Tzu-li　張澤黎
Chao Kung-pi　趙公璧
Chen-hua Shih-yeh Yu-hsien Kung-szu
　振華實業有限公司
Ch'en I-k'an (Ch'en Chi-yen)　陳儀侃
　(陳繼儼)
Ch'en Min-sheng　陳敏生
Chen-nan kuan　鎮南關
Ch'en Ta-chao (Chun Ti Chu)　陳大照
chen-t'an　偵探
Ch'en T'ien-shen (Chan Tin Shan)
　陳天申
Ch'eng Wei-nan　程蔚南
Cheng-wen she　政聞社
Ch'i-Ming pao　啓明報
Chiang Kuan-yün　蔣觀雲
Chih-kung t'ang (Chee Kung Tong)
　致公堂
Chih-ne wen-t'i chih chen chieh-chüeh　支那
　問題之真解決
chih-shih　執事
Chin-lan yü-so　金蘭寓所
Chin Lung　金龍
Chin-shan Kwang-tung Yin-hang
　金山廣東銀行
Chin-shan ta-pu Chung-hua tsung hui-
　kuan ko shen-shih t'ung-chih　金山大
　部中華總會舘各紳士同志
Chiu-kuo hui　救國會
Ch'iu Shu-yüan (Koo Seok-wan)
　邱菽園
Ch'ou-hsiang Chü　籌餉局

ch'ü-k'uei　渠魁
Chu Mao-ts'ai　朱茂才
"Chua-li-chua-hsia"　抓李抓䰖
chün-chu kuei-tsu　君主貴族
chün-ch'üan　君權
chung　忠
chung-ai　忠愛
Chung-ho t'ang　中和堂
Chung-hsi jih-pao (*Chung Sai Yat Po*)
　中西日報
Chung-hua hui-kuan　中華會舘
Chung-hua kung-so　中華公所
Chung-hua kuo-min kung-hui　中華國
　民公會
Chung-hua Shih-yeh Kung ssu　中華實
　業公司
Chung-hua tsung hui-kuan　中華總會舘
Chung-kuo jih-pao　中國日報
Chung-kuo Wei-hsin hui　中國維新會
Chung-kuo Yu-ch'uan Yu-hsien Kung-
　ssu　中國游船有限公司
Chung Pao-hsi　鍾寶僖
Chung Sai Yat Po (*Chung-hsi jih-pao*)　中西
　日報
Chung Shui-yang　鍾水養
Chung Yü (C. K. Ai)　鍾宇
Chü-yüeh tsung-chü　拒約總局
Chung-shan (see also Hsiang-shan)
　中山 (See also 香山)
e　惡
fei-tang　匪黨
Feng Cheng-ch'u ("Little Pete"; Feng
　Ching)　馮正初
Feng-shan　鳳山

fu-hsing 復興

Hakka (K'o-chia) 客家

Han-chien 漢奸

Ho Ch'i-tung (Ho Ch'i?) 何啓東(何啓？)

Ho-ho hui-kuan 合和會舘

Ho Kai (Ho Ch'i; perhaps same as Ho Ch'i-tung?) 何啓

Ho K'uan 何寬

Ho-p'ing Hui 和平會

Ho T'ing-kuang 何廷光

Hsiang-shan (Heung-shan) 香山

hsiang-tzu 香主

hsiao-k'ang 小康

Hsiao Yü-tzu 蕭雨諡

Hsieh Ch'iu 謝秋

Hsieh-sheng t'ang (Hsieh-sheng tsung kung-hui) 協勝堂(協勝總公會)

Hsien-cheng tang 憲政黨

Hsin Chung-kuo pao 新中國報

Hsin-hui (Sun-wui) 新會

Hsin Kwangtung 新廣東

Hsin-ning (Sun-ning) 新寧(新寧)

Hsin-ta-lu yu-chi 新大陸遊記

hsin-tang 新黨

Hsü Chih-ch'en 許直臣

Hsü Shih-ch'in (Hsü Ch'in) 徐士芹 (徐勤)

Hsü Wei-ching 徐為經

Hua-ch'i T'ang-jen hui 花旗唐人會

Hua-ying jih-pao 華英日報

Huang (Wong) 黃

Huang Ch'ao-wu 黃超五

Huang Chi-yao 黃吉耀

Huang Hsüan-lin 黃宣林

Huang K'uan-cho (Wong Foon-chuck) 黃寬焯

Huang Liang (Wong Leong) 黃亮

Huang Po-yao 黃伯耀

Huang San-te (Wong Sam Duck) 黃三德

Huang Yün-su 黃芸蘇

hui-fu Chung-hua 恢復中華

hui-kuan 會舘

Hung Ch'üan-fu 洪全福

Hung-men 洪門

Hung-men ch'ou-hsiang chü 洪門籌餉局

Hung-shun t'ang 洪順堂

i 義

I-hsing hui 義興會

I-hsing kung-szu 義興公司

i-hui 議會

i-yuan 議員

jeh-hsüeh ch'ing-nien 熱血青年

jen 仁

Jen-ho hui-kuan (Yan Wo Company) 人和會舘

Jih-hsin pao 日新報

Jun Wah Mining Company (Chen-hua shih-yeh kung-szu) 振華實業公司

K'ai-p'ing (Hoi-ping) 開平

Kan-ch'eng Hsüeh-hsiao 干城學校

kan-ssu t'uan 敢死團

K'ang 康

Kang-chou hui-kuan (Kong Chow Company) 岡州會舘

K'ang T'ung-pi 康同璧

K'ang T'ung-wei 康同薇

Ko-chih shu-yüan 格致書院

Ko-lau Hui 哥老會

ko-ming 革命

ko-ming chih-shih 革命志士

Ko-ming chün 革命軍

Ko-ming tang 革命黨

K'o-shang hui-kuan 客商會舘

K'uang (Kwong) 鄺

Kuang-fu hui 光復會

K'ung Yang 孔陽

Kuo-an Hui-kuan 國安會舘

kuo-min 國民

Kuo-min chiu-chi chü 國民救濟局

Kuo-min hsien-cheng hui 國民憲政會

Kwok Won Yat Po (*Kuo-hun jih-pao*) 國魂日報

Li 李

Li Ch'i-hui (Dr. Li Khai Fai) 李啓輝

Li Fu-chi (Lee Fuk Ki) 李福基

Li Shih-nan 李是男

Liang 梁

Liang Ch'i-t'ien 梁啓田

Liang Yin-nan 梁陰南

Liu Ch'eng-yü 劉成禺

Liu Hsing (Lew Hing) 劉興

Liu Shih-chi 劉士驥
Lu Feng-shan (Look Poong Shan) 陸蓬山
Lu Hsin 盧信
Lung-chi pao 隆記報
Lung-kang ch'in-i kung-so (Lung Kung Tin Yee Association) 龍岡親義公所
Ma Hsiao-chin 馬小進
Mao Wen-ming 毛文明
min-chu 民主
min-ch'üan 民權
min-chün 民軍
Min-sheng pao 民生報
min-tang 民黨
min-ts'ai hsien-cheng, hsien-cheng min-ts'ai 民財憲政, 憲政民財
Nan-hai (Nam hoi) 南海
Ning-i shang-wu kung-so 寧邑商務公所
Ning-yang hui-kuan (Ning Yeung Company) 寧陽會舘
Ou Chü-chia 歐榘甲
Pa-shu 巴梳
P'an-yü (Pun-yu) 番禺
pao-chiao 保教
Pao-chiu Ta-Ch'ing Kuang-hsü huang-ti hui 保救大淸光緒皇帝會
Pao-huang Hui 保皇會
Pao-kuo Hui 保國會
Pao-shang chü 保商局
Pao-shang hui 保商會
Piao-hsüeh-ti (Boise) 表雪地
p'ing-chün ti-ch'üan 平均地權
p'ing-ho shou-tuan 平和手段
Ping-kung t'ang 秉公堂
Punti 本地
Sai Gai Yat Po (*Shih-chieh jih-pao*) 世界日報
San-ho hui 三和會
San-i (Sam Yap; Sam Yup) 三邑
San-shui 三水
San-tien hui 三點會
shan-t'ang 善堂
shang 商
Shang-wu kung szu 商務公司
Shao-i kung-so 昭益公所

Shao-nien Chung-kuo ch'en-pao (*Young China*) 少年中國晨報
Shao-nien hsüeh-she 少年學社
Shao-nien hsüeh-she hsün-k'an 少年學社旬刊
Shen pao 申報
shen-shang 紳商
Sheng-fa kung-szu 生發公司
Shih-chieh jih pao (*Sai Gai Yat Po*) 世界日報
shih-hsing min-sheng chu-i 實行民生主義
shu-fu 叔父
So-yüan t'ang (Soo Yuen Benevolent Assn.) 遡源堂
Sun 孫
Sun Mei (Sun Te-chang) 孫眉(孫德彰)
Sun Wen Yin-chih 孫文銀紙
Sung Chü-jen 宋居仁
Szu-i (Sai Yap; Ssu Yup) 四邑
Ta Ch'ing shu-yüan 大淸書院
Ta-Han pao 大漢報
ta-ko 大哥
ta-lao 大老
Ta-lung-t'ou 大龍頭
ta-t'ung 大同
Ta-t'ung hsüeh-hsiao 大同學校
Ta-t'ung jih-pao (*Tai Tung Yat Po*) 大同日報
T'ai-shan (Toi-shan; formerly Hsin-ning) 台山 (formerly 新寧)
T'an Chin-yung chih shih 譚錦鏞之事
T'an-shan hsin-pao 檀山新報
T'an Shu-pin (Dr. Tom Shee Bin) 譚樹彬
tang 黨
T'ang 唐
T'ang Ch'iung-ch'ang 唐瓊昌
T'ang Chueh-tun 湯覺頓
T'ang Hsiung 唐雄
T'ang Ts'ai-chih 唐才質
T'ao Ch'eng-chang 陶成章
te 德
Teng I-yün 鄧翼雲
Teng Yin-nan (Teng Sung-sheng) 鄧蔭南(鄧松盛)

Ti-kuo Hsien-cheng tang 帝國憲政黨
T'ien-p'ing 天平
T'ien-ti hui 天地會
Tsao-ch'ing hui-kuan (Shew Hing
  Company) 肇慶會舘
Tseng Ch'ang-fu (Tseng Fu?) 曾長福
  （曾福？）
Tseng T'ing-hui 曾庭輝
Ts'ui-sheng t'ang (Suey Sing Tong)
  萃勝堂
tso-fan 作反
Ts'ui T'ung-yüeh 崔通約
tsun ti-kuo 尊帝國
tsung 總
tsung-li 總理
tsu-shui 租稅
T'ung-hsing kung-szu 同興公司
T'ung-yüan hui (Chinese American
  Citizens' Alliance) 同源會
Tzu-li Chün 自立軍
tzu-yu 自由
Tzu-yu hsin-pao 自由新報
Wang Tzu-kuang 王子匡
wei-hsin 維新
Wei-hsin Hui 維新會

Wei-hsin pao 維新報
Wei Ting-kao 魏鼎高
Wen-hsien pao 文憲報
Wen-hsing pao (*Mon Hing Po*) 文興報
Wen Hsiung-fei 溫雄飛
wen-ming 文明
Wen jung pao 文榮報
Wen Sheng-ts'ai 溫生財
wu-chün wu-fu 無君無父
Wu P'an-chao (Ng Poon Chew)
  伍盤照
wu-yeh yu-min 無業遊民
Wu Yü-yen 伍于衍
Ya-ching (pen name of Wu Yü-yen)
  亞競
Yang-ho hui-kuan (Yeong Wo
  Company) 陽和會舘
Yang Wei-pin 楊蔚彬
Yang Wen-na 楊文納
Yang Wen-pin 楊文炳
Yang-wen Cheng-wu Szu 洋文政務司
Yeh En (Yip On, Yeh Hui-po) 葉恩
  （葉惠伯）
Yü (Yee) 余
Yu Lieh 尤列

BIBLIOGRAPHY

A SHORT ESSAY ON SOURCES

The literature on Chinese in the Americas, on Chinese political parties, and on overseas Chinese for the period in question is voluminous. Furthermore, this literature is growing as new research is conducted on various aspects of all three topics. As an aid to the interested reader, I shall point out the works that I have found to be broadest and most useful. Preference has been given to works in the English language.

On the topic of Chinese in North America, the two best and most comprehensive works are Thomas Chinn, H. Mark Lai, and Philip P. Choy, eds., *A History of the Chinese in California: A Syllabus* (San Francisco: Chinese Historical Society of America, 1982), and Edgar Wickberg et al., *From China to Canada: A History of the Chinese Communities in Canada* (Toronto: McClellan and Stewart, Ltd., 1982). The first, which in fact reaches beyond California, emphasizes the nineteenth and early twentieth centuries. The second, somewhat better integrated, is slightly weighted towards the present century. Rose Hum Lee's *The Chinese in the United States of America* (Hong Kong: University of Hong Kong Press, 1960) and Corinne Hoexter's *From Canton to California: The Epic of Chinese Immigration* (New York: Four Winds Press, 1976) also deserve mention as general works. Ping Chiu, *Chinese Labor in California, 1850–1880* (Madison: State Historical Society of Wisconsin, 1963), and Charles McClain, "The Chinese Struggle for Civil Rights in 19th Century America," in *Law and History Review* 3 (1985), although somewhat specialized, are also worth consulting. On the topic of negotiations between China and the United States relative to Chinese Exclusion, and its effects on Chinese in the United States, see Henry Shih-shan Tsai, *China and the Overseas Chinese in the United States, 1868–1911* (Fayetteville: University of Arkansas Press, 1983), and Michael H. Hunt, *The Making of a Special Relationship: The United States and China to 1914* (New York: Columbia University Press, 1983). Finally, Him Mark Lai, *A History Reclaimed* (Los Angeles: Asian American Studies Center of the University of California, Los Angeles, 1986) is a good, annotated bibliography of extant Chinese-language materials written by and about Chinese in America.

There is no really good work devoted exclusively to the Chinese in Hawaii, but Andrew W. Lind, *Hawaii's People* (Honolulu: University of Hawaii Press, 1955), contains much relevant demographic information. For overseas Chinese in all of the "Americas," including North and South America and Hawaii, the best single source is the handbook by Ch'en K'uang-min, *Mei-chou hua-ch'iao t'ung-chien* (New York: Overseas Chinese Culture Publishing Co., 1950). Liang Ch'i-ch'ao, *Hsin-ta-lu yu-chi*, written in 1903 and published in Shen Yün-lung, ed., *Chin-tai Chung-kuo shih-liao tsung-k'an* (Taipei: Wen-hai Ch'u-pan She, 1967), and its shorter companion, *Hsia-wei-i yu-chi* (written in 1900), contain excellent, detailed information on Chinese in North America and Hawaii. I have translated a small portion of the *Hsin-ta-lu yu-chi* in *BC Studies* 59 (Autumn 1983): L. Eve Armentrout Ma, "A Chinese Statesman in Canada, 1903: Translation from the Travel Journal of Liang Ch'i-ch'ao."

On the subject of the activities and development in the Americas of the early Chinese political parties, there is abundant data on the Pao-huang hui/Hsien-cheng tang and its principal leaders, K'ang Yu-wei and Liang Ch'i-ch'ao, in Jung-pang Lo, *K'ang Yu-wei, a Biography and a Symposium* (Tucson: University of Arizona Press, 1967). Liang Ch'i-ch'ao's aforementioned *Hsin-ta-lu yu-chi* should also be consulted. Shanghai Shih Wen-wu Pao-kuan Wei-yüan Hui, ed., *K'ang Yu-wei yü Pao-huang hui* (Shanghai: Jen-min Ch'u-pan She, 1982), contains much valuable primary material on these topics. Robert Worden, "A Chinese Reformer in Exile: The North American Phase of the Travels of K'ang Yu-wei, 1899–1909" (Ph.D. thesis, Georgetown University, 1972), gives details of K'ang's trips to North America. Also, my "A Chinese Association in North America: The Pao-huang Hui from 1899 to 1904," in *Ch'ing-shih wen-t'i* 3, no. 9 (November 1978), covers the early development of that party.

Sun Yat-sen has been the subject of many books and articles. Perhaps the most relevant for our purposes here is Harold Z. Schiffrin's early book, *Sun Yat-sen and the Origins of the Chinese Revolution* (Berkeley: University of California Press, 1968). Schiffrin's later book, *Sun Yat-sen: Reluctant Revolutionary* (Boston: Little, Brown and Co., 1980), and C. Martin Wilbur's *Sun Yat-sen: Frustrated Patriot* (New York: Columbia University Press, 1976) also deserve mention. As for the political parties with which Sun was associated, especially the Hsing-Chung hui and T'ung-meng hui, apart from biographies of Sun the best works on the topic are the several (Chinese-language) books by Feng Tzu-yu, along with Jeffery Garrigus Barlow's (English-language) "Vietnam and the Chinese Revolution of 1911" (Ph.D. thesis, University of California, Berkeley, 1973). A book and an article by Ching Hwang Yen can also be consulted with profit: *The Overseas Chinese and the 1911 Revolution* (Oxford University Press, 1976) and "Overseas Chinese Nationalism in Singapore and Malaya, 1877–1912" (*Modern Asian Studies* 16, part 3). Both concentrate on Southeast Asia. Chang Ch'i-yün, ed., *Kuo-fu ch'üan-shu* (Taipei: Kuo-fang Yen-chiu Yüan, 1963) is the best published source of primary material.

The several articles in Mary Clabaugh Wright, ed., *China in Revolution: The First Phase, 1900–1913* (New Haven: Yale University Press, 1971), provide a good overview of the late Ch'ing, its collapse, and the revolution of 1911 as seen separate from the political parties. Jerome B. Grieder, *Intellectuals and the State in Modern China: A Narrative History* (New York: The Free Press, 1981), contains a good, general discussion of the intellectual context in which the revolution took place (with analyses of the proposals of K'ang, Liang, and Sun). Those interested in a modern (mainland) Chinese view of the 1911 revolution presented in the English language will find it in several of the articles in Eto Shinkichi and Harold Z. Schiffrin, eds., *The 1911 Revolution in China* (Tokyo: Tokyo University Press, 1984).

General works on overseas Chinese emphasize Chinese in Southeast Asia, since that is where most of them lived (and still do live). G. William Skinner's *Chinese Society in Thailand: An Analytical History* (Ithaca: Cornell University Press, 1957), William E. Willmott's *The Chinese in Cambodia* (University of British Columbia Press, 1967), Edgar Wickberg's *The Chinese in Philippine Life, 1850–1898* (New Haven: Yale University Press, 1965), and Maurice Freedman's "Immigrants and Associations: Chinese in Nineteenth Century Singapore," in *Comparative Studies in Society and History* 3 (1960–1961) are standard works on this topic. Lawrence W. Crissman, in "The Segmentary Structure of Urban Overseas Chinese Communities," in *Man*, n.s., 2, no. 2 (June 1967), has provided an interpretive framework for the development of the social structure of overseas Chinese communities. It is only fair to mention that his interpretation has been questioned by this author in my "Urban Chinese at the Sinitic Frontier: Social Organizations in United States' Chinatowns, 1849–1898," in *Modern Asian Studies* 17, no. 1 (1983). Finally, Sing-wu Wang, in his recent *The Organization of Chinese Emigration, 1848–1888* (San Francisco: Chinese Materials Center, 1978), has dealt with the means by which Chinese emigrated from China in the nineteenth century, with the emphasis on emigration to Southeast Asia.

NOTE ON ARRANGEMENT

In some cases it has been difficult to separate published works according to language, for a number of works are written partly in English and partly in Chinese. Where this is the case, I have classified them according to whichever language predominates. Where an author writing in Chinese has given his work an English language title, I have used it. If an author of a published Chinese-language work has chosen his own romanization for his name, I have followed the author's rendering. I have not divided archival material according to language.

WESTERN LANGUAGE SOURCES

Ai, Chung Kun. *My Seventy-Nine Years in Hawaii*. Hong Kong: Cosmorama Pictorial Publishers, 1960.

Armentrout, L. Eve (see also Armentrout-Ma, and Ma). "American Involvement in Chinese Revolutionary Activities, 1893–1913." M.A. thesis, California State University, Hayward, 1972.

———. "The Canton Rising of 1902–1903: Reformers, Revolutionaries, and the Second Taiping." *Modern Asian Studies* 10, no. 1 (January 1976).

———. "Conflict and Contact between the Chinese and Indigenous Communities in San Francisco, 1900–1911." In Chinese Historical Society of America, eds. *The Life, Influence and the Role of the Chinese in the United States, 1776–1960*, pp. 55–70. San Francisco: Chinese Historical Society of America, 1976.

Armentrout-Ma, L. Eve (see also Armentrout, and Ma). "A Chinese Association in North America: the Pao-huang hui from 1899 to 1904." *Ch'ing-shih wen-t'i* 3, no. 9 (November 1978).

———. "Big and Medium Businesses of Chinese Immigrants to the United States, 1850–1890: An Outline." *Bulletin (of the Chinese Historical Society of America)* 13, no. 7 (September 1978).

———. "Chinese in California's Fishing Industry, 1850–1950." *California History* 60, no. 2 (Summer 1981).

———. "Urban Chinese at the Sinitic Frontier: Social Organizations in United States Chinatowns, 1849–1898." *Modern Asian Studies* 17, no. 1 (February 1983).

Barlow, Jeffery Garrigus. "Vietnam and the Chinese Revolution of 1911." Ph.D. thesis, University of California, Berkeley, 1973.

Barth, Gunther. *Bitter Strength: A History of the Chinese in the United States, 1850–1870.* Cambridge, Massachusetts: Harvard University Press, 1971.

Bodde, Derk. *China's Cultural Tradition.* New York: Holt, Rinehart and Winston, 1957.

Chan, Anthony B. *Gold Mountain: The Chinese in the New World.* Vancouver: New Star Books, 1983.

Chang, Hao. *Liang Ch'i-ch'ao and Intellectual Transition in China, 1890–1907.* Cambridge, Massachusetts: Harvard University Press, 1971.

Chapin, Frederick. "Homer Lea." Joshua B. Powers Collection, Hoover Institution for War, Revolution and Peace, Stanford, California. Mimeo.

Cheng, Shelley. "A History of the T'ung-meng hui (1905–1912)." Ph.D. thesis, University of Washington, 1961.

———. "The Provincial Groupings of the T'ung-meng Hui." University of Washington Modern Chinese History Project, Seattle, 1962. Mimeo.

Chesneaux, Jean. *Les sociétés secrètes en Chine.* Paris: René Juilliard, 1965.

Chinn, Thomas W., H. Mark Lai, and Philip P. Choy, eds. *A History of the Chinese in California: A Syllabus.* San Francisco: Chinese Historical Society of America, 1973.

Chiu, Ping. *Chinese Labor in California, 1850–1880: An Economic Study.* Madison: State Historical Society of Wisconsin for the Department of History, University of Wisconsin, 1963.

Chong, Key Ray. *Americans and Chinese Reform and Revolution, 1898–1922: The Role of Private Citizens in Diplomacy.* Lanham, Maryland: University Press of America, 1984.

Chung, Sue Fawn. "The Image of the Empress Dowager Tzu-hsi." In Paul A. Cohen and John E. Schrecher, eds. In *Reform in Nineteenth-Century China.* Cambridge, Massachusetts: East Asian Research Center of Harvard University, 1976.

Coolidge, Mary Roberts. *Chinese Immigration.* New York: Henry Holt and Co., 1909.

Courtney, William J. *San Francisco's Anti-Chinese Ordinances, 1850–1900.* San Francisco: R and E Research Associates, 1971.

Crane, Daniel M., and Thomas A. Breslin. *An Ordinary Relationship: American Opposition to Republican Revolution in China.* Miami: University Presses of Florida, 1986.

Crissman, Lawrence W. "The Segmentary Structure of Urban Overseas Chinese Communities." *Man*, n.s. 2, no. 2 (June 1967).

Cullin, Stewart. *The Gambling Games of the Chinese in America*. Las Vegas: Gambler's Book Club, 1972.

————. "The I Hing or 'Patriotic Rising' "; "Chinese Secret Societies"; and "Customs of Chinese in America," an 1887 series of articles reprinted as one work. San Francisco: R and E Research Associates, 1970.

Daily Alta. San Francisco, 1852.

Dillon, Richard. *The Hatchet Men: San Francisco's Chinatown in the Days of the Tong Wars, 1880-1906*. New York: Ballantine Books, 1962.

Dinegar, Captain Avery, and (?) Kolb. "The Bitter Tea of Homer Lea." Joshua B. Powers Collection, Hoover Institution for War, Revolution, and Peace, Stanford, California. Mimeo.

Dobie, Charles Caldwell. *San Francisco's Chinatown*. New York: D. Appleton-Century, 1936.

Eastman, Lloyd E. *Family, Fields and Ancestors: Constancy and Change in China's Social and Economic History, 1550-1949*. New York: Oxford University Press, 1988.

Eng Ying Gong and Bruce Grant. *Tong War!* New York: N. L. Brown, 1930.

Esherick, Joseph W. *Reform and Revolution in China: The 1911 Revolution in Hunan and Hubei*. Berkeley: University of California Press, 1976.

Eto, Shinkichi, and Harold Z. Schiffrin. *The 1911 Revolution in China*. Tokyo: Tokyo University Press, 1984.

Fairbank, John King. *The United States and China*. 3d ed. Cambridge, Massachusetts: Harvard University Press, 1972.

Fewsmith, Joseph. *Party, State and Local Elites in China: Merchant Organizations and Politics in Shanghai, 1890-1930*. Honolulu: University of Hawaii Press, 1985.

Freedman, Maurice. "Immigrants and Associations: Chinese in Nineteenth Century Singapore." *Comparative Studies in Society and History* 3 (1960-61).

Gasster, Michael. *Chinese Intellectuals and the Revolution of 1911: The Birth of Modern Chinese Radicalism*. Seattle: University of Washington Press, 1969.

Gibson, Rev. O. *The Chinese in America*. Cincinnati: Hitchcock and Walden, 1877.

Glick, Carl. *Double Ten: Captain O'Banion's Story of the Chinese Revolution*. London and New York: McGraw-Hill, 1945.

Grieder, Jerome B. *Intellectuals and the State in Modern China: A Narrative History*. New York: The Free Press, 1981.

Hoexter, Corinne K. *From Canton to California: The Epic of Chinese Immigration*. New York: Four Winds Press, 1976.

Hoy, William. *The Chinese Six Companies*. San Francisco: Chinese Consolidated Benevolent Association (Chinese Six Companies), 1942.

Hsiao, Kung-chuan. "K'ang Yu-wei and Confucianism." *Monumenta Serica* 18 (1959): 96–212.

Hui, Kin. *Reminiscences*. New York: San Yu Press, 1932.

Hunt, Michael H. *The Making of a Special Relationship: The United States and China to 1914*. New York: Columbia University Press, 1983.

Johnson, Chalmers. *Peasant Nationalism and Communist Power: The Emergence of Revolutionary China, 1937-1945*. Stanford: Stanford University Press, 1962.

Lai, Him Mark. "Growing Wings on the Dragon." *East-West,* 20 January 1977.
————. *A History Reclaimed.* Los Angeles: Asian American Studies Center of the University of California, Los Angeles, 1986.
Lai, Him Mark, and Philip P. Choi. *Outline History of the Chinese in America.* San Francisco: Chinese American Studies Planning Group, 1973.
Lea, Homer. *The Valor of Ignorance.* New York and London: Harper & Bros., 1909.
Lee, C. Y. *Days of the Tong Wars.* New York: Ballantine, 1974.
Lee, Rose Hum. *The Chinese in the United States of America.* Hongkong: Hongkong University Press, 1960.
Levenson, Joseph R. *Liang Ch'i-ch'ao and the Mind of Modern China.* Cambridge, Massachusetts: Harvard University Press, 1959.
Liang, Phoebe Meng Hsuan. "The Influence of K'ang Yu-wei and Liang Ch'i-ch'ao in the Making of New China." M. A. thesis, University of Hawaii, 1933.
Liew, K. S. *Struggle for Democracy: Sung Chiao-jen and the 1911 Chinese Revolution.* Berkeley and Los Angeles: University of California Press, 1971.
Lind, Andrew W. *Hawaii's People.* Honolulu: University of Hawaii Press, 1980.
Liu, Kwang-ching. *Americans and Chinese: A Historical Essay and a Bibliography.* Cambridge, Massachusetts: Harvard University Press, 1963.
Lo, Jung-pang. *K'ang Yu-wei, a Biography and a Symposium.* Tucson: University of Arizona Press, 1967.
Los Angeles Times. 1903.
Lowe, Pardee. *Father and Glorious Descendant.* Boston: Little, Brown & Co., 1943.
Lyman, Stanford M. *Chinese Americans.* New York: Random House, 1974.
Lyman, Stanford M., W. E. Willmott, and Berching Ho. "Rules of a Chinese Secret Society in British Columbia." *Bulletin of the School of Oriental and African Studies* 27, part 3 (1964): 530–539.
Ma, L. Eve Armentrout (see also Armentrout, and Armentrout-Ma). "The Big Business Ventures of Chinese in North America, 1850–1930." In Jinny Lim, ed. *The Chinese American Experience.* San Francisco: Chinese Historical Society of America and Chinese Culture Foundation of San Francisco, 1984.
———— and Jeong-Huei Ma. *The Chinese of Oakland: Unsung Builders.* Oakland: Oakland Chinese History Research Committee, 1982.
————. "A Chinese Statesman in Canada, 1903: Translation from the Travel Journal of Liang Ch'i-ch'ao." *BC Studies (British Columbia Studies)* 59 (Autumn 1983).
————. "Fellow-Regional Associations in the Ch'ing Dynasty: Organizations in Flux for Mobile People. A Preliminary Survey." *Modern Asian Studies* 18, no. 2 (June 1984).
————. "Short Biography of Mr. Taam Wu, Head of the Chee Kong Tong." *Annals of the Chinese Historical Society of the Pacific Northwest* (Fall 1984).
————. "Social Organization of Chinatowns in North America and Hawaii in the 1890s." In Lee Lai To, ed., *Early Chinese Immigrant Societies: Case Studies from North America and British Southeast Asia,* pp. 159–185. Singapore: Heinemann Asia, 1988.
McClain, Charles. "The Chinese Struggle for Civil Rights in Nineteenth Century America." *Law and History Review* 3 (1985).
————. "Of Medicine, Race and American Law: The Bubonic Plague Outbreak

of 1900." *Law and Social Inquiry: Journal of the American Bar Association* 13, no. 3 (Summer 1988).

McClellan, Robert. *The Heathen Chinese.* Cleveland: Ohio State University Press, 1971.

Mann, Susan. *Local Merchants and the Chinese Bureaucracy, 1750-1950.* Stanford: Stanford University Press, 1987.

Michael, Franz. *The Taiping Rebellion.* Seattle and London: University of Washington Press, 1972.

Morgan, W. P. *Triad Societies in Hong Kong.* Hongkong: Government Press, 1960.

Nee, Victor G., and Brett de Bary Nee. *Longtime Californ': A Documentary Study of an American Chinatown.* New York: Pantheon Books, 1972.

New York Tribune. 1900.

Pang, Loretta O. Q. "The Chinese Revolution: Its Activities and Meaning in Hawaii." Honors B.A. thesis, University of Hawaii, 1963.

Png Poh Seng. "The Kuomintang in Malaya, 1912-1941." *Journal of Southeast Asian History* 2, no. 1 (March 1961): 1-32.

Pomerantz, Linda. "The Chinese Bourgeoisie and the Anti-Chinese Movement in the United States, 1850-1905." *Amerasia* 11, no. 1 (Spring/Summer 1984): 1-34.

Price, Don C. *Russia and the Roots of the Chinese Revolution, 1896-1911.* Cambridge, Massachusetts: Harvard University Press, 1974.

Rankin, Mary Backus. *Early Chinese Revolutionaries: Radical Intellectuals in Shanghai and Chekiang, 1902-1911.* Cambridge, Massachusetts: Harvard University Press, 1971.

Rhoads, Edward J. M. *China's Republican Revolution: The Case of Kwangtung, 1895-1913.* Cambridge, Massachusetts: Harvard University Press, 1975.

Roosevelt, Theodore. *African and European Addresses.* New York and London: G. P. Putnam's Sons, 1910.

San Francisco Examiner. 1900.

San Francisco Examiner and Chronicle. 1973.

San Francisco Morning Call. 1900.

Saxton, Alexander. *The Indispensable Enemy: Labor and the Anti-Chinese Movement in California.* Berkeley and Los Angeles: University of California Press, 1971.

Schiffrin, Harold Z. *Sun Yat-sen and the Origins of the Chinese Revolution.* Berkeley and Los Angeles: University of California Press, 1968.

————. *Sun Yat-sen: Reluctant Revolutionary.* Boston: Little, Brown and Co., 1980.

Sellers, Charles, Henry May, and Neil R. McMillen. *A Synopsis of American History.* Vol. 2. Chicago: Rand McNally, 1974.

Senate of the State of California. *Chinese Immigration: The Social, Moral, and Political Effect: Testimony (1876).* Sacramento: Government Printing Office, 1876.

Skinner, George W. *Chinese Society in Thailand: An Analytical History.* Ithaca: Cornell University Press, 1957.

————. "Marketing and Social Structure in Rural China," part 1. *Journal of Asian Studies* 24, no. 1 (November 1964).

Smythe, Joan E. "The Tzu-li Hui: Some Chinese and Their Rebellion." *Papers on China* 12 (December 1958): 51-68.

Sung, Mrs. William Z. L. "A Pioneer Chinese Family." In Chinese Historical

Society of America, ed. *The Life, Influence and the Role of the Chinese in the United States, 1776-1960*, pp. 287-291. San Francisco: Chinese Historical Society of America, 1976.

Tang, Vincent. "Chinese Women Immigrants and the Two-Edged Sword of Habeas Corpus." In Jinny Lim, ed. *The Chinese American Experience: Papers from the Second Annual Conference on Chinese American Studies*, pp. 48-56. San Francisco: Chinese Historical Society of America and Chinese Culture Center of San Francisco, 1982.

Thompson, L. G., trans. *Ta T'ung Shu: The One World Philosophy of K'ang Yu-wei*. London: Allen and Unwin, 1958.

Trauner, Joan B. "The Chinese as Medical Scapegoats in San Francisco, 1870-1905." *California History* 62, no. 1 (Spring, 1978): 70-87.

Tsai, Shih-shan Henry. *China and the Overseas Chinese in the United States, 1868-1911*. Fayetteville: University of Arkansas Press, 1983.

United States Department of State. *Papers Relating to the Foreign Relations of the United States, 1902*. Washington, D.C.: Government Printing Office, 1903.

Wakeman, Frederic, Jr. *The Fall of Imperial China*. New York: The Free Press, 1975.

————. "Les sociétés secrètes du Guangdong (1800-1856)." In Jean Chesneaux, Feiling Davis, and Nguyen Nguyet Ho, eds. *Movements populaires et sociétés secrètes en Chine aux XIXieme et XXieme siècles*, pp. 90-116. Paris: Librarie François Maspero, 1970.

————. *Strangers at the Gate: Social Disorder in South China, 1839-1861*. Berkeley: University of California Press, 1966.

Wang, Sing-wu. *The Organization of Chinese Emigration, 1848-1888*. San Francisco: Chinese Materials Center, 1978.

Wickberg, Edgar. *The Chinese in Philippine Life, 1850-1898*. New Haven: Yale University Press, 1965.

Wickberg, Edgar, et al. *From China to Canada: A History of the Chinese Communities in Canada*. Toronto: McClelland and Stewart, Ltd., 1982.

Wilbur, C. Martin. *Sun Yat-sen: Frustrated Patriot*. New York: Columbia University Press, 1976.

Willmott, William E. *The Chinese in Cambodia*. Vancouver: University of British Columbia Press, 1967.

Worden, Robert. "A Chinese Reformer in Exile: The North American Phase of the Travels of K'ang Yu-wei, 1899-1909." Ph.D. thesis, rough draft, Georgetown University, 1971.

Wright, Mary Clabaugh. "Introduction: The Rising Tide of Change." In Mary Clabaugh Wright, ed. *China in Revolution: The First Phase, 1900-1913*, pp. 1-63. New Haven: Yale University Press, 1971.

Wynne, Mervyn Llewelyn. *Triad and Tabut*. Singapore: Government Printing Office, 1941.

Yen, Ching Hwang. "The Overseas Chinese and Late Ch'ing Economic Modernization." *Modern Asian Studies* 16, no. 2 (April 1982).

————. *The Overseas Chinese and the 1911 Revolution*. Kuala Lumpur: Oxford University Press, 1976.

————. "Overseas Chinese Nationalism in Singapore and Malaya, 1877–1912." *Modern Asian Studies* 16, no. 3 (July 1982).

Yong Ching Fatt. "A Preliminary Study of Chinese Leadership in Singapore, 1900–1941." *Journal of Southeast Asian History* 9, no. 2 (September 1968): 258–285.

Yu, Renqiu. "Chinese American Contributions to the Educational Development of Toisan, 1910–1940." *Amerasia* 10, no. 1 (Spring/Summer 1983): 47–72.

CHINESE LANGUAGE SOURCES

Anonymous. *Chung-kuo pang-hui shih* 中國幫會史 (History of Chinese secret societies). Shanghai: Hsien-tai Ch'u-pan Kung-szu, 1969.

Chang Ch'i-yün 張其昀, ed. *Kuo-fu ch'üan-shu* 國父全書 (Collected letters of Sun Yat-sen). Taipei: Kuo-fang Yen-chiu Yüan, 1963.

Chang Dai Chow 鄭帝秋, ed. *Ket On Society 100th Anniversary August 17, 1969*. Honolulu: Ket On Society, 1969.

Chang P'eng-yüan 張朋園. *Liang Ch'i-ch'ao yü Ch'ing-chi ko-ming* 梁啓超與清季革命 (Liang Ch'i-ch'ao and the 1911 revolution). Taiwan (Nan-kang): Chung-yang Yen-chiu Yüan Chin-tai Shih Yen-chiu So, 1964.

Chang Ts'un-wu 張存武. *Chung-Mei kung-yüeh feng-ch'ao* 中美工約風潮 (History of the Chinese-American labor immigration treaties). Taipei: Chung-yang Yen-chiu Yüan Chin-tai-shih Yen-chiu So, 1966.

Ch'en Ju-chou 陳汝舟. *Mei-chou hua-ch'iao nien-chien* 美州華僑年鑑 (Yearbook of overseas Chinese in the Americas). New York: Chung-kuo Kuo-min Wai-chiao Hsüeh Hui, 1946.

Ch'en K'uang-min 陳匡民. *Mei-chou hua-ch'iao t'ung-chien* 美州華僑通鑑 (History of the overseas Chinese in the Americas). New York: Overseas Chinese Culture Publishing Co., 1950.

Chong Yit-Sun 張奕善. "Tung-nan-ya hua-jen i-min chih yen-chiu" 東南亞華人移民之研究 (A study of the Chinese immigrants in Southeast Asia). *Nanyang University Journal* 南洋大學學報 3: 211–238.

Chung-hua Min-kuo K'ai-kuo Wu-shih-nien Wen-hsien Pien-tsuan Wei-yüan Hui 中華民國開國五十年文獻編纂委員會, eds., *Chung-hua Min-kuo k'ai-kuo wu-shih-nien wen-hsien* 中華民國開國五十年文獻. Ser. 1, parts 9–10 (vols. 2 and 3) of *Ko-ming chih ch'ang-tao yü fa-chan [Hsing-Chung Hui]* 革命之倡導與發展[興中會] (The planning and execution of the revolution [Hsing-Chung hui phase]). Taipei: Cheng-chung Shu-chü, 1964.

Chung Sai Yat Po (Chung-hsi jih-pao) 中西日報 (China and the West daily news). 1900–1912.

Feng Ai-ch'un 馮愛群. *Hua-ch'iao pao-yeh shih* 華僑報業史 (History of overseas Chinese newspapers). Taipei: Taiwan Student Bookstore, 1967.

Feng Tzu-yu 馮自由 and Ch'en Shao-pai 陳少白. *Chung-hua Min-kuo k'ai-kuo-ch'ien ko-ming shih* 中華民國開國前革命史 (A history of the revolutionary movement in China prior to the founding of the Republic). Taipei: Shih-chieh Shu-chü, 1971.

Feng Tzu-yu 馮自由. *Hua-ch'iao ko-ming k'ai-kuo shih* 華僑革命開國史 (Overseas Chinese and the revolution of 1911). Taiwan: Shang-wu Yin-shu Kuan, 1953.

————. *Ko-ming i-shih* 革命逸史 (Relaxed reflections on the 1911 revolution), Vols. 1–8. Shanghai: Shang-wu Yin-shu Kuan, 1947.

Fu Ch'i-hsüeh 傅啓學. *Kuo-fu Sun Chung-shan hsien-sheng chuan* 國父孫中山先生傳 (Collected writings of Sun Yat-sen). Taipei: Chung-hua Min-kuo Ko-chieh Chi-nien Kuo-fu Pai-nien Yen-chiu Ch'ou-pei Wei-yüan Hui, 1968.

Hsieh Shu-hsin 謝樹新, ed. *K'o-chia yüan-liu* 客家源流 (Origin of the Hakkas). In *Chung-yüan wen-hua ts'ung-shu* 中原文化叢書 (Compendium on Chinese culture). Taichung: Ming-kuang-t'ang Yin-shu-chü Yu-hsien Kung-ssu, 1967.

Hsin Chung-kuo pao 新中國報 (New China news). 1903–1908.

Huang Chen-wu 黃珍吾. *Hua-ch'iao yü Chung-kuo ko-ming* 華僑與中國革命 (Overseas Chinese and the Chinese revolution). Taipei: Kuo-fang Yen-chiu Yüan, 1963.

Huang Chia-mo 黃嘉謨. "Mi-lu hua-ch'iao te ai-kuo huo-tung" 秘魯華僑的愛國活動 (The patriotism of overseas Chinese in Peru). *Ta-lu tza-chih* (Mainland miscellany) 42, no. 11 (June 1971).

Huang Fu-luan 黃福鑾. *Hua-ch'iao yü Chung-kuo ko-ming* 華僑與中國革命 (Overseas Chinese and the revolution of 1911). Hong Kong: Ya-chou Ch'u-pan She Yu-hsien Kung-ssu, 1954.

Huang San-te 黃三德. *Hung-men ko-ming shih* 洪門革命史 (The Triads' contribution to the revolution of 1911). San Francisco: N.p., 1925.

Huang Ting-chih 黃鼎之. "Ku-pa te San-min yüeh shu-pao she" 古巴的三民閱書報社 (The San-min Reading Society of Cuba). In Chung-kuo she-hui k'o-hsüeh-yüan chin-tai-shih yen-chiu-so, chin-tai-shih tse-liao pien-chi ch'u-pan she [hereafter, CASS] 中國社會科學院近代史研究所, 近代史資料編輯組編社, ed. *Hua-ch'iao yü hsin-hai ko-ming* 華僑與辛亥革命 (Overseas Chinese and the 1911 Revolution), pp. 312–330. Peking: Chung-kuo She-hui K'o-hsüeh Ch'u-pan She, 1981.

Kwok Won Yat Po (*Kuo-hun jih-pao*) 國魂日報 (New era newspaer). 1908.

Lai, Him Mark 麥禮謙. "Mei-kuo hua-ch'iao chien-shih" 美國華僑簡史 (Short history of Chinese in the United States). *Shih-tai pao* 時代報 (Current age news), September–November 1980.

Li Shao-ling 李少陵, ed. *Ou Chü-chia hsien-sheng chuan* 歐榘甲先生傳 (Biography and selected writings of Ou Chü-chia). Taipei: Li Shao-ling, Inc., 1950.

Liang Ch'i-ch'ao 梁啓超. "Hsia-wei-i yu-chi" 夏威夷遊記 (Record of a trip to Hawaii). In *Yin-ping-shih wen-chi* 飲冰室文集 (Collected writings from an ice-drinker's studio), chüan 37, pp. 185–186. N.p., n.d.

————. *Hsin-ta-lu yu-chi* 新大陸遊記 (Record of a trip to the New World). In Shen Yün-lung 沈雲龍, ed., *Chin-tai chung-kuo shih-liao tsung-k'an* 近代中國史料叢刊 (Collection of documents on recent Chinese history). Taipei: Wen-hai Ch'u-pan She, 1967.

Liu Po-chi 劉伯驥. *Mei-kuo hua-ch'iao shih* 美國華僑史 (A history of the Chinese in the United States of America). Taipei: Liu Ming Wen-hua Shih-yeh Kung-ssu, 1976.

Lo Hsiang-lin 羅香林. *K'o-chia shih-liao hui-p'ien* 客家史料匯篇 (Historical sources for the study of the Hakkas). Hong Kong: Institute of Chinese Culture, 1965.

Lung Doo Benevolent Society 隆都從善堂, ed. *Lung Doo Benevolent Society Diamond Jubillee Edition*. Hong Kong: Lung Doo Benevolent Society, 1966. (Note: In spite of the English title, most of the material is in Chinese.)

Lu Pao-ch'ien 陸寶千. *Lun Wan-Ch'ing Liang-kuang te T'ien-ti hui cheng-ch'üan* 論晚清兩廣的天地會政權 (An analysis of the rebel government of the T'ien Ti hui in South China). Taipei: Academia Sinica, 1975.

Mon Hing Po (Wen-hsing pao) 文興報 (Literary flourishing news). 1900.

Ou Chü-chia 歐榘甲. "Hsin Kwangtung" 新廣東 (New Kwangtung). In Li Shao-ling 李少陵, ed. *Ou Chü-chia hsien-sheng chuan* 歐榘甲先生傳 (Biography and selected writings of Ou Chü-chia). Taipei: Li Shao-ling, Inc., 1950.

Overseas Chinese Penman's Club, eds. *The Chinese of Hawaii*. Honolulu: Overseas Chinese Penman's Club, 1929. (Note: In spite of the English title, much of the material is in Chinese.)

Ow, Yuk 區寵賜, Lai Him Mark 麥禮謙, and P. Choy, 胡垣坤, eds. *A History of the Sam Yup Benevolent Association of the United States, 1850–1974*, or *Lü-Mei San-i tsung hui-kuan chien-shih* 旅美三邑總會館簡史. San Francisco: Sam Yup Benevolent Association, 1975.

Sai Gai Yat Po (Shih-chieh jih-pao) 世界日報 (World news daily). 1908–1912.

Shanghai Shih Wen-wu Pao-kuan Wei-yüan Hui 上海市文物保管委員會, ed. *K'ang Yu-wei yü Pao-huang hui* 康有為與保皇會 (K'ang Yu-wei and the Pao-huang hui). Shanghai: Jen-min Ch'u-pan She, 1982.

Shao-nien Chung-kuo ch'en-pao 少年中國晨報 (Young China). 1910–1912.

Shih-chieh jih-pao 世界日報 (World news daily). 1979. (Current publication separate from the former *Sai Gai Yat Po/Shih-chieh jih-pao*, a Pao-huang hui newspaper).

So-yüan chi-k'an 遡源季刊. 1973–1978.

Special Magazine/Book to Commemorate the Fortieth Anniversary of the *Chung Sai Yat Po*. Unpublished manuscript, Chinese Historical Society of Anerica Archives, 1940.

Ta-t'ung jih-pao (Tai Tung Yat Po) 大同日報 (Great harmony news). 1904–1908.

Ting Wen-chiang 丁文江. *Liang Jen-kung hsien-sheng nien-p'u ch'ang-p'ien ch'u-kao* 梁任公先生年譜長編初稿 (Chronological biography and letters of Liang Ch'i-ch'ao). Vol. 1. Taipei: Shih-chieh Shu-chü, 1958.

Tsung-ku t'e-k'an 鐘鼓特刊 (A call to arms). 1961.

Wei-hsin pao 維新報 (Reform news). 1904.

Wen Hsiung-fei 溫雄飛, "Hui-i hsin-hai-ch'ien Chung-kuo T'ung-meng hui tsai Mei ch'eng-li te kuo-ch'eng" 回憶辛亥前中國同盟會在美成立的過程 (Reminiscences about the founding of the American branch of China's Tung-meng hui). In CASS, ed. *Hua-ch'iao yü hsin-hai ko-ming* 華僑與辛亥革命 (Overseas Chinese and the 1911 Revolution), pp. 179–192. Peking: Chung-kuo She-hui K'o-hsüeh Ch'u-pan She, 1981.

———. "Hsin-hai-ch'ien wo tsai T'an-hsiang-shan T'ung-meng hui han *Tzu-yu hsin-pao* kung-tso te hui-i" 辛亥前我在檀香山同盟會和自由新報工作的回憶. (Reminiscences about my work for Honolulu's T'ung-meng hui and *Tzu-yu hsin-pao* before the 1911 Revolution). In CASS, ed. *Hua-ch'iao yü hsin-hai ko-ming* 華僑與辛亥革命 (Overseas Chinese and the 1911 Revolution), pp. 223–252. Peking: Chung-hua She-hui K'o-hsüeh Ch'u-pan She, 1981.

Wu Hsien-tzu 伍憲子. *Chung-kuo Min-chu Hsien-cheng tang tang-shih* 中國民主憲政黨黨史 (History of the Chinese Constitutionalist Party). San Francisco: Chinese Constitutionalist/Reform Party, 1952.

ARCHIVAL MATERIALS

Adee, Alvery A., Second Assistant Secretary of State, to the Secretary of the Treasury, 24 April 1899 (with enclosure). Enclosure in letter to the author from National Archives, 25 June 1971.

Ai, C. K. (Chung Yü), Ho Fon (Ho K'uan), Wong Leong (Huang Liang), K. F. Li, M.D. (Dr. Li Ch'i-hui), et al., to Secretary of State John Hay, 26 February 1902. Hawaii State Archives.

Bow Wong Progressive Association. Brief Translation of the Rules and Regulations of the Bow Wong Progressive Association (Royal Protective Union) of the Hawaiian Islands, 17 March 1900. Hawaii State Archives.

Brown, Edmund G., Jr., Secretary of State, California, to the author, 10 March 1971.

Brown, Joshua K., Chinese Inspector, Honolulu, to Secretary of the Treasury, 19 February 1900. Enclosure in letter to the author from National Archives, 25 June 1971.

Chien chiao yin-hang t'ieh-lu ku-yu ke fei-ch'ang t'e-li chang-ch'eng 兼招銀行鐵路股優給非常特利章程 (Rules/petition to encourage investors to purchase stock in the bank and railway), 1910. (Written by K'ang Yu-wei.) University of California, Berkeley, Asian American Studies Library Archives.

Chinese Empire Reform Association. Articles of Incorporation of the Chinese Empire Reform Association (San Francisco branch), 2 November 1899. California State Archives. Office of California Secretary of State. Document 16022.

Chinese Empire Reform Association. Proclamation (in Chinese) of Chinese Empire Reform Association (Pao-huang hui), 1903. University of California, Berkeley, Asian American Studies Library Archives.

Chung-kuo shang-wu kung-szu chiao-ku chien-ming chang-ch'eng 中國商務公司招股簡明章程 (Rules for the public stock offering of the Chinese Commercial Corporation), 1903. University of California, Berkeley, Asian American Studies Library, Archives.

Cooper, Henry Ernest. Acting Governor Henry Ernest Cooper to Secretary of State John Hay, 20 April 1902. Hawaii State Archives.

Cooper, Henry Ernest. Acting Governor Henry Ernest Cooper to Secretary of State John Hay, 29 April 1902. Hawaii State Archives.

Cooper, Henry Ernest. Exhibit "F," Statement of Mr. Li Cheung, Official Chinese Interpreter. Enclosure in report by Acting Governor of Hawaii Henry Ernest Cooper to Secretary of State of the United States, 29 April 1902. Hawaii State Archives.

Dole, E. P. Deputy Attorney General E. P. Dole to the Executive Council of the Republic of Hawaii, 9 March 1900. Hawaii State Archives.

Dunn, James R. Office of Special Agent Treasury Department, Office of the Collector of Customs, San Francisco, Chinese Bureau, Inspector in Charge, James R. Dunn, to Postmaster of Sanderson, Texas, 24 October 1899. Immigration and Naturalization Service, Chinese E Files, National Archives.

Eckley, William H., to Governor Frank W. Higgins, 25 May 1905. Enclosure in letter to the author from National Archives, 25 June 1971.

Flint, Charles R., to Oscar H. Straus, Secretary of Commerce and Labor, 23 May 1907. Enclosure in letter to the author from National Archives, 25 June 1971.

Gibbs, Major George W., to General Homer Lea, 6 January 1905. Joshua B. Powers Collection, Hoover Institution for War, Revolution, and Peace, Stanford, California.

Hawaii. Executive Council. Meeting of the Executive Council of the Government of Hawaii, 12 April 1900. Hawaii State Archives.

Henshall, William A., lawyer for Bow Wong Progressive Association, to the President of the Republic of Hawaii, 20 March 1900. Hawaii State Archives.

Ho-p'ing hui chih li 和平會之例 (Peace Preservation Society Rules.) Author's collection.

Hsien-cheng tang lieh-wei t'ung-chih i-hsiung chün-chien 憲政黨列位同志義兄均鑒 (Notice to members of the Hsien-cheng tang/Pao-huang hui), 1904. University of California, Berkeley, Asian American Studies Library Archives.

Jackson, J. P., Collector of the Customs, San Francisco, to Commissioner-General of Immigration, 12 September 1900. Immigration and Naturalization Service, Chinese E Files, National Archives. (Documents 14487, 14212-3-C, 1891-C, 1991-C, 12748-C) National Archives.

K'ang Yu-wei chih Chang Pin-ya tzu-pien han 康有為致張炳雅自辯函 (Letter of explanation/defense from K'ang Yu-wei to Chang Pin-ya), 1907. University of California, Berkeley, Asian American Studies Library Archives.

Kim, Joseph Goo. Statement of Joseph Goo Kim (with enclosure), submitted to Executive Council of the Republic of Hawaii, 5 April 1900. Hawaii State Archives.

Lai, H. Mark (president, Chinese Historical Society of America), to the author, 17 November 1975.

Lea, Homer. "Miscellaneous writings of Homer Lea." Joshua B. Powers Collection, Hoover Institution for War, Revolution, and Peace, Stanford, California.

Li Fuk Ki (Li Fu-chi) to K'ang Yu-wei, 9 September 1900. British Foreign Office, Public Records Office of Great Britain Foreign Office, 17, 1718, 850. "China. Chinese Revolutionaries in British Dominions: Sun-Yat-sen, Kang-yu-wei, etc," pp. 413–414.

Li Fuk Ki (Li Fu-chi) to K'ang Yu-wei, 11 September 1900. British Foreign Office, pp. 414–419.

Lin (Sin?) to K'ang Yu-wei, 24 October 1900. British Foreign Office, pp. 419–422.

Lo Fêng-luh to British Foreign Office, 7 February 1900. British Foreign Office, pp. 259–260.

Lo Fêng-luh to Lord Salisbury, 7 February 1900. British Foreign Office, pp. 253–254.

Mei-chou Chung-hua Ti-kuo Hsien-cheng hui pin 美洲中華帝國憲政會稟 (Petition to the Ch'ing government from the Hsien-cheng tang/Pao-huang hui of the Americas), 1909. (Signed by Chao Wan-sheng 趙萬勝 and Feng Ching-ch'üan 馮鏡泉.) University of California, Berkeley, Asian American Studies Library Archives.

Mei-kuo Cheng-pu Ti-kuo Hsien-cheng hui chien-lou ku-fen-pu 美國正部帝國憲政會建樓股份布 (United States Headquarters [in San Francisco] of the Chinese Constitutionalist Party: List of contributors). Chinese Historical Society of America, archives.

Mei-shu T'an-hsiang-shan pao Kuang-hsü Huang-ti hui chih li 美屬檀香山保光緒皇帝會之例 (Rules and regulations of the Hawaii branch of the Pao-huang hui). Enclosure in statement of Joseph Goo Kim, 5 April 1900. Hawaii State Archives.

Pao-huang hui Kan-ch'eng hsüeh-hsiao hsiao-shih 保皇會干城學校校史 (Materials on the history of the Pao-huang hui's Western Military Academy [Kan-ch'eng hsüeh-hsiao]), 1905. University of California, Berkeley, Asian American Studies Archives.

Pao-huang hui kung-i kai-ting hsin-chang 保皇會公議改定新章 (Convention to rewrite the rules of the Pao-huang hui), 1905. University of California, Berkeley, Asian American Studies Library Archives.

Petition to Charter a Chinese-American Educational Association, 2 February 1905. Joshua B. Powers Collection, Hoover Institution for War, Revolution, and Peace, Stanford, California.

Powers, Joshua B., Collection. Hoover Institution for War, Revolution and Peace, Stanford, California.

Report submitted by Lo Shang (Captain of left wing of Kwangtung army) on Hung Ch'un-fuk's uprising, pp. 558–560.

Sargent, J. W. Memorandum for the Secretary from J. W. Sargent, Department of Commerce and Labor, Bureau of Immigration, 6 April 1906. Letter to the author from National Archives, 25 June 1971.

Smith, Abraham E. United States Consul, Abraham E. Smith, Victoria, to Honorable Thomas W. Cridler, Assistant Secretary of State, Washington, D.C., 14 April 1899 (with enclosure). Enclosure in letter to the author from National Archives, received 25 June 1971.

Tom Chue Phom (Tom Chhui Pak) to K'ang Yu-wei, 8 August 1900. British Foreign Office, pp. 414–421.

Wong Leong (Huang Liang) to Secretary of State John Hay, 4 March 1902. Hawaii State Archives.

Wu T'ing-fang, Minister to the United States, to the United States Secretary of State, 31 January 1900. Enclosure in letter to the author from National Archives, 25 June 1971.

"X" to "My Dear Sir," 25 September 1910. Joshua B. Powers Collection, Hoover Institution for War, Revolution, and Peace, Stanford, California.

Yang Wei-pin, Chinese Consul, to E. A. Mott Smith, Minister for Foreign Affairs, Republic of Hawaii, 17 March 1900. Hawaii State Archives.

Ying-shu Chia-na-ta chi-sheng Hsien-cheng tsung hui pin 英屬加拿大七省憲政總會稟 (Petition to the Ch'ing court from Canada's Hsien-cheng tang/Pao-huang hui), 1910. (Signed by Lin Li-kuang 林理滉 and Chiang Nai-t'ung 蔣奈同.) University of California, Berkeley, Asian American Studies Library Archives.

Yün-kao-hua pu Hsien-cheng hui pu-kao shu 雲高華部憲政會佈告書 (Proclamation of Vancouver's Hsien-cheng tang/Pao-huang hui), 1909. (Includes supporting proclamation by Honolulu's Hsien-chung hui/Pao-huang hui branch, and Hsü Ch'in's original accusation.) University of California, Berkeley, Asian American Studies Library Archives.

Yü-to-li Chung-hua hui-kuan kuei-t'iao 域多利中華會舘規條 (Rules of Victoria's Chung-hua hui-kuan). Author's collection.

INDEX

Production Notes

This book was designed by Roger Eggers.
Composition and paging were done on the
Quadex Composing System and typesetting
on the Compugraphic 8400 by the design
and production staff of University of
Hawaii Press.

The text typeface is Baskerville
and the display typeface is Gill Sans.

Offset presswork and binding were done by
Vail-Ballou Press, Inc. Text paper is
Writers RR Offset, basis 50.